Multiculturalism

The Essence of Indian Culture

Purnima Singh

Vitasta

Let Knowledge Spread

Published by
Renu Kaul Verma
Vitasta Publishing Pvt Ltd
2/15, Ansari Road, Daryaganj
New Delhi - 110 002
info@vitastapublishing.com

ISBN 978-93-82711-63-6
© Purnima Singh, 2017
Reprint 2019
MRP 695
Cover and layout by Vits Press
Printed by Thomson Press (India) Ltd.

*I dedicate this book to
our brave martyred soldiers and to those
serving the nation selflessly*

Acknowledgements

I consulted several primary and secondary sources, public libraries and archives to gather relevant material for almost a decade. I wish to extend my sincere gratitude to the director, librarian and staff of National Archives, Patna, A N Sinha Library and Khuda Buksh Library, Patna, Nehru Memorial Museum Library and Deen Dayal Research Institute Library, New Delhi.

Content

Author's Note

In course of writing my previous book on Indian culture, I was fully exposed to the intricacies of cultural India. It gave me an opportunity to assess the vastness of Indian culture and its deep rooted traits as well as the process of its evolution through the ages.

I could understand that the glory of Indian culture lies in its huge capacity to accommodate and assimilate diversities. It was during this exercise that the seeds of the present work, *Multiculturalism: The Essence of Indian Culture,* was conceived.

Indian culture has emanated from our ancient civilisation that was nurtured by our great sages and philosophers, whose wisdom and postulations enriched cultural ethos of India. With the passage of time, Indian culture incorporated the traits of aggressors and amalgamated different racial and linguistic stocks to emerge as a cohesive society with the doctrine of 'Sarve bhavantu sukhinah, sarve bhavantu niramaya' and tolerance towards each groups.

However, amidst cohesion, conflict situations also flared up with ethnic and communal tensions, struggle between haves and have-nots, war for geographical boundaries and tussle between two religious groups over supremacy of their respective faiths.

Thus, multiculturalism has become a potent political and social tool for policy-makers and political authorities to provide an ideal situation in which all communities and groups respect each other and strived for their rational attainment and contented existence.

In successive chapters, I have attempted to elucidate on the concept of multiculturalism, its significance and inevitability for Indian society. I have dwelt upon both supportive and critical arguments of various social and political thinkers on multiculturalism and critically analysed the liberal-pluralist approach enunciated by many political scientists.

Patna

September 2016 **Purnima Singh**

Introduction

MULTICULTURALISM, as a body of thought in political philosophy, is all about the proper responses of society while dealing with the cultural and religious diversities of its components. Mere 'toleration' of group differences, theorists say, are not enough when it comes to treating members of minority groups as equal citizens. Rather, 'recognition and positive accommodation of group differences' are required through what noted political scientist Will Kymlicka terms 'group-differentiated rights'.

Multiculturalism is seen by its advocates as a fairer system that allows people to truly express who they are within a society that is more tolerant and which adapts apparently seamlessly to the then-existent social issues. The argument used is that since culture is not one definable social reality based on one race or religion, it follows that it is the result of a multiplicity of factors that change as the world around changes. Thus, it would be safe to categorise multiculturalism as a public policy approach for managing cultural diversity in a multiethnic society, officially stressing mutual respect and tolerance for cultural differences within a country's borders.

Multiculturalism is closely associated with what can safely be referred to as 'identity politics', 'the politics of difference' and 'the politics of recognition', all of which share a commitment to revaluing disrespected identities and changing dominant patterns of representation and communication that marginalise certain groups. Multiculturalism is also a matter of economic interests and political power as it demands remedies to economic and political disadvantages that people suffer as a result of their minority status.

While some group-differentiated rights could be held by individual members of minority groups—as may be the case of individuals granted exemptions from generally applicable laws in consideration of their religious beliefs or those who seek language accommodations in schools or in voting—other group-differentiated rights are held wholly by some communities or rather by its members severally and properly termed 'group rights' as in the case of indigenous groups or minority nations that claim the right to self-determination. In the latter instance, multiculturism is closely allied with notions of nationalism. Regular instances of physical violence against Indian blue collar workers and students in Australia (over 8,000 taxi drivers of Asian origin staged a mass sit-in in Melbourne to protest the death by bludgeoning of a fellow cabbie in 2006 and another murderous attack occurred in 2010 when an Indian student was hit on the head by a petrol bottle by white Australians while alighting from a local train in Adelaide) over the past couple of years, is one such example of aggressive nationalism and racism. The resounding turnout of Blacks, Hispanics, Latinos, Asians and women in a country which till recently was considered a citadel of White conservatism in favour of Barack Obama, a Black American, as President of the USA(minorities such as Blacks, Hispanics and Latinos are expected to equal and surpass the native White majority by 2050) and the ban on women from entering the sanctum sanctorum of the famed Haji Ali shrine in Mumbai by the Haji Ali Trust are two other instances in recent decades that leave a sense of disquiet in their wake. Such intolerance and fragmentation of the given societies are beginning to compel policymakers and academics to voice their misgivings over the efficacy of multiculturalism to ensure a level playing field for society's components.

Essentially a work of in-depth research, *Multiculturalism: The Essence of Indian Culture,* attempts to explore the vexed issue of 'multiculturalism',, both as a politico-philosophical concept as also a sociological phenomenon that became popular currency towards the latter part of the 21st century. The mixing up of diverse and varying forms of cultures and social mores within a specified region or territory was largely the result of the transmigration of people in search of better livelihood prospects. The tendency to settle down in another place or region was further fuelled by the desire in people to be integrated into the society they wished to be part of, largely on account of holding on to their religious and cultural views that may not have gone down well with the social set-up they were a part of earlier. It also explores the theoretical aspects of multiculturalism as it seeks to explain in sociological terms the process of migration and cultural assimilation of the minority by the larger society.

It presents to the reader both, the theoretical as well as the practical, aspects of multiculturalism, as it exists in India today given its unique 'unity in diversity' character, apart from focusing on how the phenomenon could further strengthen a country whose ancient wisdom and cultural traditions have largely succeeded in threading India and the Indian people into a common strand.

Indian sages and saints, with their tradition of wisdom and philosophies that have given to the world three great religions, have also given the Indian people the strength to peaceably sustain India's unity in diversity. Their philosophies have further taught us that everything in this material world is in some distinct yet mysterious way inextricably bound with *dharma* or that way of life that is a strong and supple spiritual thread that balances man and materialism and thus holds this country together as one. India's essential spiritualism often finds mention in the *Vishnu Purana*, something that reflects well on the wealth of our universally acknowledged cultural heritage:

अत्रापि भारतं श्रे ठं जम्बूद्वीपे महामुनेय।
तो हि कर्म भूरेबा ह्मतोऽन्या भोग भूमयः।।22।।
अत्र जन्मसहस्राणां सहस्त्रैरपि सप्तम।
कदाचिल्लभते जन्तुर्मानु यं पुण्य स०चयात्।।23।।

In the Jambudweep also, Bharatvarsha is the supreme because this is 'karmabhoomi', apart from this the other countries are 'bhogbhoomi'. Birth in this country as human being is achieved only after doing great works and 'punya' for thousands and thousands births.

It was Swami Vivekananda, who in his address to the World Religious Congress in Chicago (1893), aptly summed up India's distinctly unique position as a leader of nations and men, largely on the basis of its cultural traditions and ancient wisdom. 'This is the motherland of philosophy, spirituality, and of ethics, of sweetness, gentleness and love. These still exist, and my experience of the world leads me to stand on the firm ground and make the bold statement that India is still the first and foremost of all the nations of the world in these respects', he had then said.

Exhorting the gathering that included religious leaders from around the world to learn how to reconcile social and religious differences from the Indian way of life, Vivekananda went on to propound one of his most favoured ideas—the concept of pure blood-lines, blood so pure, so as to be strong enough to brook no diseased germs within. 'If it flows strong and pure and vigorous, everything is right. Political, social or any other material defects, even the poverty of the land, will all be cured if the blood-line is pure', he had stressed in his seminal address that made the world sit up and look anew at India.

Vivekananda expounded the thesis that the world was waiting for a 'complete' civilisation, waiting for the marvelous inheritance of a race of people so spiritual in nature and character that India still represented, despite centuries of decadence, degradation and misery. Extolling India's spiritual heights Vivekananda had then pointed to a largely material world that was waiting for the spiritual treasures that India represented. 'We talk here, we quarrel with each other; we laugh at and ridicule everything holy, for it is little that we do understand... that millions the world over were stretching out their hands for a little sip of that nectar that our forefathers have preserved in this land of India.'

The first chapter of the book explores the theoretical aspects of multiculturalism as it exists in India. In the Indian context, multiculturalism does not represent mere differentiation or the diversity of our culture or cultural pluralism. Multiculturism in India is defined by a far larger concept—that of according equality, justice and respect to the huge diversity of its people. Here, there is no question of the 'tyranny of the majority' or the 'tyranny of the minority'. In

India, the foremost concern is the maintenance of unity and harmony between its many stocks of people. Sardar Patel (1875-1950), in his address at the Karachi Congress of 1931, had rightly observed: As Hindu, I adopt my predecessor's formula and present the minorities with a Swadeshi fountain pen and paper and let them write out their demands. And I should endorse them. I know that it is the quickest method. But it requires courage on the part of the Hindus. What we want is a heart unity, not patched-up paper unity that only comes when the majority takes courage in both the hands and is prepared to change places with the minority.

Shere-e-Punjab Lala Lajpat Rai (1865-1928), among the earliest of Indian nationalists, was of the view that there was no conflict between the various Indian races. 'Mother India', he once said, 'knows and recognises no race distinctions' But he was quick to add, soon thereafter, that there was no denying the conflicts that existed between India's various religious streams. He, however, termed this conflict of opinions as more artificial than real, 'manufactured by interested parties'. In one of his speeches, Lajpat Rai stressed eloquently on this unique facet of Indian culture and tradition when he pointed out that, 'if Mother India is proud of Nanak, she is also proud of a Chisti. If she had an Asoka, she had had an Akbar too. If she had a Chanakya, she also had Kabir. If she had had a Harsha, she had had too a Sher Shah Suri. If she had Vikramaditya, she had a Shahjahan also. And if there were Mohammad Alauddin Khilji and Mohmmad Tughlaq, she had had their Hindu prototypes as well'.

The seminal works of three contemporary liberal philosophers: John Rawls (*A Theory of Justice*, 1971), Joseph Raz (*The Morality of Freedom*, 1986), and Will Kymlicka (*Liberal Theory of Minority Rights*, 1995), which, stressing different liberal principles, respond to the phenomenon of cultural diversity and suggest possible ways of handling it at the level of the state, social structures and moral grounds. The overall concern here is to examine whether contemporary liberal thought is able to face the challenge of a multicultural society.

In his definitive book, *Rethinking Multiculturalism*, Bhikhu Parekh sees the source of insufficiency of the pluralist perspectives in their tendency to give differences an ontological status, to treat diversity as self-contained and self-sufficient, and, finally, to see cultures as static units, internally homogeneous and sedate.

While **Giovan Battista Vico** (1668-1744) appreciated the plethora of diverse social formations and cultures, his historiographic vision, nevertheless, provided grounds for the comparison of diversity otherwise incompatible. This allowed him to see Europe as a beacon of blissful plenitude. **Montesquieu**, on the other hand, shares Vico's preoccupation with diversity, but his insights sought to transgress the confines of intra-cultural perspectives. He was primarily interested in social and political institutions of both European and non-European societies. Diversity raises questions about why societies and polities differ, what determines the differences, and how to handle these in terms of judgment and evaluation. It is apt here to take note of the fact that Montesquieu (1689-1755) declined from passing judgments, which he called normative questions, because these would fall beyond the logic of explanatory action—the effort to demonstrate the origins and causes of difference. However, Montesquieu's pioneering multicultural perspective was cut short by his attempts to explain differences through what he termed the physical and moral causes, often overlapping, and surprisingly attributed to climatic influences.

Herder, in turn, rested his recognition of diversity on the organic view of culture. Human nature did not come prior to that, nor was it transcendental to culture; on the contrary, Herder (1744-1803) saw it as 'pliant clay' moulded by culture. Human nature, the environment and the common experiences of the members of society together formed an organic whole, an inimitable and unique culture, which Herder developed into his concept of a *Kulturnation*—the *Volk*—stemming from a common bearer, with progenitors sharing the imaginary, expressed through the national language. For Herder language was more than a mere conveyor of communication—it expressed the very idea of the *Volk*, its spirit and imagination. Herder's understanding of the familial constitution of the national community is literally genetic—the nation should avoid being diluted (ie. cross-bred with another culture). The source of insufficiency of pluralist perspectives, according to Herder, is their tendency to give difference an ontological status; to treat diversity as self-contained and self-sufficient, and finally to see cultures as static units—internally homogeneous and sedate—which is both facile and simplistic.

The discrepancies that exist between the claims of incompatibility of cultures, and therefore, impossibility or redundancy of inter-cultural judgment and the historiographic projects which, in the case of the following three contemporary liberal philosophers, further exposes their failure to appropriate liberalism critically in defence of multiculturalism.

Rawls vacillates between his initial urge to provide a shared theory of a human person, developed into a comprehensive philosophical doctrine, and an ideologically neutral, practical set of tools which he calls a 'workable basis of social cooperation for democratic liberal societies' which would surpass comprehensive doctrines dividing society into separate cultural units. Rawls' theory fails to get past its metaphysical entanglements and liberalism becomes the depository of the 'essentials of democratic society'.

Raz concentrates on the teleological understanding of human life driven largely by the pursuit of well-being. He defines Western society as shaped and determined by the idea of personal autonomy (from the personal to the interpersonal and institutional level). Although it is not a universal value, confined as it is specifically to Western society as its constitutive force, it nevertheless occupies a central position in Raz's theory and, ultimately, becomes a yardstick with which to measure any culture's worth (understood as recognition of the right to personal autonomy). Parekh, however, underlines the inevitable ethnocentric bias of Raz's theory, especially where he puts up the thesis that non-liberal cultures (here exemplified only by Asian immigrants to Great Britain), in fact, alienate their members who, not knowing the liberating force of autonomy, remain embedded in their cultures only out of ignorance.

In his appreciation of cultural diversity, Raz not only does not set perspectives for cultural interaction, but sees the very fact of diversity as conditioned (a culture's value depends on its ability to contribute to its individual member's well-being, a concept in itself rather difficult to measure).

Kymlicka's definition of cultural community largely coincides with that of the nation; he bases his theory of the 'minority rights' on the concept of national units as the most complete cultural achievement, thereby rejecting the assimilationist approach, which Kymlicka feels impinges upon the principle of justice which demands that minorities and majority should enjoy equal rights and a share of autonomy. National majority and minority differ only in quantitative terms, not qualitative ones, which means that they operate within the same logic. According to the same principle of justice and the logic of social structures, national minorities have the most right to cultural claims and other forms of pressure on the state. Likewise, individual immigrants, the least. Kymlicka explains this bizarre polarity in the following way: national minority remains a discrete cultural and social unit, and, since culture is defined via nation and community, it fares better than an individual immigrant who, by an act of immigration, subscribes automatically to the new culture and nation, which now become for him his 'host' culture and nation.

Despite their many salutary, even ground-breaking propositions, none of the three liberals are quite able to elaborate a theory which would genuinely appreciate diversity as a value *per se*, not only the value of separate cultures. Also, the 'other' culture, recognised in its differences, must be run by liberal principles for the state to tolerate it. This, in effect, would imply that differences cannot be contentious in relation to the state structure. As a result, diversity is severely limited in its political potential; indeed, it stands reduced to 'merely' a cultural realm.

The book's second chapter confines itself to the issue of Hinduism being the cornerstone of the edifice of multiculturalism in modern-day India, arguing as it does, about the efficacy of Hinduism as being most suited to assist in the consolidation and spread of multicultural norms in an as hugely diversified country as India. It also briefly profiles the basic philosophical tenets of the other major religions practiced in India, besides describing the work of their founders through a comparative analysis that is both, jargon-free as also illuminating. It also delves into the problems that have beset the Indian state of late.

The second and third chapters, aptly titled 'Diversities Unlimited: An Asset' and 'The Genesis of Sustaining Multiculturalism in India' seeks to advance the argument that it is because India is a truly multicultural society, it exists without those disturbing socio-politico-cultural warts that are today visible in most countries of the world. *The third chapter* presents the real treasures of India's multicultural foundations, represented by our rich spiritual and cultural heritage. It also advances the thesis of India's and Indians' belief in the 'principles of spiritual science, unity, truth, harmony, tolerance, non-violence, brotherhood and sacrifice'. It is our strong cultural heritage which has kept India together as a nation and even now continues to bind us all into a single spiritual thread.

The fact is that such socio-religious thinkers as Jesus, Prophet Mohammed, Shankaracharya, Kabir, Nanak, Bankim Chandra Chattopadhyay, Ramakrishna, Vivekananda, Tagore, Gandhi, Aurobindo, Iqbal, have all advanced thoughts and philosophies that seek to project India as being a harmonious society through the ages. It is precisely these reflections on society, morality and values that have continued to project India as a propagator of peace and a harbinger of truth and sound moral values that bind people rather than divide them into cultural ghettos.

Rabindranath Tagore (1861-1941), in one of his treatises entitled 'The Religion of Man', says… the consciousness of this unity is spiritual, and our effort to be true to it is our religion. It ever waits to be revealed in our history in a more and perfect illumination. He further reinforces this argument in his book on nationalism, that 'in India our difficulties being internal, our history has been the history of continual social adjustment and not that of organised power for defense and aggression'. The book has advanced the thesis that since religion has a direct connect with *dharma* (or the way of life as practiced by Indians), it is religion alone that is the basis of our unique multiculturalism. Religion, according to me, is to serve humanity; indeed the reason for and being of every religion is the search for truth.

Given the present crisis of values and morality, the ancient texts of India offer numerous eye-openers for those who associate religion with creed and dogma. The story of 'Sabari' in the *Ramcharitmanas* is a perfect example of a benign caste system that binds all classes of people into a strong single strand, all on the basis of religion and the belief that we are all born equal, that it is deeds alone that either raise or lower an individual's esteem in society.

कंद मूल फल सुरस अति दिए राम कहुँ आनि।
प्रेम सहित प्रभु खाए बारंबार बखानि ।।34।।

She brought and offered to Sri Ram the most delicious bulbs, roots and fruits. The Lord partook of them praising them again and again.

—Goswami Tulsidas' *Ramcharitmanas*

पानि जोरि आगें भइ ठाढ़ी।
प्रभुहि बिलोकि प्रीति अति बाढ़ी ।।
केहि बिधि अस्तुति करौं तुम्हारी।
अधम जाति मैं जड़मति भारी ।।1।।
अधम से अधम अधम अति नारी।
तिन्ह महँ मैं मतिमंद अधारी ।।
कह रघुपति सुनु भामिनि बाता।
मानउँ एक भगति कर नाता।।2।।
जाति पाँति कुल धर्म बड़ाई।
धन बल परिजन गुन चतुराई।।
भगति हीन नर सोहइ कैसा।
बिनु जल बारिद देखिअ जैसा ।।3।।
नवधा भगति कहउँ तोहि पाहीं।
सावधान सुनु धरू मन माहीं।।
प्रथम भगति संतन्ह कर संगा।
दूसरि रति मम कथा प्रसंगा ।।4।।

Joining her palms she stood before Him; as she gazed upon the Lord her love waxed yet more ardent. 'How can I extol You, lowest in descent and the dullest of wit as I am? A woman is the lowest of those who rank as the lowest of low. Of women again I am the most dull-headed, O Destroyer of sins.' Answered the Lord of Raghus: Listen , O good lady, to My words. I recognise no other kinship except that of Devotion. Despite caste, kinship, lineage, piety, reputation, wealth, physical strength, numerical strength of his family, accomplishments and ability, a man lacking in Devotion is of no more worth than a cloud without water. Now I tell you the nine forms of Devotion; please listen attentively and cherish them in your mind. The first in order is fellowship with the saints and the second is marked by a fondness for My stories...

—Goswami Tulsidas' *Ramcharitmanas*

गुर पद पंकज सेवा; तीसरि भगति अमान।
चौथि भगति मम गुन गान करइ कपट तजि गान ।। 35 ।।

Humble service of the lotus feet of one's preceptor is the third form of Devotion, while the fourth type of Devotion consists in singing My praises with a guideless purpose.

—Goswami Tulsidas' *Ramcharitmanas*

मंत्र जाप मम दृढ़ बिस्वासा।
पंचम भजन सो बेद प्रकासा।।
छठ दम सील बिरति बहु करमा।
निरत निरंतर सज्जन धरमा ।।1।।
सातवँ सम मोहि मय जग देखा ।
आठवँ जथालाभ संतोषा।
मोतें संत अधिक करि लेखा ।।
सपनेहुँ नहिं देखइ परदोष ।।2।।
नवम सरल सब मन छलहीना।
मम भरोस हियँ हरष न दीना।।
नव महुँ एकउ जिन्ह कें होई।
नारि पुरूष सचराचर कोई ।।3।।
सोइ अतिसय प्रिय भामिनि मोरें।
सकल प्रकार भगति दृढ़ तोरें।।
जोगि बृंद दुरलभ गति जोई।
तो कहुँ आजू सुलभ भइ सोई ।।4।।

...Muttering my Name and unwavering faith constitutes the fifth form of adoration revealed in the Vedas. The sixth variety consists in the practice of self control and virtue, desisting from manifold activities and ever pursuing the course of conduct prescribed for saints. He who practices the seventh type sees the world full of Me without distinction and reckons the saints as even greater than Myself. He who cultivates the eighth type of Devotion remains contented with whatever he gets and never thinks of detecting other's faults. The ninth form of Devotion demands that one should be guideless and straight in one's dealings with everybody, and should in his heart cherish implicit faith in Me without exultation or depression. Whoever possess any one of these nine forms of Devotion, be a man or woman or any other creature—sentient or insentient—is most dear to Me, O good lady. As for yourself you are blessed with unflinching devotion of all these types. The prize which is hardly won by Yogis is within your easy reach today. The most incomparable fruit of seeing Me is that the soul attains its natural state.

—Goswami Tulsidas' *Ramcharitmanas*

कहि कथा सकल बिलोकि हरि मुख हृदयँ पद पंकज धरे।
तजि जोग पावक देह हरि पद लीन भइ जहँ नहिं फिरे।।
नर बिबिध कर्म अधर्म बहुमत सोकप्रद सब त्यागहू।
बिस्वास करि कह दास तुलसी राम पद अनुरागहू।।

After telling the whole story, she gazed on the Lord's countenance and imprinted the image of His lotus fleet on her heart; and casting her body in the fire of Yoga she entered Sri Hari's state wherefrom there is no return. 'O men, abandon your varied activities, sins and diverse creeds, which all give birth to sorrow and with genuine faith', says Tulsidas, ' be devoted to the feet of Sri Rama'.

—Goswami Tulsidas' *Ramcharitmanas*

जाति हीन अघ जन्म महि मुक्त कीन्हि असि नारि।
महामंद मन सुख चहसि ऐसे प्रभुहि बिसारि ।।36।।

> The Lord conferred final beatitude even on a woman who was
> not only an outcaste but a very mine of sin; you seek happiness,
> my most foolish mind, by forgetting such a master!
>
> —Goswami Tulsidas' *Ramcharitmanas*

Sabari was known by the name of the tribe (Sabaras) to which she belonged. Though low-born, she had already acquired some status in her immediate society for her piety and devotion. It is because of her exalted status that the poet Tulsidas had chosen to call her abode a 'hermitage'. This can easily serve as an illustration of the catholicity of the great Hindu religion, which, though rigid in social matters, does not fail to give proper recognition to individual merit and virtue.

The great writer-philosopher Bankim Chandra Chattopadhyay (1838-1894), in his work *Deb'tattva o Hindu Dharma*, typifies two kinds of Hindus—one who wishes to live in accordance with the *shastras*, observes all rituals, reads the scriptures, performs his daily worship but proves highly immoral in his dealings with his fellow brethren. The other does not care for authority-related *shastras*, but is true and righteous. The first individual's conduct is derived from *acara (aachar)* or conduct; Bankim Chandra, however, supported the second type of Hindu and emphasised that *dharma* should rather mean morality and not mere 'ritualistic conduct'.

> Alama Iqbal, the Pakistani poet, is reported to have said that
> 'the Quran considers it necessary to unite religion and state,
> ethics and politics in a single revelation much in the same way
> as Plato does in the *Republic*. Islam, in short, represents an
> ideal of a harmonious organic structure and wants to unite the
> sacerdotium and the emporium'. For Iqbal, religion is to shape
> all phases of life. Hence 'politics and administration should be
> organised on a spiritual basis—In an Islamic state, the individual
> and the government cannot be discussed in isolation'.
>
> —*Modern Indian political thought* by VP Verma

The book's fourth chapter, which deals with the challenges faced by multiculturalism in India, provides the reader with the practical socio-economic-political crises gripping India today. Mahatma Gandhi, in the aftermath of India's independence from British rule (1947), had pointed to one painful political reality of free India, that 'though the Congress had won political freedom, it had yet to win economic, social and moral freedom... These freedoms are harder than the political, if only because they are constructive, less exciting and not spectacular'. Jawaharlal Nehru (1889-1964) too, while spelling out his vision for a free India, had remarked that political freedom would be only 'a means to an end, that end being the raising of the people to higher levels and hence the general advancement of humanity'.

India today has numerous issues of social crisis, which in turn, have adversely affected the pace of the country's development. Some of the most critical areas that spring to mind and which have a direct bearing upon the pace of India's development are its ever-widening gap between the haves and the have-nots, its mind-numbing poverty, scourges such as child labour, a faulty education system that places a premium on learning by rote rather than have its children learn to develop livelihood skills besides assisting them in their ability to think for themselves, issues of gender disparity that today are a matter of great concern, the free-wheeling attitude that 'everything goes' and nothing can be done to cap the all-pervasive corruption, the haunting spectre of communalism, the recent trend for pitched calls for regionalism, the issue of terrorism from across the borders, the instances of ethnic violence, environmental issues that are fast becoming a stumbling block for a country such as India that could well have been happily done away with.

All such issues threaten to put multiculturalism under siege and tend to severely strain the capacity of the political executives to nurture multiculturalism in a country like India that still faces challenges to its nation-building process from the assertive preponderant community.

The fifth and concluding chapter of the book attempts to answer the query as to why multiculturalism is the essence of Indian culture and nation. It is clear that 'multiculturalism', as we understand the concept, forms the backbone of the Indian civilisation and that India cannot survive as a 'nation' without accommodating the various diversities. Tagore once rightly pointed out that 'we should remember Gandhi's views, which if we follow, can be helpful in tackling our vast diversity'. He was, of course, referring to what Gandhi had all along stressed upon, the fact of 'how man can feel honoured by the humiliation of their fellow being'. Gandhi had also often emphasised that 'an eye for an eye will make the whole world blind'. Negative sentiments, the book stresses, could never be the rock on which multiculturalism rests, for such sentiments could only lead to the clash of civilisation rather than usher in the harmony of civilisation.

Tagore, way back in the early 1900s, had realised that 'the spirit of India has always proclaimed the ideal of unity. This ideal of unity never rejects anything, any race or culture. It comprehends all and it has been the highest aim of our spiritual exertions to be able to penetrate all things with one soul, to comprehend all things as they are and not keep out anything in the whole universe… to comprehend all things with sympathy and love. This is the spirit of India'. Interestingly, he had added, the West 'is guided by the impulse of competition' whose end is the gain of wealth for individuals.

The Theoretical Conundrum

MULTICULTURALISM sprouted as a philosophical concept and tradion as part of the pragmatism movement towards the end of the 19th Century in Europe and the United States and, thereafter, as political and cultural pluralism by the turn of the 20th Century. Its birth and subsequent growth was partly in response to the new wave of European imperialism in sub-Saharan Africa and the massive immigration from southern and eastern Europe to the United States and Latin America. Philosophers, psychologists, historians and early sociologist such as Charles Sanders Pierce, William James, George Santayana, Horace Kallan, John Dewey, WEB Du Bois and Alain Locke developed concepts of cultural pluralism from which emerged what we understand today as 'Multiculturalism'. *In A Pluralistic Universe* (1909), William James espoused the idea of a 'plural society' wherein he termed pluralism as 'crucial to the formation of philosophical and social humanism to help build a better, more egalitarian society'.

Conceptually and theoretically, multiculturalism entails the appreciation, acceptance and/or promotion of multiple cultures applied to the demographic make-up of a given specific place, usually at the organisational level, ie. schools, businesses, neighbourhoods, cities or nations. In the political context, it has come to mean the advocacy of extending equitable status to distinct and disparate ethnic and religious groups without the promotion of any specific ethnic, religious and/or cultural community values. As a 'cultural mosaic' it is often contrasted with the concepts of assimilation and social integration and has come to represent a 'salad bowl' instead of a 'melting pot'. Contemporary society, going by the difference in its understanding of multiculturalism, has given birth to two different and seemingly inconsistent strategies. The first focuses on the interaction and communication between the different cultures that make it up. The second strategy is centered round a society's cultural uniqueness and diversity. Cultural isolation, for instance, can help protect the uniqueness of a local and self-limiting culture and also contribute to a wider global cultural diversity. The policy of 'cultural exception', introduced by France in the General Agreement on Tariffs and Trade (GATT) negotiations in 1993 is a perfect instance of a specific demographic area or region trying to protect its own cultural traditions and historical inheritances.

These different aspects of multiculturalism are not totally distinct from each other. Rather, the variegated understanding and strategies, at times, actually complement each other to generate new cultural phenomena that embody the ideologies of individual cultures as also the relationship that exists between them. The term 'transculturation', coined by Cuban anthropologist Fernando Ortiz (in 1940), indicates the 'transaction' of one culture with another. Mary Louise Pratt coined the phrase 'the contact zone' to describe cultural disharmony, clashes and operations. In the cultural environment they represent, cultures are not only interacted upon but have the capacity of existing in isolation. The two strategies work in tandem and so can be applied to different aspects of cultures which then coalesce to create fresh and absolutely new forms of cultures. Multiculturalism, thus, can be defined in ways that go beyond human activities to impart a vivid multi-dimensional understanding of cultural interaction, cultural isolation and all other social or cultural phenomenon that can possibly exist between the two extremes.

Historically, support for modern multiculturalism stems from changes in Western societies after World War II, in what Susanne Wessendorf calls the 'human rights revolution', in which the horrors of institutionalised racism and ethnic cleansing became almost impossible to ignore. Also, with the collapse of the European colonial system as colonised nations in Africa and Asia successfully fought for their independence and pointed fingers at the racist underpinnings of the colonial system; and, in the United States in particular, with the rise of the Civil Rights Movement, which criticised ideals of assimilation that often led to prejudices against those who did not act according to Anglo-American standards, led to the development of academic ethnic studies programmes as a way to counteract the neglect of contributions by racial minorities in classrooms. History shows that multiculturalism in Western countries was seen as a useful set of strategies to combat racism, to protect minority communities of all types, and to undo policies that had prevented minorities from having full access to the opportunities for freedom and equality promised by the liberalism that has been the hallmark of Western societies since the Age of Enlightenment.

Scholars like C James Trotman argue that multiculturalism is valuable because it 'uses several disciplines to highlight neglected aspects of our social history, particularly the histories of women and minorities... and promotes respect for the dignity of the lives and voices of the forgotten. By closing gaps, by raising consciousness about the past, multiculturalism tries to restore a sense of wholeness in the post-modern era that fragments human life and thought'.

Tariq Modood says that multiculturalism 'is most timely and necessary' in the early years of the 21st Century, 'and... we need more, not less', since it is 'the form of integration' that best fits the ideal of egalitarianism, and has 'the best chance of succeeding' in the post-9/11, post-7/7 world, and has remained 'moderate and pragmatic'.

Bhikhu Parekh is not in agreement with what he terms 'tendencies' to equate multiculturalism with racial minoritism, 'demanding special rights' and to see it as promoting a 'thinly veiled racism'. On the contrary, he suggests that multiculturalism is, in fact, 'not about minorities' but 'is about the proper terms of relationship between different cultural communities', which means that the standards by which the communities resolve their differences. For example, 'the principles of justice' must not come from only one of the cultures but must come 'through an open and equal dialogue between them'.

As a policy, multiculturalism attempts to highlight the unique characteristics of the various and different cultures as they relate to one another in nations. The word was first used in 1957 to describe Switzerland, but came into common currency in Canada in the late 1960s, and thereafter spread to other English-speaking countries as they were in the throes of societal churnings that multiculturalism brought about there. The sociologist, Harrison White, hit it right when he said that multiculturalism spelt out a theory, albeit vague, about the foundations of a culture rather than a practice that subsumes cultural ideas.

Looked at broadly, the term is often used to describe societies (especially nations) which have many distinct cultural groups, usually as a result of immigration. This can lead to anxiety about the stability of the national identity, yet can also lead to cultural exchanges that benefit such diverse groups. Such exchanges range from major accomplishments in literature, art and philosophy to relatively token appreciation of variations in music, dress and new foods.

On a lesser scale, the term can also be used to refer to specific districts in cities where people of different cultures co-exist. The actions of city planners can result in some areas remaining mono-cultural, often due to pressure groups active in the local political arena, or indeed the direct actions of these pressure groups or a society's general prejudices such as racism or homophobia. Mono-cultural districts can often be referred to positively or negatively, as ghettos. Gay ghettos could well be a positive force for some, but other forms of ghettos like those created by the Nazis, or those in South Africa during that country's dark and terrible 'apartheid era' can never be any force but a negative one.

Multiculturists take for granted that it is 'culture' and 'cultural groups' that are to be recognised and accommodated. Yet multicultural claims include a wide range of claims involving religion, language, ethnicity, nationality and race. Culture, as Susan Song says in *The Stanford Encyclopedia of Philosophy,* 'is a notoriously overbroad concept, and all these categories have been subsumed by or equated with the concept of culture'.

Multiculturalism can also be a prescriptive term which describes government policy. In dealing with immigrant groups and their cultures, there are four essential approaches and these are:

Monoculturalism: In most Old World nations, notably with the exception of the UK, culture is very closely linked to nationalism, thus government's policy is to assimilate immigrants. These countries have in place policies that aim to socially integrate the immigrant groups with the national culture. This is typical of nations that define themselves as 'one and indivisible' and do not recognise the existence of other nations within their midst.

Leading Culture (German-Leitkultur): This societal model was developed in Germany by the orientalist Bassami. In his book, *Europa Ohne Identität* (Europe with no identity), communities within a country are permitted an identity but then they need to support the core concepts of the leading culture on which a particular society is based. In the West, these concepts are democracy, the separation of the Church and the State, enlightenment and civil society.

Melting Pot: In the United States the traditional view is one of a melting pot where all the immigrant cultures are mixed and amalgamated without state intervention. However, many States have different language policies within the Union. Immigrants maintain their own cultures even as they consciously attempt at becoming Americans.

Multiculturalism: In comparison to the above two approaches, multiculturalism is a view or policy that advocates immigrants and others to preserve their cultures within the different cultures by interacting peacefully within a nation. Today, this is the official policy of Canada, Australia and the UK. However, contrasting views on the Australian model articulate a fundamental shift that identifies a singular homogenised culture, derived from a heterogenous society. Multiculturalism has been described as preserving a 'cultural mosaic' of separate ethnic groups and is often contrasted with a 'melting pot' that mixes them. It has also been described as the 'salad bowl' model.

No country aligns itself completely with one or another of these categories. For example, France has made efforts to impart French culture to new immigrant groups, while Canada still has policies that encourage assimilation.

Some, such as Diane Ravitch, use the term multiculturalism differently, describing both the melting pot and Canada's cultural mosaic as being multicultural and refer to them as 'pluralistic and particularist' multiculturalism. In her terminology, pluralistic multiculturalism views each culture or sub-culture in a society as contributing unique and valuable cultural aspects to the whole or fuller culture and is partial in preserving the existing distinctions between cultures.

Multiculturalism was incorporated into the official policies of several nations during the 1970s for reasons that varied from country to country. In Canada, it was adopted in 1971 following the Royal Commission on Bilingualism and Biculturalism, a government body set up in response to the grievances of Canada's French-speaking minority (concentrated in the province of Quebec). The report of the Commission advocated that the Canadian government recognise Canada as a bilingual and bicultural society and adopt policies to preserve this character.

Progressive: Conservative Party leader John Diefenbaker saw multiculturalism as an attack on his vision of an unhyphenated Canadianism. It did not satisfy the growing number of young Francophones who gravitated towards Quebec's nationalism. While many Canadians of British descent disliked the new policies of biculturalism and official bilingualism, the strongest opposition to this new biculturalism came from Canadians of neither English nor French descent, the so-called 'Third Force' Canadians. Biculturalism was hardly in sync with local realities in the western provinces, where the French population was tiny in comparison with such groups as the Ukrainian Canadians, arguably the single most important ethnic group, in modifying the policy of biculturalism. To accommodate such large groups, the Canadian government had to affect a policy shift, opting for 'bilingualism and biculturalism' to 'bilingualism and multiculturalism'.

The Liberal Party government of Pierre Trudeau promulgated the 'Announcement of Implementation of Policy of Multiculturalism within Bilingual Framework' on 8 October 1971, which was the precursor of the Canadian Multiculturalism Act that received Royal assent on 21 July 1988. Symbolically, the legislation affirmed that Canada was a multicultural nation. On a more practical level, federal funds began to be distributed to ethnic groups to help them preserve their cultures. Projects typically funded included folk dancing competitions and the construction of community centres. This led to criticisms of the policy being motivated by electoral considerations. After its election in 1984, the Progressive Conservative government of Brian Mulroney did not reverse these policies, although these had earlier been criticised by the Tories as being inconsistent with 'unhyphenated Canadianism'. This policy has been supported by every subsequent government and was added to Canada's 1982 constitution, in section 27 of the Canadian Charter of Rights and Freedoms.

Important government multicultural policies the world over can and do include such parameters as:

- Dual citizenship.
- Government support for newspapers, television and radio in the minority languages.
- Support for minority festivals, holidays and celebrations.
- Acceptance of traditional and religious dresses in schools, the military and society in general. Support for arts from cultures around the world.
- Programmes to encourage minority representation in politics, education and the work force.

While multiculturalist policies, at times, can be seen as opposing cultural assimilation, the policies of countries such as Canada do support structured assimilation. Immigrant groups are encouraged to participate in the larger society, learn the majority languages and enter the labour force.

Different scholars have defined multi-culturalism in their own fashion. In a query posed by *BBC News Online* for a shorter definition of multiculturalism, Professor Sir Bernard Crick said: I see no incompatibility between multiculturalism and Britishness. Britishness must be part of multiculturalism. 'Who are we British?', he asked. For a long time, UK has been a multicultural state composed of England, Northern Ireland, Scotland and Wales and also a multicultural society... made up of a diverse range of cultures and identities and one that emphasises the need for a continuous process of mutual engagement and learning about each other with respect, understanding and tolerance.

Dual identities, thus, have been a commonplace occurrence even before the advent of large-scale immigration. Crick went on to add that 'to be British means that we respect the laws, the parliamentary and democratic political structure, traditional values of mutual tolerance and respect for equal rights'. However, he had clarified that Britishness did not mean a single culture. 'Integration is the coexistence of communities and unimpeded movement between them. It is not assimilation. Britishness is a strong concept but not all-embracing.'

According to Ruth Lea, 'There are two ways in which people interpret multiculturalism. The first one is the more common way and that is, every culture has the right to exist and there is no over-arching thread that holds them together. That is the multiculturalism, we think, is so destructive because there is no thread to hold society together. It is that multiculturalism that Trevor Phillips has condemned and, of course, we too do. There is another way to define multiculturalism, which I would call diversity—where people have their own cultural beliefs and happily coexist. But there is a common thread of Britishness or whatever you want to call it, to hold society together. And that is clearly what I would support because you do accept that people have different cultures and you accept them. It is a positive acceptance not a negative tolerance'.

Multiculturalism, according to the Lord Bhikhu Parekh Commission report of 2000, titled, *The Future of Multi-ethnic Britain*, which raised quite a storm by questioning the racist character of the term 'Britishness', 'is sometimes taken to mean that different cultural communities should live their own ways of life in the self-contained manner. This is not its only meaning.... Multiculturalism basically means that no culture is perfect or represents the best life and that it can therefore benefit from a critical dialogue with other cultures. In this sense, multiculturalism requires that all cultures should be open, self-critical and interactive in their relations with each other'. *(The Future of Multi-ethnic Britain,* Runnymede Trust 2000.)

Karen Chouhan (Chief executive of the 1990 Trust, a Black-led human right organisation) has said, 'Multiculturalism is not dead, in fact it has been re-asserted by government policy in the form of valuing diversity'. Neither is it incompatible with an appreciation or knowledge of British cultures. To suggest otherwise would mean turning the clock back on the 'race debates of the past thirty years'.

Most minority ethnic communities have made substantial contributions to the making of Britain and have made huge efforts to learn British history and language, and engage in civic society despite encountering social exclusion and racism in practically every area of public policy and practice. Let's not lose sight of this or how far we have to go. Tackling racial disadvantage is the best way to engender a sense of belonging, being valued is a two-way street.

According to Parekh, 'Multiculturalism is best understood neither as a political doctrine with a programmatic content, nor a philosophical school with a distinct theory of man's place in the world but as a perspective on, or a way of, viewing human life. Its central insights are three, each of which is sometimes misinterpreted by its advocates and needs to be carefully reformulated if it is to carry conviction'.

Human beings, first, are culturally embedded, in the sense that they grow up and live within a culturally structured world and organise their lives and social relations in terms of a culturally derived system of meaning and significance. This does not mean that they are determined by their culture, in the sense of being unable to rise above its categories of thought and critically evaluate its values and system of meaning, but rather that they are deeply shaped by it and can overcome some but not all of its influences. And, if need be, necessarily view the world from within a culture, be it the one they inherit and uncritically accept or reflectively revise or in rare cases, one they consciously adopt.

Second, different cultures represent different systems of meaning and vision of the good life. Since each realises a limited range of human capabilities and emotions and grasps only a part of the totality of human existence, it needs other cultures to help understand itself better, expand its intellectual and moral horizon, stretch its imagination and save it from narcissism so as to guard it against the obvious temptation to absolutise itself, and so on. This does not mean that one cannot lead a good life within one's own culture, but rather, other things being equal, one's way of life is likely to be richer if one also enjoys access to others and that a culturally self-contained life is virtually impossible for most human beings in the modern module and interdependent world. Nor does it mean that all cultures are equally rich and deserve equal respect, that each of them is good for its members or that, they cannot be compared and critically assessed. All it means is that no culture is wholly worthless, that it deserves at least some respect because of what it means to its members and the creative energy it displays, that no culture is perfect and has a right to impose itself on others and that cultures are best changed from within.

Third, every culture is intrinsically plural and internalises within itself a continuing conversation between its different traditions and strands of thought. This does not mean that it is devoid of coherence and identity, but that its identity is plural, fluid and open. Cultures grow out of conscious and unconscious interactions with each other, define their identity in terms of what they take to be their significant other, and are, at least, partially multicultural in their origins and constitution. Each carries bits of the other within itself and is never wholly sui generis. This does not mean that it has no powers of self-determination and inner impulses. Rather, it is porous and subject to external influences which it assimilates in its now autonomous ways.

The converse is just as true. Closed cultures cannot and do not wish or need to talk to each other. Since each defines its identity in terms of its differences from others or what it is not, it feels threatened by them and seeks to safeguard its integrity by resisting their influences and even avoiding all contacts with them. A culture cannot be at ease with differences outside it unless it is at ease with its own internal differences. A dialogue between cultures requires that each should be willing to open itself up to the influences of and learning from others. This presupposes that it is self-critical and willing and able to engage in a dialogue with itself.

According to Parekh, a multiculturalist perspective is composed of the creative interplay of these three important and complementary insights—the cultural embeddedness of human beings, the inescapability and desirability of cultural plurality and the plural and multicultural constitution of each other.

Gurpreet Mahajan points to the fact of 'plural, diverse and multicultural' being terms that are commonly used 'to describe societies that comprise different religions, races, languages and cultures'. In everyday conversation these words are applied interchangeably, the assumption being that each of these expressions represent the same thing—namely, the presence of many different communities. While it is true that plural, diverse and multicultural point to the existence of 'many', it is less realised that they embody three quite distinct conceptions of 'many'. The idea of multiplicity and difference, which they incorporate, are dissimilar in significant ways. Far from being synonyms they are discrete concepts with distinct meanings, contextual parameters and symbolic spaces. It is this dissonance in meaning that we need to apprehend if we are to understand both, the discourse on multiculturalism and its relevance in contemporary political theory.

Plurality suggests the presence of many but it does not stipulate anything about the nature of many. How multiple forms are structured and how they relate to one another are aspects on which the idea of plurality is silent. Consequently, the many that it suggests could be the manifold representations of the 'one'; they could even be reducible to a single unified whole. Alternately, the 'many' may be separate and unequal entities. As such, they may occupy different positions along a continuum; at times the many may be hierarchically arranged. All these possibilities can be envisaged within the framework of a broader plurality. Thus, for instance, the existence and worship of many different gods makes Hinduism a plural religion even though the many are, in the ultimate analysis, reducible to one supreme God.

Similarly, we may speak of a multiracial society as a plural society even when the different races are related to each other in a relationship of domination and subordination. Then again, we may see different caste communities in India as a sign of its plurality, even though these castes are hierarchically arranged. In another context, we could refer to plural associations and plural centres of power within society, each of which seek to influence the centre—the 'one' that constitutes the core. We may associate the presence of many interest groups in a society with pluralism even when some groups are relatively powerless. Even when the lobbying groups are all members of one and the same class, the presence of several groups is seen as an indicator of its plural character. This is the idea of pluralism that political theorists used in their study of industrialised Western societies, and it is on the basis of this understanding that they distinguished between a totalitarian and democratic polity. Here again, plurality symbolised the presence of more than one, but that is all.

The existence of 'many' became a sign of democracy in the 20th Century because the presence of one, for instance—one ideology, one political party, one electoral candidate—was regarded to be a sign of state coercion. Hence, the presence of many—associations, interest groups, political parties and so on—was seen as a minimum condition of freedom. The fact that these many entities may express one and the same ideology was an aspect that did not bother most. While this reading of democracy was insensitive to structures of inequality that continued to exist in these societies despite the presence of a multitude of groups, it was correct in one small respect: the presence of many is a precondition for the recognition of difference. We need to acknowledge the presence of many before we can speak of difference and diversity.

To say this is not to suggest a necessary connection between the concept of plurality and diversity. Plurality merely suggests the presence of many; diversity points to the existence of many that are different, heterogeneous and often incommensurable. It was this notion of difference and diversity that German historians developed in the mid-18th Century. Theorists of Enlightenment in England and France noted the existence of plural cultures and civilisations. However, in keeping with their understanding of plurality, they arranged these cultures' hierarchy. The history of humankind, in their view, represented progress—from the dark ages to the civilised, enlightened present. In making this assessment, the philosophers used their contemporary sensibilities to judge all other cultures, and it was from the perspective of their own historical world that other civilisations in the past, as well as existing non-industrial, absolutist regimes, seemed to be lagging behind.

German historians, from Herder to Ranke (1795-1886), used the idea of cultural diversity to question this judgement of the Enlightenment. They argued that human history was constituted by discrete and heterogeneous cultures, each with its own values, morality and aesthetic norms as also political and economic structures. Thus, each culture was 'in itself a whole' complete, with its own centre of happiness. 'Can it be that thousands are made for one? All the generations which have passed away merely for the last? Every individual, only for the species, that is for the image of the abstract name? The All Wise sports not in this manner: he invents no fine-spun shadowy dreams: he lives and feels in each of his children with paternal affection, as though it were the only creature in the world.'

To emphasise the authentic and unique nature of each culture, Herder represented them as 'children' of God who were destined to carve their own distinct identity and future. Subsequent historians and philosophers drew upon this idea of diversity to point to the heterogeneity and incommensurability of different epochs and civilizations. However, the peculiarity of this framework was that it accommodated diversity only historically. That is, it maintained that history is defined by a succession of diverse cultures or values, but each culture manifests a single idea. Thus, while each era was characterised by a defined 'spirit' or *volkgeist,* historical succession provided evidence of difference and diversity.

German historicist tradition elucidated the distinction between plurality and diversity. Since then the idea of 'irreducible difference' or diversity has been used in a variety of theoretical contexts. Occidentalists invoke this concept of diversity when they stress the difference between civilisations of Asia and West Europe and argue that the former embody a set of values which are admirable in themselves. Advocates of ethno-social science also anchor their arguments in this conception of diversity or non-collapsible difference. They maintain that each society is unique in terms of its internal structure, institutions and values. Consequently, it must be studied on its own terms. That is, through the language and values internal to it, instead of those imported from outside.

At another level, this conception of diversity surfaces in the writings of contemporary liberals. The presence of different, and even incommensurable, epistemologies, perspectives, lifestyles, ideas and moral values is, for them, the crucial test of tolerance and democracy in society. To protect this diversity of thought and belief, they favour a procedural republic and give priority to rights. To the extent that some liberals protested the *fatwa* issued by Ayatollah Khomeini (1998) that sought to suppress this diversity of views (coming, in this case, from Salman Rushdie).

Observes Gurpreet Mahajan: The concept of multiculturalism endorses the idea of difference and heterogeneity that is embodied in the concept of diversity. In its discussion of diverse communities it distinguishes between the majority community and the minorities. That is, diverse cultural communities are categorised as majority or minority. In a modern democratic polity, the state is usually identified with the majority culture, while communities that differ from it are designated as minorities. In emphasising the irreconcilable differences between the majority and minority cultures multiculturalism locates incommensurable differences within the boundaries of the state. In other words, diversity is no longer pushed outside the boundaries of the nation state. Further, as diverse communities co-exist within the state, multiculturalism raises the issue of their equality. It asks whether the different entities, constituting the many, are granted an equal status within the polity.

Amartya Sen visualises multiculturalism in a different perspective. He writes that, 'the demand for multiculturalism is strong in the cotemporary world... one of the central issues is how human beings are seen. Should they be categorised in terms of inherited traditions, particularly the inherited religion of the community in which they happen to have been born, taking that un-chosen identity to have automatic priority over other affiliations involving politics, profession, class, gender, language, literature, social involvements and many other connections? Or should they be understood as persons with many affiliations and associations whose relative priorities they must themselves choose (taking the responsibility that comes with reasoned choice).'

Also, should we assess the fairness of multiculturalism primarily by the extent to which people from different cultural backgrounds are 'left alone', or by the extent to which their ability to make reasoned choices is positively supported by the social opportunities of education and participation in civil society, he asks. 'There is no way of escaping these rather foundational questions, if multiculturalism is to be fairly assessed', he concludes. Elsewhere, Sen poses the query whether multiculturalism is nothing but the tolerance of the diversity of cultures? Does it make a difference as to who chooses the cultural practices... whether they are imposed on young children in the name of 'the culture of the community' or whether they are freely chosen by persons with adequate opportunity to learn and to reason about alternatives? What facilities do members of different communities have, in schools as well as in the society at large, to learn about the faiths and non-faiths of different people in the world and to understand how to reason about choices that human beings must, if only implicitly, make?

'One important issue concerns the distinction between multiculturalism and what may be called "plural mono-culturalism". Does the existence of a diversity of cultures, which might pass one another, like ships in the night, count as a successful case of multi-culturalism? Since, in the matter of identity, Britain is currently torn between interaction and isolation, the distinction is centrally important (and even has a bearing on the question of terrorism and violence)', he writes.

Indian and British food can genuinely claim to be multicultural. By contrast, having two styles or traditions co-exist side by side, without the twain meeting, must really be seen as plural monoculturalism. The vocal defense of multiculturalism that we frequently hear these days is very often nothing more than a plea for plural monoculturalism. If a young girl in a conservative immigrant family wants to go out on a date with an English boy that would certainly be a multicultural initiative. In contrast, the attempt by her guardians to stop her from doing this (a common enough occurrence) is hardly a multicultural move, since it seeks to keep the cultures separate. And yet, it is the parents' prohibition, which contributes to plural monoculturalism, that seems to garner the loudest and most vocal defense from alleged multiculturalists, on the ground of the importance of honoring traditional cultures as if the cultural freedom of the young women were of no relevance whatever; as if the distinct cultures must somehow remain in secluded boxes.

Being born in a particular social background is not in itself an exercise of cultural liberty, since it is not an act of choice! In contrast, the decision to stay firmly within the traditional mode would be an exercise of freedom if the choice were made after considering other alternatives. In the same way, a decision to move away—by a little or a lot—from the standard behavior pattern arrived at after reflection and reasoning, would also qualify as such an exercise. Indeed, cultural freedom can frequently clash with cultural conservatism, and if multiculturalism is defended in the name of cultural freedom, then it can hardly be seen as demanding, unwavering and unqualified support for staying steadfastly within one's inherited cultural tradition.

Sen says, the second question relates to the fact that while religion or ethnicity may be an important identity for people (especially if they have the freedom to choose between celebrating or rejecting inherited or attributed traditions), there are other affiliations and associations that people also have reason to value. Unless it is defined very oddly, multiculturalism cannot override the right of a person to participate in civil society, or to take part in national politics, or to lead a socially non-conformist life. No matter how important multiculturalism is, it cannot lead automatically to giving priority to the dictates of traditional culture over all else. Sen further argues that the central issue was identifieda long time ago with great clarity by Emperor Akbar in his observations on reason and faith in the 1590s. Akbar was born a Muslim and died a Muslim, but he insisted that faith cannot have priority over reason since one must justify—and if necessary, reject—one's inherited faith through reason.

Attacked by traditionalists who argued in favour of instinctive faith, Akbar told his friend and trusted lieutenant, Abul Fazl, a formidable scholar with much expertise in different religions: The pursuit of reason and rejection of traditionalism are so brilliantly patent as to be above the need of argument. If traditionalism was proper, the prophets would merely have followed their own elders (and not come with new messages). Reason had to be supreme, in Akbar's view, since even in disputing reason, we would have to give reasons.

Sen adds that convinced that he had to take a serious interest in the diverse religions of India, Akbar arranged for recurring dialogues involving not only people from mainstream Hindu and Muslim backgrounds in sixteenth century in India, but also Christian, Jews, Parsees, Jains and even the followers of 'Carvaka'—a school of atheistic thinking that had robustly flourished in India for more than two thousand years from around the sixth century BCE. Rather than taking an 'all or nothing' view of a faith, Akbar liked to reason about particular components of each multifaceted religion. Arguing with Jains, for example, Akbar would remain skeptical of their rituals but was convinced by their argument for vegetarianism and even ended up deploring the eating of flesh in general, despite the irritation this caused among those who preferred to base religious belief on faith rather than reasoning. He stuck to what he called 'the path of reason', the *Rah e Aql*, and insisted on the need for open dialogue and free choice. Akbar also claimed that his own liberal Islamic beliefs came from reasoning and choice, not from blind faith or what he called 'the marshy land of tradition'.

The essence of Indian culture is multiculturalism. India is both an exporter as well as importer of its culture. India represents a kind of economic, cultural, political and above all, spiritual synthesis of different religions. There are numerous examples that all of Indian society's components share each other's joys and sorrows in equal measure. Hindus frequent Sufi shrines and Muslims celebrate Hindu religious festivals with equal gusto. Indian culture, therefore, has capacity to absorb different cultures in a peaceful manner. Quite rightly therefore, it has been said that Indian culture is like a beehive of interlocking cells.

Manmohan Malhoutra, in his article, Multiculturalism: The historical Indian experience: The East-West Dialogue', correctly points out that 'Politically, Islam in India, represented subjugation. Culturally, it generated outstanding creative achievement and synthesis. The centuries of Muslim rule impacted all aspects of Indian life—our art and architecture, our music and dress, our manners and cuisines, our language and aesthetic sensibility—producing a composite Indo-Islamic culture. Scholars, poets and architects arrived from Turkey, Iran, Iraq, Afghanistan and Tajikistan. Persian emerged as the court language, producing in time a hybrid Indo-Persian language called Urdu. Hindus found positions at the highest levels of the administration. Royal marriages between Hindu princesses and Muslim princes were not uncommon. Sufism attracted many Hindus. The poet Kabir (1440-1518), a Hindu by birth but a Muslim by upbringing, represented a kind of spiritual fusion between Islam and Hinduism, and Sufi shrines and Hindu festivals attract equal devotion from Hindus and Muslims in India today. Guru Nanak, the founder of the Sikh faith, was profoundly influenced by the Islamic ideals of equality and social service. At a time when the inquisition was rampant in Europe, the 16th century Mughal emperor Akbar was both practicing and preaching tolerance. He brought together representatives from every sect of Islam and from Hinduism, Buddhism, Zoroastrianism and Christianity for all night debates in the hope of fashioning a new universal religion. He was the first and certainly the greatest practitioner of what is now called 'inter-faith' dialogue. Centuries ahead of his time, he foreshadowed contemporary secularism by laying down that 'no man should be interfered with on account of his religion and anyone is to be allowed over to a religion that pleases him'.

Gurpreet Mahajan in her book, *Accomodating Diversity*, asks: Why should we care about diversity? How should we deal with the cultural diversities present in our society? Should these diversities be accommodated? If so, what institutional arrangements are needed to accommodate the many kinds of differences and diversities that exist in society? Especially Indian society. In recent times these questions have been raised and debated by theorists of multiculturalism.

Diversity has been valued for a variety of reasons in recent times. The liberals associated the absence of differences with tyranny and totalitarianism. On a more positive side they linked the presence of differences and diversity with vitality and creative energy. Armed with the understanding that truth can only be arrived at though a contestation of different ideas and viewpoints, these theorists perceived the presence of different views and perspectives to be an essential condition for good life. Space for the articulation and expression of differences was further seen as a necessary condition of being free; liberty was valuable so that individuals could pursue what they regarded to be good and desirable, and by extension, the state was expected to refrain from endorsing a substantive conception of the good life. Plurality of values was thus valued and considered to be the hallmark of a free society.

For the liberals, it is the diversity of ideas, beliefs, perspectives and ideologies that would usher in a democratic society, a society that would have no space for received orthodoxies. Superstition, tradition and religion would give way to a diversity of lifestyles and new communities would emerge from these chosen ways of life. A market-based economy was an ally in this project, reinforcing the availability of different commodities and goods. Differences and diversity were thus cherished within the liberal paradigm. However, the diversity that was prized stemmed from the priority accorded to individual choice and autonomy. So, ways of life that treasured a different set of goods such as care, collective life, harmony and order, or were pre-committed to some substantive conception of the good life or derived what is desirable from some set of religious beliefs or tradition—elements that were not freely chosen—were devalued. For this reason, even though liberalism offered a strident defence of plurality and difference, it was not hospitable to all forms of life. Despite its proclaimed neutrality it remained a particular conception of the good life, one that was hostile to, and certainly not accommodative of, all non-individual-centered ways of life.

Communities that did not share the liberal way of life and constituted minorities in liberal democracies could not survive with the flourishing of liberal diversity. Protecting them required valuing diversity of cultures, and not just diversity at the level of the individual. Theorists of multiculturalism spoke for these minorities and it was to provide them equal treatment that they valued cultural diversity. Their conception of diversity as well as the reasons for defending it was significantly different from that of the liberals. Liberals had valued diversity of ideas and perspectives at the level of the individual. Multiculturalists spoke of cultures, not individuals; the diversity they wanted to protect was diversity of cultures and, with it, diversity of values and ways of life endorsed by different cultures.

Protecting the diversity of cultures was intended to promote equal treatment for people belonging to different cultural communities. If, for instance, the medium of instruction in state-run schools was the language of the majority, protecting cultural diversity implied finding ways to ensure that the language of the other cultural communities— the minorities—receive a similar treatment. The children of these minorities can also be taught in their mother-tongue or have the option of learning that language. If the laws relating to marriage, property, suicide reflect the orientation of the majority community, then the cultural concerns of the minorities must receive a similar consideration. The public domain should make space for, and allow visibility, to the cultures of the minority communities.

Diversity, namely, cultural diversity, was valued minimally for the sake of promoting equality. But while dealing with marginalized minorities that were compelled to assimilate into the dominant culture, multiculturalism in its most assertive form made a plea for protecting the existing diversity of cultures in our society by initiating policies that enabled communities to live in accordance with their own customs, practices, institutional structures and conceptions of good. To put it in another way, while the concern for equality informs the need to accommodate cultural diversity, it is by no means the only reason for which cultural diversity is valued. Indeed, many theorists of multiculturalism maintain that diversity is itself a valued good, important for leading a good life and for creating a good society. Cultural diversity, for them, is necessary not simply for minimising the disadvantages that cultural minorities face, but for our collective well-being, as well. The presence of different cultures allows us to rethink and reassess our own conceptions—our way of life, projects that we embark upon and the institutions we have created and live with. Different cultures gives us options in terms of which we might consider our present world and revise/rethink the choices that we have made; it also opens us to the possibility of organising our lives and society differently. It is the presence of such cultural differences that opens us to critically evaluate our inheritances, our dominant way of thinking and organising society. Cultural diversity thus enriches our lives and the society in which we live. It must, therefore, be valued and protected.

A few theorists go a step further to argue that cultural diversity is intrinsically valuable. Instead of judging and comparing with our own culture and civilization, we should accept the fact that cultures that have organised the lives of a people over time, must have some intrinsic worth, even if it is not so readily visible to us. Besides, we are not in a position to determine the relative worth of each culture. This could only be known at the end of history. So we must, as it were, embrace the available diversity of cultures and respect differences; if we cannot contribute to the richness provided by cultural diversity we must, at least, be willing to protect it and ensure its survival.

This is perhaps the strongest defence of cultural diversity that is offered by multiculturalists. But such arguments that offered what might be called a difference-based defence of cultural diversity are significantly different from those that attend to cultural differences in order to promote equality. Although some theorists of multiculturalism draw on both difference-based as well as equality-based arguments for defending cultural diversity, privileging one over the other hardly gives us a true picture. They eventually yield two fairly different kinds of policies; if the difference-based understanding is more inclined to accommodate community institutions and structures and endorse community practices even when they restrict options for external and internal others, the equality-based defence is more attentive to issues of intra-group equality while advocating measures to promote inter-group equality. As such, what is important in this framework is not the protection of a given minority culture, but the availability of choices and options for the individual—the option to live in accordance with a given way of life or to abandon it.

The distinction between difference-based and equality-based arguments becomes more evident when we turn to the arguments proffered by Peter Emberly and Anne Phillips, later in the volume. Emberley recognises that the differences are, in this sense, 'messy, inconvenient and quarrelsome'. Yet, they are needed for conflict, and tension is a source of creativity. We need, as it were, 'chaos within ourselves to give birth to a dancing star'. It is this productive dimension of diversity that makes plurality of cultures valuable.

The search for concrete alternatives and expressions of difference took Emberley to small communities in India that were (and, to some extent, continue to be) organised through norms and principles that are strikingly different from those of liberalism and its accompanying model of free market economy. Although these communities are responding to the changes occurring around them and the opportunities thrown up by the expansion of the market, they still retain elements of their pre-modern worldview, and, for Emberley, engaging with the difference they embody holds the possibility of 'mutual renewal'

The desire to look for, and perhaps even protect, non-liberal ways of life remains an undercurrent in much of multicultural theorisation. Homogenisation imposed by the market economy had been a central concern of theorists that were influenced by Hegel and Heidegger. In the social sciences, members of the Frankfurt School, particularly Herbert Marcuse, pointed to the new kind of homogeneity ushered in by the capitalist consumer society. The latter offered multiplicity of goods and a bewildering variety of the same commodity to choose from. The large supermarkets, for instance, offered ten varieties of potato chips and tomato sauce, the same spices packed, branded and sold under different names, a range of electronic goods and gadgets that were changing faster than we could keep pace with, yet the society was woven around the same organising principle. It was a 'one-dimensional society' and it produced through its many different activities and institutions the 'one-dimensional man' wedded to more and more consumption, profit-making and maximising one's interest.

Although this is an intellectual tradition to which many analysts return when they point to the homogenising forces of globalisation and the loss of control that small communities face over their produce and environment, this process of homogenisation has not been a central concern of theories of multiculturalism. Theorists of multiculturalism often refer to, and try to protect, marginalised communities such as the indigenous populations whose way of life is governed by principles that are different from that of liberalism and free market economy. Most of the time these theorists are concerned about the fate of diverse languages, cultural practices, and institutional arrangements and it is these that they seek to protect from external interventions. Hence, they consider policies that are likely to ensure the survival of these diversities without necessarily questioning or rejecting the capitalist economy.

Accommodating diversities and ensuring the survival of marginalised cultures poses several difficulties. The most serious one pertains to the cost that accommodation is likely to be placed upon the internal and external members. If, for instance, the culture of the Francophone population in Quebec is to be protected then, as many multiculturalists argue, French must be the official language of the region, the children of the Francophone population must attend French-medium schools and immigrants coming to live in the region must be prepared to send their children to schools where French is the medium of instruction. Such measures that are absolutely necessary for protecting the French culture will most certainly place constraints upon both internal and external members. The Francophone population will not have the option of sending their children to English-medium schools, so the choices of the internal members will be restricted. Likewise, limitations will also be placed on external members as only those immigrants would be permitted to settle in Quebec who can assimilate and adopt the culture of the regional majority.

Costs of this kind are unavoidable when policies are framed to protect and ensure the survival of a minority culture. There is also the danger that policies of accommodation might privilege the voice of the dominant sections of the community as also the prevailing community practices. Since almost all cultures tend to place women in a subordinate position this would mean that vulnerable groups like women would be disadvantaged by policies of multicultural accommodation. It is concerns of these kinds—about the fate of internal and external members—which compel us to shift attention from protecting minority cultures to minimising disadvantages faced by minorities. It is only when the prevailing norm imposes unacceptable costs upon members of minority communities that differences need to be accommodated, even when that entails some form of special consideration.

If it is the presence of inequality and disadvantage then that must receive our attention, and it is this concern that prompts Anne Phillips to affirm the need for special consideration. However, all forms of special consideration rebel against the liberal notion of equality and the accompanying norm of treating all persons alike; hence, they always require some justification. Anne Phillips recognises this and argues that in a society marked by vast inequalities the assertion of political equality is necessary but never enough. When group-based exclusions exist, as in the case of women in almost all societies, we need special measures aimed at equalising, or at least improving, the position of these subordinated groups. It is our concern for equality that warrants and justifies the deviation from the principle of identical treatment.

While acknowledging the necessity of group-specific mechanisms, Phillips reminds us that there are dangers that accompany even the most 'moderate' forms of such policies. Many a times policies chosen to redress systemic inequalities end up redefining cultures, stereotyping individuals and reinforcing differences that are themselves a source of disadvantage. These problems need to be recognised, not simply dismissed in order to formulate policies that are truly 'transformative' in nature and have the potential of breaking the cycle of disadvantage and inequality. For this reason, she advocates special consideration for women and not cultural communities as protecting cultures is likely to disadvantage women. At least implicitly, she accepts that the inclusion of women is likely to bring in a new perspective and experiences that will enrich public policy.

The idea that the pursuit of equality may at times require special consideration for some is now accepted by many liberals. From Rawls to Dworkin, contemporary liberals recognise that in the absence of a level playing field, equality of opportunity cannot exist, and it is to rectify this that they accept the need for special measures. However, special consideration here is intended to ensure equality of opportunity and not equality of outcomes in real terms, and most often it takes the form of affirmative action policies. Typically, multicultural accommodation differs significantly from such policies of affirmative action. While both support the occasional need for special consideration (and deviation from the liberal norm of identical treatment) multicultural policies are aimed at checking coercive homogenization and assimilation. Affirmative action, on the other hand, tries to ensure that victims of the policy of segregation can now be part of the mainstream and enjoy the same opportunities as all others in society.

The difference between affirmative action and multiculturalism can be presented and recognised in yet another way. Affirmative action has a moral anchor in Rawls' conception of justice as fairness. Multiculturalism, by comparison, begins by noting the limitations of liberal neutrality and the idea of justice as fairness. Affirmative action policies work with Rawls' assumption about the interchangeability of citizens; hence it tries to make identities irrelevant in the long run. Theorists of multiculturalism question the desirability of erasing cultural identities. For them, these identities are not only important to the individual and their sense of who they are—the state too, explicitly or implicitly, reflects these identities. In most cases it reflects the cultural orientation of the majority and it is this that poses a problem for minority communities. When, for instance, the state makes Sunday the weekly day-off, it implicitly at least, acknowledges the preferences of the Christian community that observes Sunday as the day of rest. And, it is this decision to declare Sunday as a holiday that disadvantages devout Muslims and Jews who may wish either to have the time-off to offer prayers on Friday afternoon or observe Saturday as the Sabbath.

So, while Rawlsian fairness pushes us in the direction of erasing all markers of identity by making Sunday a working day, multicultural accommodation suggests that Sunday as the day-off may be retained, while making exceptions to include the concerns of minorities.

Multiculturalism privileges the policy of even-handedness and in so doing, takes into account, at least implicitly, the history of the society and the groups that we are dealing with and seeking equality.

The notion of even-handedness, articulated by Joseph Carens, appears particularly attractive in India where secularism is often associated with maintaining an equal distance from all communities. Many scholars writing about the distinctiveness of the Indian notion of secularism argue that in the West, secularism implied the separation, if not the absence of religion from the political and public domain. In contrast in India, religion was not seen just as a mark of individual identity, but also as a positive moral and social influence. So it was pushed into the public realm. The nature of Indian religions was also not conducive to such private-public distinction. Hence, religion remained, and continues to be, visible in the public area. Being secular, therefore, took on a different meaning in the Indian context. It implied a commitment to fair and equal treatment to all religions—*sarva* dharma *sambhava*.

The notion of evenhandedness begins by acknowledging the near impossibility of erasing all cultural markers in the public domain; whether it is the policy on language or monogamy, suicide or euthanasia, public holidays or symbols of the state, a cultural orientation is bound to be present. So, to ensure that minority religious groups are not unduly disadvantaged it tries to accommodate their concerns. Accommodation is here made with a view to minimising disadvantages and protecting diversity.

The notion of equidistance (from all communities) also recognises the presence of multiple communities. It also accepts the impossibility of restricting religion to the private domain. It also rejects the possibility of separating religion entirely from the state. Hence, in order to be fair to different communities, particularly the minorities, it consciously tries to accommodate the existing plurality. In fact, when we are dealing with such issues as state funding for community-run schools then it too, like the principle of evenhandedness, suggests that if the state is supporting schools run by one community then it must also consider giving funds to schools run by other communities. It would also suggest that community-administered schools should receive the same consideration as state-administered schools. However, this is where the similarity ends.

Equidistance underlines the need to not align the state with any one religion, but beyond that it does not offer a framework or a vantage point from which accommodation should take place. Evenhandedness, by comparison, underlines the need to accommodate with a view to minimising disadvantages and reflecting diversity. This difference becomes sharply evident when we turn to such issues as the language policy of the state. Here the principle of equidistance is not very helpful as it does not offer any suggestions about how the state should identify an official language that can be the language of administration as also the medium of instruction in schools. As equidistance is hardly a feasible option in such situations, this principle is of little assistance when we are dealing with issues of linguistic diversity. Evenhandedness, on the other hand, suggests that the state policy on language must give due consideration to the claims of minorities within the territory. Even when the language of the majority is privileged, primary schools should provide instructions in the minority language, or teach the language of the minorities in schools, at least as an option, so that the minorities interested in the fare of their languages or those wanting to impart their language and culture to their children, can do so.

Evenhandedness, thus, approaches issues and problems from the perspective of accommodating differences and minimising disadvantages. It accepts the inevitability of the majority (whether it is defined with reference to the nation, state as a whole or a given region/state within that whole) preference marking state policy; so all it does is to bring in and accommodate the concerns of the minority/minorities. In other words, it recognises the difficulties of being equidistant from all communities on all matters. So it attempts to accommodate minorities, given the inevitability of the majority prevailing in a given context and tries to minimise disadvantages rather than ensure near-neutrality of the state.

This distinction between the notion of even-handedness and equidistance needs to be recognised in order to understand and appreciate some of the differences between secularism and the notion of multicultural accommodation. While both aim to minimise and eliminate discrimination, they approach this issue with a different understanding of state, equality, religion and culture.

One must now turn to the two questions that the actual task of accommodation raises—namely, which groups of communities should be accommodated and through what forms of special consideration. Theorists of multiculturalism harbor significant differences on both questions. Nevertheless, the discussion of these issues has to a considerable extent been structured by the framework provided by Will Kymlicka. Looking primarily at the North American experience, Kymlicka distinguished between two kinds of minorities—national minorities (communities with a distinct language and 'societal culture'; that is, a set of more or less complete and separate institutions; social, political, economic and legal—who have lived on a particular territory for a long period of time and see that territory as their homeland) and immigrants (communities that have voluntarily left their homeland and come to another country in search of better opportunities and life conditions). The claims of national minorities are, in this framework, stronger and they can justifiably claim, and be given, the right to self-government as well as the right to separate representation.

Immigrants, who choose to leave their homeland and come to another country, cannot however claim the same kind of special consideration. They can, at best, ask for some cultural rights, such as, the right to put up signboards on their shops in their own language. They cannot expect recognition of their community institutions, or subsidies to run separate schools or other institutions. Rights of this kind could only be granted to national minorities and if these national minorities were concentrated in some part of territory, they could be given the right to self-government. This could be in the form of creating a separate federal unit with special powers (as is the case of Quebec in Canada) or it could create new structures, such as reservations for the indigenous people. If these groups were not territorially concentrated then they could perhaps be given special and separate representation in key decision-making bodies so that their culturally distinct perspective and interest is represented and protected.

The distinction that Kymlicka makes between national minorities and immigrants is not entirely a satisfactory one. As his critics are quick to point out, this distinction may have some relevance when we are dealing with first generation immigrants, but it cannot adequately apply to the second or third generation immigrants. In the case of the latter, the younger generation only knows the country in which they are living and they see it as their homeland. So why should their rights not be at par with those of other national minorities? Indeed, how long must a community live on a territory for it to be seen as a national minority and not just an immigrant. There is, in addition, the case of political refugees and people driven out of their homeland due to prolonged conflict or conditions of abysmal poverty and chronic hunger. Should they be denied the right to live in accordance with their cultural beliefs?

These problems notwithstanding, Kymlicka's framework underlined the necessity of differentiating between different minorities and their claims. It also pointed out that special consideration to some, particularly in the form of such special rights as separate representation or the right to self-government, does not mean that all minorities should be given the same rights. Distinctions can legitimately be made and indeed they need to be made. History matters here; history of the group that is making the claim, its relation to the state, are all elements of the context that are, as Joseph Carens argued, relevant for distinguishing between the claims of different communities.

In India, the political leadership as well as the members of the Constituent Assembly saw religious, linguistic and cultural diversity as being an essential part of the mosaic that was India; diversity was considered to be a part of the Indian civilisation and heritage, a social norm of her existence rather than an anomaly that needed to be explained. Hence, diversity was not only acknowledged, it was seen as being a defining feature of who we are as a people. Consequently, little time was spent on justifying its value for the society. However, in the new framework of democracy and the accompanying commitment to equality, issues of difference and diversity received a fresh articulation. The decision to treat all persons as equals meant that persons belonging to different communities must be equally free to pursue their own beliefs and social-cultural practices. The peculiarity of this conception of equality was that it saw individuals as citizens as well as members of different communities—religious, social, and cultural. It also associated freedom to pursue one's own way of life as a condition of equal treatment.

The link between equality and freedom surfaces over and over again in the discussions about difference and diversity. This is an aspect that comes through in the work of Rinku Lamba who examines the writings of two nineteenth century social activists and reformers—Jyotiba Phule and Ranade—both of whom were fighting for the equal treatment of the lower castes who had been excluded and coercively segregated from the rest of society. The manner in which the concerns of freedom and equality came together is particularly important as the struggle for the inclusion of previously excluded populations in post-independence India has almost entirely been in the language of equality and rarely ever linked with the question of freedom. Perhaps this is because of the centrality accorded to the twin categories of group and backwardness/ marginalisation. Eventually what has happened is that freedom as a value has been pushed further in the background, significantly affecting the functioning of democracy. However, this is an issue that must be left aside for the present. What needs nevertheless to be noted is that in India, questions of difference and diversity have in recent times been pegged around the idea of equality and justice rather than equality and freedom. Since freedom figures so infrequently in contemporary discourses on difference and diversity, it is interesting to draw attention to writings that used a vocabulary where self-determination and freedom remain the recurrent motif.

The framework that India adopted to accommodate different kinds of diversities and difference is a question that Sarah Joseph attempts to address in her work. What needs to be mentioned here is that accommodation and protection of difference took many different forms. At the most basic level the Constitution of India assured equal treatment by giving all persons as members of the political community, or as citizens, the same rights to participate in the political process and enjoy the same kinds of civil liberties. This was supplemented by separate and special considerations, and at times, special rights for minorities.

A distinction was made between the communities—religious, linguistic and tribal— with a distinct culture and societal institutions and previously excluded populations like the victims of the practice of untouchability. For treating as equal all religious communities and individuals as members of different religious communities as equal, the Constitution provided all persons the liberty to profess, propagate and practice their religion (Article 25). After protecting religious liberty of all individuals, the Constitution attended to the concerns of religious communities and gave them the right to set up their own charitable trusts and religious institutions (Articles 26). Religious minorities received additional attention and were given the right to establish their own educational institutions for promoting their culture and language (Articles 29 and 30).

These rights were intended to accommodate the concerns of different religious communities, to protect their liberty and to allay the fears of the minorities. On the positive side, religious communities were being assured that they will all be treated as equal. This was supplemented by the tacit agreement that the Indian state will have no religion of its own and it will continue with community-based personal laws. These were fairly strong assurances and they provided each religious community with a certain amount of space and autonomy to function vis-à-vis each other, and to some extent, even the state. Paradoxically however, enough of these provisions also envisaged a role for the state, thereby entailing a great responsibility upon the state to ensure equal treatment to all the religious communities.

The state was expected to fulfill this expectation by acknowledging the plurality of religious practices. That is, recognising that people of different religions do things differently: they hold different things sacred, dress differently, observe different practices, and at times, exhibit different visible markers of their identity on their person. In addition to accommodating such differences, the state was obliged to facilitate the observance of religious practices; to see, for instances, that members of a religious community could take the dip in the Ganges on the occasion of the Kumbh Mela or take out a procession though streets and public places. Religious and cultural diversities of this kind were to be acknowledged and accommodated, as part and parcel of the commitment to treat all religious communities, or persons as members of different communities, as equal. If we look back at the functioning of the Indian state since independence, it is evident that it has been remarkably successful in accommodating diversity in such a manner. In fact, the ease with which it has been done can only be appreciated and understood fully when we look at the challenges that are currently being faced in this regard by many liberal democracies in the West.

Besides accommodating the practice of diversity in the public arena, the Indian state was also expected to support and facilitate the functioning of religious and other minority educational institutions—institutions that were all equally eligible to receive funds from the state. Again, the record of the last six decades shows that minority educational institutions have grown and flourished. A commitment to secularism has not stood in the way of religious communities and groups establishing their own educational institutions. In fact, the number and scope of these minority institutions, of all religions, has steadily grown. Although the initial justification for setting up these institutions was to provide space to communities to promote their language and culture, the state has allowed minority educational institutions at all levels of education, from primary schools to professional colleges offering degrees in medicine and engineering—areas hardly involved in the promotion of any given language or culture of the identified minorities. The Supreme Court too has, in its interpretation of the relevant clauses, emphasised the phrase 'can impart education of their choice' (Article 29) rather than the initial rationale of promoting the language and culture of the minority. These are ways in which the state has not only accommodated religious differences, but also has given space to different religious communities to be visible participants in the public domain.

The Supreme Court of India has over the years supported this reading of the Constitution. In its judgment on the Gowda Saraswat Brahmin case, it stated that while religious rituals and norms could be used to decide who performs what ceremony, in principle no temple (recognised as a place of Hindu worship) could close its doors to members of the lower caste. Here, and in several other instances, the framework of equality brought in the state and allowed it to regulate and intervene in the functioning of religious institutions.

The Constitution has allowed state intervention in secular aspects of religious institutions: the state could regulate financial and administrative functioning of religious institutions, even those that were set up as trusts and recognised as religious bodies. The concern for equality further expanded the space for the state's involvement and intervention in matters of religion. At one level, the right to religious practice given to all communities to live in accordance with their own way of life allowed the state to be involved in facilitating the observance of these practices; in ensuring that no hindrances are placed by others in society to the observance of these practices; and above all, seeing that the collective performance of religious practices does not create conflict and violent confrontations between communities.

Besides being involved in religious matters in this way, the concern for equality—equality of women and lower castes—allowed for a stronger kind of intervention by the state in religion. To promote equality for women, some legislation had already been initiated under the colonial rule; there was a law against the practice of sati and campaigns against child marriage and the regime of prohibitions against widow remarriage. Although the Constitution protected the space for such interventions in the future, in post-independence India, the state has shown a reluctance to legislate a uniform civil code to ensure equality for women, even though a commitment in this regard was made in the Constitution in the form of the Directive Principles of State Policy.

This issue of equality and the uniform civil code was taken up by V SriRanjani who shows that even in the Constituent Assembly, when discussions on the uniform civil code took place, there was a strong sentiment that that space should remain for the continued existence of community personal laws, and the latter be done away with only with the consent of the communities. There was thus, a continuous tension between two dimensions of the concern for equality: if the equality of all religions (and the accompanying assurance to minorities that they will be treated as equal) pushed in one direction, equality for women pushed in another. Eventually, the balance tilted in favour of religious communities and the minorities. The uniform civil code remained a desired goal rather than a matter of right; more importantly, the individual was placed squarely in one religious community or another. SriRanjani underscores this point through her analysis of the Constituent Assembly debates and subsequent judicial pronouncements. As she argues, the rights eventually accorded by the Constitution voiced the sentiments of the religious communities and, at best, those of believers—people who placed themselves in one community or another. No room remained for the agnostics or the atheists.

The individual was wedged between two actors—religious community and the state. On the one hand, religious liberty, particularly the liberty to observe the practices of a community, pushed in the direction of accommodating the concerns of communities, the majority and the minorities; on the other, the state became the arbiter of disputes between communities. The latter placed some constraints upon the exercise of religious liberty as claims of religious belief and practice were open to state scrutiny. Thus, even as community concerns were accommodated and religious diversity was recognised, religion became a matter of constant public concern, scrutiny and state intervention. Over the years the state has used this space for intervention in many different ways, often dictated by political compulsions and interests rather than any principle. It has intervened to oversee and sometimes, administer trusts of major Hindu temples, reform the Hindu personal laws to make them more gender just and ban books and films that seem to offend the sentiments of religious communities. The courts have also used the available space to interpret religious texts so as to determine what is or is not 'essential' to the practice of a religion.

At the same time the state has refrained from intervening in the personal laws of the minorities, leaving it to the communities to deliberate and change their personal laws at their own pace. It has often also overlooked 'inflammatory' political speeches targeting some communities and failed to hold perpetrators of communal violence (the single most important impediment to communal harmony) accountable. In the absence of a strong affirmation of the primacy of the individual over the community, the state has come to exercise a great deal of power—power to negotiate with religious communities, power to take up certain religious and cultural concerns voiced by the members of a community. Only the individual lost out and remained vulnerable to the influence and power exercised by the community and the state.

Rohit Wanchoo points to this reality. He notes that in India, as also in many other parts of South Asia, the category of the group was accepted more readily. But why did this happen? Why did the political leadership that had itself fought the colonial administration and demanded basic civil liberties and political rights, allow the individual to be submerged into the community, whether it was the cultural religious community or the political community? Part of the explanation is that the colonial rule had solidified religious community identities through its policies of community-based electorates and representation. This is an aspect that Wanchoo elucidates in detail. One might add to it another element, the fact of religious and cultural communities becoming the rallying point or a source of solace and solidarity for the people of India in the public arena. As the locus of collective life, communities became vehicles of political mobilisations and they came also to articulate their own concerns and fears, many of which were propped up by the policies initiated by the British Raj. It is not, therefore, surprising that religious communities came to occupy a central positions; the leadership of these communities was in a position to bargain and see that their main concerns and interests were factored in, if not accommodated. But was the protection granted to religious and cultural practices enough for ensuring the equality of all religious communities?

Clearly it was not. Even though religious diversity was acknowledged and recognised, minority religious communities did not always feel secure. Sporadic but repeated inter-community riots and violence left members of different communities vulnerable as their lives, family and property remained insecure. The state, which was only too keen to support religious community practices, remained rather slow and reluctant to intervene in such incidents of communal violence. At any rate, it remained ineffective in checking the repeated occurrence of such episodes of inter-community riots. Although judicial commissions of inquiry were set up after riots, the perpetrators of violence remained by and large unpunished.

Repeated incidents of violence and systematic targeting of a community created a new form of ghettoisation, as community members relocated themselves and began to live in close proximity of one another for the sake of personal safety and security. Accommodation of religious diversity was expected to make minority communities secure and confident in the larger society—an element that would eventually allow them to critically engage with their own community practices. Inter-community violence however, undermined just this. As a consequence community solidarities have strengthened, but not necessarily in the space for internal reflection. This has adversely affected the claims and struggles for the equal status of women in almost all communities.

At the time of independence, it was assumed that accommodation of religious diversity would allow a category of the citizenry to remain more or less undifferentiated in the political and public arena. Religious identities would be recognised and accommodated in society and in the public arena, but the state would not make distinctions between individuals on grounds of their religious identity. As citizens all would be, in a matter of speaking, the same. There was a greater degree of agreement on this at the time of independence and this is why it was relatively easy for the Sub-Committee on Minorities to withdraw its claims for separate representation. However, in post-independence India, the differences in the experiences of communities has created fissures and even though separate representation is not a strong demand, the decision of the Constitution-makers to not consider separate representation for religious communities, has become a subject of debate. More importantly, minority communities, often, particularly when they are concentrated in a given space, have started to use their vote as a collective weapon to give themselves a de facto voice in the political process.

Political parties too tend to treat minority populations as a block vote and in an attempt to woo them attend to their demand—mostly religious and cultural. This is to some extent changing as development related concerns (namely, issues of education, employment in public institutions, health care, and other such issues) are being raised and the government is trying to accommodate the demands of minorities by looking at their position in society. Perhaps the most striking example in India of this in recent times is the Sachar Committee Report.

The accommodation of linguistic diversity through a framework of recognition and power-sharing within the framework of federalism revealed the limits of pursuing policies that are aimed simply at valuing diversity. Policies, at all times, need to be devised with a view to minimising disadvantages rather than protecting diversity. Diversity is valuable, but policies aimed at protecting it have to be tempered by a regime of rights for internal minorities. For without it, majoritarianism could easily take over and undermine the rights of minorities as equal citizens.

How should independent India deal with tribal communities and cultures that lived in the Northeast and in many other parts of the country? Should all tribal cultures be protected in a way similar to the hill tribes of the Northeast? Should the special policies initiated by the British continue, at least in the Northeast? Should tribal communities have the right to continue with their own cultural way of life, their own customary laws and social practices? These questions engaged the political leadership of the country at the time of independence. There was a strong opinion, expressed by Verrier Elwin among others, which advocated protective isolation of the tribal communities, particularly those living in the Northeast, so that they are not adversely affected by the laws, that are by and large unsuitable for them, and can continue with modes of organisation that are distinct to them.

Eventually this thinking was not accepted in its entirety. There were several reasons for this. India had many tribal communities (some estimates placed the number at four hundred) with different forms of social organisation, economic systems and degree of isolation or integration with the other communities in the region. While some had chosen to live by their own social and economic practices, others had been pushed out into remote areas and had, as a consequence, lost out. They were, in comparison to other groups in the area, lagging behind in every respect. A section of the leadership felt that these tribal communities could not be left to themselves. The Indian state had an obligation to provide basic infrastructure and other necessary facilities to all the people, and this included the tribal communities. In regions like the Northeast, which enjoyed special protection under the colonial rule, special provisions could be made to protect them from the influx of external members as they may exploit the resources on which these communities depended.

Both kinds of concerns, with regard to the tribal communities, were ultimately accommodated by avoiding the extremes of complete segregation on the one side and assimilation on the other. The Constitution tried to integrate these communities and include them without compelling them to conform to the norms of the outside world. Accordingly, a twofold arrangement was accepted. All tribal communities, identified as the scheduled tribes, were given separate representation, in proportion to their size in the total population, in legislative bodies. At the same time, Inner Line policies continued in those areas of the Northeast where the tribal communities were territorially concentrated and which had previously enjoyed this status. In addition to these provisions, under the Sixth Schedule of the Constitution, Autonomous District Councils were set up in identified hill regions of the state of Assam to give tribal communities some degree of autonomy to govern themselves and manage their own pattern of social and economic life. Autonomous District Councils were a sub-federal institutional arrangement involving tribal village councils in the deliberation of such crucial elements as use of land, jhum cultivation and regulation of water resources, canals, and other such elements. In other words, the provisions of the Sixth Schedule gave tribal communities some degree of autonomy to govern themselves on matters that concerned them deeply.

The instrumentations of self-governance were further strengthened in the post-independence period when separate States were carved out of the State of Assam. While the State of Nagaland was formed in 1956, four new States were formed in 1972—Arunachal Pradesh, Meghalaya along with Tripura and Manipur, which were previously Union Territories. Special provisions were made for Nagaland, and subsequently, Mizoram under Article 371 A and G respectively. Through the provisions of this Article, religious and social practices as well as the customary law of these communities was protected. These structures of asymmetric federalism that were created to accommodate several tribal communities in the Northeast resemble the institutional arrangements advocated by many theorists of multiculturalism to accommodate minority populations. The question, however, is whether these arrangements have been successful in protecting the minorities? The framework of self-governance devised in India for tribal communities had some space for external interventions, particularly interventions by the central government. The state could acquire land for development purposes—a provision that has been used, and some would say misused—to take over tribal lands. The laws of the Union prevailed even in the case of conserved forests. Thus, on the crucial issue of land, even as the community rights were recognised, certain exemptions existed, and over the years this has been the subject of considerable friction and conflict with the central government.

The case of tribal cultures and communities throws up another problem. While theories of multiculturalism take tribal cultures to constitute a typical instance of communities with a distinct culture and identity (and it is for them particularly that they suggest accommodation through some form of right to self-governance), what is often overlooked is the stand of the tribal communities in history. While some aspects of social and economic life of tribal communities in the Northeast continue to be quite distinct, other aspects of their cultural existence, such as language and religion, have changed significantly. Under colonial rule the missionaries had a strong presence in this region. They created educational, social and religious institutions which continue to play a crucial role. So even though identities are often constructed in the language of cultural difference and distinctiveness, the influence of the Church, and more specifically the creation of a new class—one that is different from the traditional elite—cannot be discounted. In fact, in some regions it has created sources of internal conflict that cannot be adequately dealt with through the institutions created for purposes of self-governance.

If we look at the Indian experience in its totality, perhaps the single most important lesson that emerges is that accommodation is an on-going process. No doubt multiculturalism is the essence of Indian culture but to maintain a balance in a multi-lingual, multi-ethnic and multi-religious country is not an easy task. India, at present, has about a billion Hindus, 150 million Muslims (the second largest Muslim population in the world), 24 million Christians and 24 million Sikhs. In addition to English and Hindi, they speak 20 major languages and some 22,000 dialects. This huge population is further sliced and diced by caste and region. The four major castes have 4,000 sub-castes. There are also many tribal groups with distinct ethnic and cultural identities. Each of India's twentynine States has its own centuries-old flourishing culture with further internal diversities. There are many challenges to multicultural India like poverty, illiteracy, terrorism (internal as well as external), regionalism, corruption etc. which need to be tackled amicably without differentiating on grounds of religion, language and ethnicity.

There are many Western scholars who have criticised multiculturalism. In English Canada, the noted critics of multiculturalism include such scholars as Kenneth Mc Roberts, Neil Bissoondath and Daniel Stoffman. In his, *Selling Illusion: The cult of Multiculturalism in Canada*, the Trindad and Tobago-born Bissoondath argues that official multiculturalism limits the freedom of minority members by confining them to cultural and geographic ghettos. He further says that cultures are very complex and must be transmitted through close family and kin relations. To him, the government view of cultures as being all about festivals and cuisine is crude over-simplification, which leads to easy stereotyping.

Daniel Stoffman, however, raises serious questions about the policy behind Canadian multiculturalism and stresses the argument that multiculturalism works better in theory than in practice.

One of the earliest critics of multiculturalism in Australia was historian Geoffrey Blainey, who warned that it threatened to transform Australia into a 'cluster of tribes'. In his 1984 book, *All for Australia*, Blainey criticised multiculturalism for tending to 'emphasise the rights of ethnic minorities at the expense of the majority of Australians' and also for tending to be 'anti-British' even though 'people from the United Kingdom and Ireland form the dominant class of pre-war immigrants and the largest single group of post-war immigrants'. According to Blainey, such a policy with its 'emphasis on what is different and on the rights of the new minority rather than old majority', was unnecessarily creating division and threatened national cohesion. He argued that 'evidence is clear that many multicultural societies have failed and that the human cost of the failure has been high' and warned that 'we should think very carefully about the perils of converting Australia into a giant multicultural laboratory for the assumed benefit of the peoples of world'.

In 1999, the legal philosopher Paul Cliteur attacked multiculturalism in his book, *The Philosophy of Human Rights*. Cliteur sees non-Western cultures not as merely different but as anachronistic. He sees multiculturalism primarily as an unacceptable ideology (of cultural relativism), which would lead to acceptance of barbaric practices, including those brought to the Western world by immigrants. Cliteur lists infanticide, torture, slavery, oppression of women, homophobia, racism, anti-Semitism, gangsterism, female genital cutting, discrimination by immigrants, Sati and the death penalty and compares multiculturalism being as morally unacceptable as Auschwitze, Stalin, Polpot and the Ku Klux Klan.

Multiculturalism is difficult to define. Andrew Heywood distinguishes between two forms of multiculturalism when he writes that 'the term "multiculturalism" has been used in a variety of ways, both descriptive and normative. As a descriptive term, it has been taken to refer to cultural diversity… As a normative term, multiculturalism implies a positive endorsement, even celebration, of communal diversity, typically based on either the right of different groups to respect and recognition, or to the alleged benefits to the larger society of moral and cultural diversity'.

Critics of multiculturalism often debate whether the multicultural ideal of benignly co-existing cultures that interrelate and influence one another, and yet remain distinct, is sustainable, paradoxical or even desirable. It is argued that nation states that would previously have been synonymous with a distinctive cultural identity lose out to enforced multiculturalism and that this ultimately erodes the host nation's distinct culture.

Harvard professor of political science Robert D Putnam conducted a nearly decade-long study on how multiculturalism affects social trust. He surveyed 26,200 people in forty American communities, finding that when the data were adjusted for class, income and other factors, the more racially diverse a community was, the greater the loss of trust. People in diverse communities 'don't trust the local mayor, they don't trust the local paper, they don't trust other people and they don't trust institutions' wrote Putnam. In the presence of such ethnic diversity, Putnam maintains that 'We hunker down. We act like turtles. The effect of diversity is worse than had been imagined. And it's not just that we don't trust people who are not like us. In diverse communities, we don't trust people who do look like us'.

Ethnologist Frank Salter writes: Relatively homogeneous societies invest more in public goods, indicating a higher level of public altruism. For example, the degree of ethnic homogeneity correlates with the government's share of gross domestic product as well as the average wealth of citizens. Case studies of the United States, Africa and South-East Asia find that multi-ethnic societies are less charitable and less able to cooperate to develop public infrastructure. Moscow beggars receive more gifts from fellow ethnics than from other ethnics. A recent multi-city study of municipal spending on public goods in the United States found that ethnically or racially diverse cities spend a smaller portion of their budgets and less per capita on public services than do the more homogenous cities.

Dick Lamm, former three-term Democratic governor of the US State of Colorado, wrote in his essay, 'I have a plan to destroy America': Diverse peoples worldwide are mostly engaged in hating each other—that is, when they are not killing each other. A diverse, peaceful, or stable society is against most historical precedent.

There have been many criticisms of official multiculturalism from both the Left and the Right. Criticisms have been voiced from a variety of perspectives including the democratic, feminist, capitalist, nationalist, chauvinist, separatist, racialist and xenophobic perspectives. Critics charge that one of the dangers of pursuing multicultural social policies is that social integration and cultural assimilation can be held back. This can potentially encourage economic disparities and an exclusion of minority groups from mainstream politics. However, policies that facilitate racially proportional representation in the districts and the accommodation of bilingualism in the voting booth are claimed to do precisely the opposite: they may encourage political participation and increase minority representation in local and national political life. On the other hand, democracy can only work if there is a public debate. The fragmentation of society in several linguistic factions would ultimately lead to the loss of public debate and democratic unity. It is exactly this fragmentation that makes many doubt the viability of a democratic European Union.

One of the most forceful critics of multiculturalism was Ayn Rand, who feared the world-wide ethnic revival of the late 1960s would lead to an ethnic Balkanization, destructive to modern industrial societies. Her philosophy considered multiculturalism and monoculturalism to be culturally determinist collectivism (ie. that individual human beings have no free choice in how they act and are conditioned irreversibly by society). Philosophically, Rand rejected this form of collectivism on the grounds that: 1) it undermines the concept of free will, and 2) the human mind (according to her philosophy) is a tabula rasa at birth. But it is also true that the human mind is born without any culture, and that, nearly all societies attempt to condition their citizens culturally. What is distinct about multiculturalism is the assertion of an identity, aside from the nationally imposed identity, allowing for individuals within minority cultures to exercise more free choice than they otherwise would in a universalist society.

In her 1999 essay, later expanded into an anthology, 'Is Multiculturalism Bad for Women?' feminist and political theorist Susan M Okin argues that a concern for the preservation of cultural diversity should not overshadow the discriminatory nature of gender roles in many traditional minority cultures, that, at the very least, 'culture' should not be used as an excuse for rolling back the women's rights movement. Literature by prominent minority women authors such as Toni Morrison and Maxine Hong Kingston can be both critiques of the traditional majority and minority cultures, as well as the articulation of a multicultural vision.

One of the most articulate critics of multiculturalism is the political theorist Brian Barry who in his 2002 book, *Culture and Equality: An Egalitarian Critique of Multiculturalism,* voices the liberal Left argument that some forms of multiculturalism can divide people when they need to unite in order to fight for social justice.

Another more recent and conservative criticism, based largely upon the Nordic and Canadian experience, is presented by the administrative scientist Gunnar KA Njalsson who views multiculturalism as a utopian ideology with a simplistic and overly optimistic view of human nature, the same weakness he attributes to communism, anarchism, and many strains of liberalism. Some variants of multiculturalism, he believes, may equip non-egalitarian cultural groups with power and influence. This, in turn, may alter the values system of the larger society. This realist criticism of multiculturalism maintains that in Canada, Australia, New Zealand and the US, multiculturalism may aggravate a situation where old-stock families do not consider themselves as English, French, Scandinavian etc. while newer arrivals can claim two or more national identities. This is not borne out by historical records. Fears that minorities in the US or Canada would have divided loyalties have been a canard, for example, to intern Japanese-Americans during World War II. In fact, native-born ethnic and religious minorities in North America have high rates of out-marriage and participate fully in activities in their country of birth. They tend to identify culturally, not politically, with the home of their forbearers. The potential struggle to alter societal values is a concern mainly in European countries with monocultural policies, where religious and ethnic minorities are politically and socially marginalised—a condition that can reinforce fundamentalist strains in any culture.

If, however, cultural communities do not support the basic values of multiculturalism, such as the pluralistic freedom of religion, and are merely interested in their particular exertion of that right, the multicultural system can blow itself up; orthodox Muslims in Europe may not accept freedom of religion when it comes to non-Muslims, but do call upon that freedom when they wish to build a mosque or when they desire to wear headscarves in public. Multiculturalism, thus, fails to consolidate its own values.

Anti-racists of the Marxist persuasion view white supremacy as a system that stems from an internalised form of imperialism—that is, exploitation of other races for the accumulation of capital in the homeland. When racism is so analysed—as a problem of political economy—the logical response is to tear down its structural foundations, meaning thereby, imperialism. Multiculturalism stands in the way of such agenda because it implies that the grounds for racism in society are not economic, but cultural or ideological. Ironically, a contradictory view asserts that the pursuit of 'particularist multiculturalism' is somehow 'apartheid' by another name.

The relationship between multiculturalism and Islam is an important aspect in the overall debate on the soundness of the modern doctrine of multiculturalism, given that many Muslims are culturally opposed to the idea of nationalism, and often prefer to identify themselves as Muslims instead of Egyptians, Iranians, Moroccans, Pakistanis etc. The need of the hour, therefore, is to broaden our outlook as well as try and understand each other's feelings.

India is uniquely placed to assimilate all this diversity without a blip of discontent. The Indian government has adopted aggressive assimilation policies around recognition of diverse culture and language and inserted the word 'secular' in the preamble of the Constitution in the seventies. Many Indian States have recognised Urdu, spoken by the minorities and the Hindus as well in some parts of the country, as their second official language.

The Indian government had created the ministry of minority affairs to ensure a more focused approach towards issues relating to the minorities. It facilitates the formulation of overall policy and planning, coordination, evaluation and review of regulatory framework and development programmes for the benefit of the minority communities in the country.

India's history has been the saga of assimilation of Persian and Islamic culture with the local ancient culture when Muslim and Persian aggressors invaded the country and stayed as rulers. The historical monuments of Muslim and Mughal periods are unique example of fusion of Persian and local architecture. Urdu language is the perfect example of assimilation of Persian and the local dialect, Awadhi spoken in Uttar Pradesh.

In India, problem of immigrants is limited to bordering areas of Bangladesh and the north-east and in Tamil Nadu in the south while in the rest of the country, the longstanding minority groups coexist with the majority groups. Conflicts have erupted in some areas where conversions have taken place but preventing inter-faith riots has been the major concerns of the central and State governments.

Since independence, the successive governments in India have been seized with two issues in particular, pertaining to Muslims-personal law and uniform civil code.

The Constituent Assembly debates saw two opposing views regarding personal laws. One view was that the state should have nothing to do with personal laws. This view was prominently represented by Mehboob Ali Baig and MH Mohani. Apart from the privacy argument, it was felt that personal laws are divinely-ordained and, therefore, a human agency had no scope in changing it. The second view felt that the state had a positive though limited role to play. It was felt that the state should protect personal laws to uphold its secular character and to protect minority communities from the tyranny of the majority. This view was voiced by Pocker Sahib Bahadur and Mohd Ismail Sahib.

Regarding intervention in personal laws, suggestions ranged from reforming personal laws to replacing it by a Uniform Civil Code. Social reform and welfare was given as the main reason for reforming personal laws. Pocker Sahib admitted that he had received representations from various organisations, including those of Hindus, which characterised the provision relating to the common civil code as tyrannical. While state recognition to personal laws as laws that protect religious practices, especially that of the minority community, was sought, the apprehension with state intervention to reform personal laws was that such intervention may re-form religion in the light of such laws. The argument that religion be viewed as distinct from personal laws seemed to have threatened to render as irrelevant the dominant understanding of personal laws as laws of a religious community.

Indeed, calling upon the state to protect these laws by invoking the value of secularism underlined the assumption of personal laws as laws pertaining to a certain religious and cultural community. Extending the same assumption, laws that referred to the same civil content as personal laws without any religious references, came to be viewed as the 'other' of the personal laws in the Constituent Assembly debates. This 'other' was discussed under the label of the Uniform Civil Code.

The Uniform Civil Code, numbered as Article 35 in the Constituent Assembly debates, was worded as follows: The state shall endeavour to secure for citizens a uniform civil code throughout the territory of India. While the term 'citizen' was mentioned in Article 35, the debates in the Constituent Assembly did not focus on the term.

For those, not in favour of Article 35, the presence of a Uniform Civil Code was tolerated only as an option. This is clear from the amendment proposed by Mohammad Ismail Sahib who moved that the following proviso be added to Article 35: 'Provided that any group, section of community of people shall not be obliged to give up its own personal law in case it has such a law.' According to him, 'if anything is done affecting the personal laws, it will be tantamount to interference with the way of life of those people who have been observing these laws for generations and ages. This secular state which we are trying to create should not do anything to interfere with the way of life and religion of the people'.

Apprehending changes in personal laws in the implementation of the Uniform Civil Code, Naziruddin Ahmed insisted that any change in personal laws should be only with the consent of the community. It is to this effect that he moved the following amendment: 'That to article 35, the following proviso be added, namely – Provided that the personal law of any community which has been guaranteed by the state shall not be changed except with the previous approval of the community ascertained in such a manner as the Union Legislature may determine by law'. In other words, the presence of a Uniform Civil Code will be tolerated only if it will not override community laws and religious practices. In supporting Mohammad Ismail Sahib's amendment, B Pocker Sahib Bahadur made a case of understanding the Civil Code as a law that is exclusive of religion, not in the sense of overriding it but in the sense of having no right to interfere with religious practices and beliefs. He stated: 'In the first place, I would like to know the real intention with which this clause has been introduced. If the words 'Civil Code' are intended only to apply to matters of procedure like the Civil Procedure Code and such other laws which are uniform so far India is concerned at present well, nobody has any objection to that, but the various Civil Courts Acts in the various provinces in the country have secured for each community the right to follow their personal laws as regards marriage, inheritance, divorce, etc. But if it is intended that the aspiration of the state should be to override all these provisions and to have uniformity of law imposed upon the whole people on these matters which are dealt with by the Civil Courts Acts in the various provinces, well, I would only say, Sir, that is a tyrannous provision which ought not to be tolerated…'

An equal, if not a greater reason for apprehension than the civil aspects of the Uniform Civil Code supervening over religious practices of personal laws was such that a code may have ended up imposing the personal law of the majority community over the minority communities. Arguing for the rights of minorities, B Pocker Sahib Bahadur expressed the apprehension that 'if the framers of this article say that even the majority community is in uniform support of this… it is not so. Even assuming that the majority community is of this view, I say, it has to be condemned and it ought not to be allowed, because, in a democracy, as I take it, it is the duty of the majority to secure the sacred rights of every minority. It is a misnomer to call it a democracy if the majority rides rough-shod over the rights of the minorities. It is not a democracy at all, it is tyranny'.

The proposed amendments and views to qualify the wording of Article 35 can be grouped in the following categories:-

1. Apprehension that the enforcement of the Uniform Civil Code will result in forced assimilation as people may be forced to give up their personal laws.
2. A secular state should not interfere with the way of life and religion of the people.

3. The community needs to be assured that there will be no interference in the personal law of the community except with the prior approval of the community.

4. The Uniform Civil Code should be restricted within the ambit of property, contract, evidence etc. It should not have a supervening effect over personal laws.

5. The Uniform Civil Code may mean taking the law of one particular community as standard and, thereby discriminate against other communities.

Stressing on the term 'uniform' in India's Uniform Civil Code, KM Munshi justified its presence to 'unify and consolidate the nation by every means without interfering with religious practices.' Non-interference with religious practices for KM Munshi was to be attained by separating religion from personal law. Arguing for such a separation he stated, 'if however, the religious practices in the past have been so construed as to cover the whole field of life, we have reached a point where we must put our foot down and say that these matters are not religion, they are purely matters for secular legislation. This is what is emphasized by this article'.

He further defended it as not being tyrannical to the minority communities by observing that he was aware that many, among the majority community, also were not happy with the idea of a Uniform Civil Code. 'They feel that the personal law of inheritance, succession etc. is really a part of their religion. If that were so, you can never give, for instance, equality to women. But you have already passed a fundamental right to that effect and you have an article here which says that there should be no discrimination against sex. Look at Hindu Law; you get any amount of discrimination against women; and if that is part of Hindu religion or Hindu religious practice, you cannot pass a single law which would elevate the position of Hindu women to that of men. Therefore, there is no reason why there should not be a civil code throughout the territory of India.'

Addressing the apprehension that the Uniform Civil Code may end up imposing the practices of the majority Hindu community over the minority communities, Sir Alladi Krishnaswami Aiyyar defended the Uniform Civil Code to facilitate a unified nation in a democratic whole in the following manner: The idea is that differential systems of inheritance and other matters are some of the factors which contribute to the differences among the different peoples of India. What it aims at is to try to arrive at a common measure of agreement in regard these matters. It is not as if one legal system is not influencing or is being influenced by another legal system. In very many matters today the sponsors of the Hindu Code have taken a lead, not from Hindu Law alone, but from other systems also. Similarly, the Succession Act has drawn upon both the Roman and the English systems. Therefore, no system can be self-contained, if it is to have in it the elements of growth. Our ancients did not think of a unified nation to be welded into a democratic whole.

A similar reason was echoed by Minoo Masani who saw the Uniform Civil Code as a tool to abolish differences in personal law by which it would 'get rid of these watertight compartments… which keep the nation divided'.

Arguments in support of the Uniform Civil Code can be summed up as follows:

1. Need to unify laws that help unify the country as a secular state
2. Need to divorce religion from the rights of citizens even if it goes contrary to laws of the Hindus who constitute majority community
3. If personal laws are to be given priority, equality of women can never be attained. That will be a violation of the fundamental right of gender equality
4. The Uniform Civil Code is an attempt to have a common measure of agreement to constitute a democratic whole.

The debates indicate that arguments on personal laws oscillated between seeking legal recognition of religious practices of the community and apprehensions of state intervention in religious practices. On the other hand, debates on the Uniform Civil Code swung from invoking the need to unify a nascent nation as a secular state and implement ideas of social reform to the fear of being forced to give up religious practices and/or being subjected to the tyranny of the majority community. What's noticeable is that in its absence the choice of the individual never appears as a factor to be considered. This is so even when the term 'citizen' in Article 35 found a place in the Constituent Assembly debates.

The state, which sustains multiple numbers of ethnic groups within its boundary, is inclined, more often than not, to fabricate ethnic conflicts. Some may be in the form of majority-minority conflict, and in some contexts, it may be in the form of inter-minority scuffle. The force of cultural misrecognition was so strong that in the case of Meghalaya, that even the culturally different groups combined to fight for a common territory outside the domain of the majority domination. This was perhaps the most important reason for the tribes of Meghalaya to come together to demand a common state.

Thus, in multi-ethnic or multinational societies, giving equal respect and concern to all groups should be a worthy goal. We cannot neglect the values of 'multiculturalism' and its insights are important for democratic societies. We need to envisage a society, which offers equal opportunities and an environment conducive to peaceful co-existence of various groups within the same territory.

Mechanisms for creating such a society should be prepared on the basis of three interrelated principles. We need to take the following principles seriously because recognition through group rights is important, but since all demands cannot be fulfilled, there should be a certain basis or principles on which a particular demand or right, be accepted:

i. Survival of culture,
ii. Promotion of basic democratic values; and
iii. Equality between groups.

Survival of culture: It is a known fact that multiculturalism cherishes cultural diversity. Therefore, giving due recognition to diverse cultures is a precondition for the creation of space for equal citizenship. Contemporary liberals argue that human beings are culturally embedded in the sense that 'they grew up and live within a culturally structured world and organised their lives and social relations in terms of a culturally defined system of meaning and significance'. It would not be wrong to say that recognition of others' culture will also benefit our own culture. For different cultures represent different systems of meaning and a vision of the good life. Since each realises a limited range of human capacities and emotions, and groups encompass only a part of the totality of human existence, it needs other cultures to help it understands itself better, expand its intellectual and moral horizon, stretch its imagination, save it from narcissism, guard it against the temptation to absolutise itself.

In conflict situations, efforts have to be made to tame aggravation of sense of identity through communication with elders and mediators. The role of rational elements of the conflicting communities along with the state machinery will come into play in thwarting the situation from escalating. The success of such strategy depends on the context, perspective, and how identity relates to the situation.

Gurpeet Mahajan is of the opinion that community identity and public domain are two inseparable values. She writes, 'Community membership influences their predicaments and structures the way other people relate to them. As such, cultural identities are important.' Thus, any kind of multicultural policy should aim at preserving cultures rather than destroying them. In other words, we should recognise the importance of cultural values not only in self-development of individuals but also in creating conditions for equal citizenship. Any policy that is detrimental to the survival of cultures should not be accepted.

Promotion of basic democratic values: Even though culture is important and its survival necessary, the preservation of cultural values should not be done at the cost of basic democratic values. Both are equally important and therefore, there is a need of qualification of one value by the other. As we have seen, one of the most important factors behind the criticism of group rights is the possible violation of basic human rights. In many instances, there is violation of basic democratic values in the name of preserving culture. Preserving cultural practices may well become another way of violating their rights and consenting to patriarchal domination of society. Group rights may sometimes assist in the continued subordination of individual members of a particular community. In this way, unqualified culture can be a tool of cultural practices which undermines the basic freedom of individuals. It will be wrong to impose certain cultural practices upon individual members against their will. Thus, all multicultural policies should be based on both, individual values or rights as well as cultural values.

Equality between groups: What we are seeking today is not unequal treatment but equal treatment of all communities within a multi-nation state. Thus, any kind of multicultural policy which is devoid of the value of equality should not be accepted. This appears simple but we often forget the value of according equal treatment to all. One culture cannot be promoted at the cost of another culture. If one culture permits some practices which actually limit the interests of the other, then there is no morality in promoting such a practice. For example, forced conversions, not willful acceptance of other faith, wanton destruction of many religious places, massacres of believers of other faiths are some practices that needed to be tackled with iron hands.

Of course, there may be conditions in which certain special treatments for a particular cultural community are necessary. This kind of treatment can be resorted to when the community in question is far behind the others in terms of its development. In such arrangements, freedom of some individuals may be limited. But it is justified because it is necessary to create 'equality' between groups. The stress therefore, should be on the promotion of equality between groups.

The ultimate aim of a liberal democratic state is to make these principles complementary and to develop a way in which all these principles can coexist. A policy devoid of any one of these principles should not be accepted. There may be difficulties in a negotiating or reconciling these three principles but we will face problems when we think of and put into operation policies that miss out on any of these principles.

Looking into the institutional arrangement in India (particularly in Meghalaya), it is clear that two important values of multicultural policies have been more, or less, fulfilled by granting the minorities autonomy first, in the form of ADCs and later by creating a separate tribal State. On the one hand, it grants recognition to the values of cultures of minority communities. It was perhaps the best option at that point of time for promoting the principle of a 'survival of culture'. On the other hand, by creating a separate State, even a 'tribal State', it tries to preserve the basic democratic values of a liberal polity. Thus, it also takes care of another principle of multicultural policies namely, basic democratic values.

One may well ask 'when all the groups are given their own space for survival and autonomy and practice and preserve their customs, why should the question about the lack of equal concern be raised?' This happens because of the lack of synchronisation or cooperation between the various cultural groups. Cooperation between two cultural groups is needed for their peaceful coexistence, as the challenges of mutual distrust and animosity still linger on in some vicious minds of both the groups. They can coexist if they are willing to accept their respective faiths as an instrument of peace and human salvation rather than as a conduit through which they can compensate their feelings of inadequacy and pent-up animosity. This invisible line of tension also creates space for self-seeking leaders to politicise small matters that often lead to conflicts.

The state should respect diverse cultures. The respect for diversity implies equal space and opportunity for all cultural communities to sustain themselves. Therefore, remedying minority discrimination entails policies that ensure full and equal membership for all communities within the state. This may even involve special consideration or group rights for minorities who have been the victims of forced assimilation or exclusion. This will create a more integrated society. However, simply granting territorial autonomy will not solve the problems of ethnic conflict in all such contexts. For, assimilation of different groups and ethnic identities require increased economic activities and financial independence of individuals and their groups through state machinery.

This is why the Western model of a multi-nation federation fails in the context of Northeast India. Therefore, besides the existing institutions in the state which take care of the basic democratic values of a liberal society and ensure the value of the 'survival of culture', there should be one more body through which the 'equal concern' of all communities can be taken care of.

In his article 'Multiculturalism and the Self-liquidation of Europe', Robert Tracinski looks for the cause behind recent French riots and identifies it as European multiculturalism. Tracinski's views regarding European multiculturalism can be paraphrased as follows:

1. It draws on the theoretical framework called deconstruction, proposed by Heidegger and de Mann, both of whom had Nazi sympathies and whose philosophies had some commonalities with Nazism.

2. It is same as collectivism, which in its extreme form is the same as inversed Nazi collectivism. European multiculturalism values minority collective identity.

3. It is skeptical (about European heritage) and self-deprecating.

4. It is based on the premise that all cultures are equal, and (ironically) expresses this belief by subordinating European culture to other cultures.

5. In the context of Islam, this translates into self-imposed dhimmitude, because Islam advocates treating non-Muslims as second class people or dhimmis.

6. French Muslims cannot assimilate with a culture that is bent on self-annihilating itself.

7. The French riots are an outcome of years of misguided French tolerance which allowed Muslims to segregate themselves and turn their quarters into no-go zones for non-Muslims.

Kalavai Venkat, in his article 'Is Multiculturalism the cause of the French Riots', said that 'Jews arrived in the Malabar Coast of India. According to the traditions of the Cochin Jews, they arrived there in 72 CE, probably after the Roman destruction of the Jewish temple in Jerusalem. Hindus extended to them generous hospitality and encouraged them to retain their religion and culture. As late as 1550 CE, when the Jews were persecuted in Christian Europe, the Rajah of Cochin refused to fight a battle on Saturday (the day of the Sabbath) because on that day his Jewish soldiers would not fight'. Citing the incident, Nathan Katz (*Who Are the Jews of India?*) writes that, 'Probably India is the only country on earth so civilized, that even in war, out of deference to its esteemed Jewish soldiers, no battles were fought on the Sabbath'.

In European countries, especially where the Muslims ruled, the Jews suffered a lot at the hands of Muslims and their synagogues were destroyed. Currently, anti-Semitism is very strong in several Muslim countries due to Israel-Palestine conflict while hate crimes against Jewish and Hindu people are on the rise in Europe, Russia and Australia.

But in India, the Jews lived peaceably with the Hindus and the Muslims and there has been a great degree of syncretism over the centuries, which has created visible bridges and commonalities among all Indians.

Katz also added that Hindu India encouraged pluralism, as a result of which, every immigrant community such as Syrian Christians, Parsis and Tibetan Buddhists became part of the whole without surrendering their identities.

In India, there is no evidence that Muslims or Christians are seeking to dominate anyone. Unlike the Chinese in Southeast Asia or the Tamils in Sri Lanka, who are often accused by the majoritarian communities of unfair economic and professional dominance, Muslims pose no threat to Hindus in India. The belief that Muslims are growing at a faster pace than the Hindus has been repeatedly disproved by empirical facts and studies. Hence, the Hindus have no reason to feel intimidated by numerical preponderance of the Muslims.

In the past, two proselytising religions—Islam and Christianity—conquered India by force and both openly used their military superiority for evangelical purposes. But they failed in India, as Hindus were the overwhelming majority a thousand years ago and still remain so today. One has only to see what happened in other countries in similar situations to appreciate the difference. They had succeeded in Southeast Asia and Latin America

Prof Katz's words, in the cited book, are very pertinent: 'A crucial distinction between India and the rest of the Diaspora, however, is that in India, acculturation is not paid for in the currency of assimilation. By acculturation I mean fitting comfortably into a society while retaining one's own identity, whereas by assimilation I mean that the loss of that identity is a perceived condition for acceptance'.

Jews returned the compliment. Even though a numerically insignificant minority in India, they would emerge as Indian army generals and best goodwill ambassadors. Here, in the Jewish example, we have a testimony that multiculturalism need not result in alienation of the minority and hostility towards the host, provided the minority respects multiculturalism and strives for excellence as Jews did in India (and everywhere). The same can be said of Hindu immigrants to the West. They do maintain their religion, languages and culture but still become part of the whole and contribute tremendously to Western societies. They don't riot or bomb the tube.

The Nazis were driven by racial hatred. They had nothing but contempt for other cultures and races. Their hate-filled endeavour resulted in The Shoah. Of course, numerous scholars like Goldhagen (*A Moral Reckoning: the Role of the Church in the Holocaust and its Unfulfilled Duty of Repair*) and Carroll (*Constantine's Sword: the Church and the Jews – a History*) have demonstrated that the Nazi hatred was a mere culmination of two thousand years of Church tradition of anti-Semitism, of course with a racist twist. There is also a view that people of Europe grew wary of Jews when the Bolshevik revolution happened as Jews were noticeable in their participation in the Red cause, despite being a minority. Other factors were, of course, present.

Historically, the absence of multiculturalism has led to intolerance as seen in the Christian Bible, where the Jews are portrayed as the Children of the Devil. The Bible, too, made exclusivist claims to the absolute truth. This meant, to those who followed the Church, every other religion was false, and their practitioners devilish. So, as Netanyahu (*The Origins of the Inquisition in Fifteenth Century Spain*) documents, in medieval Christian Europe, even Murranos or Jewish converts to Christianity were suspected of secretly practicing Jewish rituals and persecuted. This tells us that any claims to absolute truth by a dominant group results in unmitigated horror for those who are unimpressed by such claims. (Exclusivism is more pronounced in Judaism than any other religion in the world. While they have no "missionary" programme, they frown upon converts and believe that one must be born of a Jewish mother in order to be recognised as a Jew.)

Multiculturalism thus, is not the problem. The lack of it, coupled with intolerance and exclusivist claims to the truth, is. But multiculturalism also requires that every constituent respects pluralism.

In spite of these criticisms, multiculturalism in India is deeply rooted in her culture. Our cultural heritage gives spiritual energy for its existence in contrast to Western culture, where there is a definite spiritual vacuum. The foundation on which multiculturalism lasts healthy and long firstly, is its true feeling of patriotism. Secondly, national interest should be given much more priority than any individual interest. Thirdly, positive tolerance and a positive belief system as well as universal brotherhood towards each other, is necessary. The main motive of multiculturalism is not 'survival of fittest' but *Surve Bhavantu Sukhinah Sarve Santu Niramayah Sarve Bhadrahipashyantu Ma Kaschit Dukha Bhoag.* It means: May all be happy. May all be healthy. May all experience what is good and let no one suffer.

The main aim of multiculturalism thus is universal brotherhood. As Swami Chidananda Saraswati stressed, 'Work for universal brotherhood and world peace as well as for humanity. Work as though this task depends upon you. Be an instrument of love, harmony and peace'. Iqbal had said somewhere that 'the mystic mode has naught except the inner changes of the heart. The talk of mullah on his creed is merely a piece of fiery art. The poet's song of zeal if bereft, is dead and struck with frost; to outward eyes he seems awake, though in thoughts completely lost'.

According to Jiddu Krishnamurthi, multiculturalism is, 'When you call yourself an Indian, Muslim, Christian, European or anything else, you are being violent. Do you see why it is violent? Because you are separating yourself from the rest of mankind. When you separate yourself by belief, by nationality, or traditions it breeds violence. So a man who is seeking to understand violence does not belong to any country, religion, political party or partial system; he is concerned with the total understanding of mankind'.

The term multiculturalism refers to peaceful coexistence of different racial, cultural and ethnic diversity and advocates a society that prefers equitable status to distinct cultural and religious groups with no one predominating and exploiting the other but encourages harmony of civilization as well as peace and unity.

References

1. *BBC News* UK, 'So what exactly is multiculturalism.htm', interviews by John Cindi.

2. Parekh, Bhikhu; *What is multiculturalism?*

3. Mahajan, Gurpreet, *Rethinking Multiculturalism.*

4. Sen, Amartya, 'The uses and abuses of multiculturalism – Chili and Liberty', the New republic Multiculturalism.htm.

5. Malhoutra, Manmohan, *Multiculturalism: the historical Indian experience East-West Dialogue.*

6. Venkat, Kalavai, 'Is Multiculturalism the cause of French Riots?', 31 January,2008.

7. Sacred space, *The Times of India*, 23rd Jan 2010

8. Taylor, Charles, (2002) *The Multicultural Path*, Sage Publications.

9. Jha, Shefali, (2002),Secularism in the Constitutional Assembly Debates, *Economic and Political Weekly*, No. 30.

10. Kymlicka, Will, (1991), *Liberalism, Community and Culture*, Oxford University Press.

11. Taylor, Charles, (1994) 'The politics of recognition in Amy Gutmann (ed.). *Multiculturalism and the politics of recognition*, Princeton University Press.

12. Phillips, Anne (2007), *Multiculturalism without culture*, Princeton University Press.

13. Madan, TN (1987), 'Secularism in its place: The journal of Asian studies'.

14. Carens, Joseph (2000), *Culture, Community and Citizenship: A contextual exploration of justice as Evenhandedness*, Oxford University Press.

15. Kymlicka, Will, *Multicultural Citizenship.*

16. Young, Iris Marion, 'Polity and Group Difference: A critique of the ideal of universal citizenship', Ethics.

17. Weiner, Myron (1978), *Sons of the soil: Ethics conflict in India*, Princeton University Press.

18. Beteille, Andre (1980), 'On the concept of Tribe', *International Social Science Jjournal*, Vol. XXXVII, No.4.

19. Haimendorf, CF. (1994), *Tribes of India*, Oxford University Press.

20. Kymlicka,Will, *Multi-nation Federalism*.

21. Tagore, Rabindranath, 'Nationalism in India in Fred Dallmayr and GN Devy (eds), *Between tradition and modernity: India's search for identity; A twentieth century Anthology*, Sage Publication.

22. Tagore, Rabindranath, 'The union of cultures' (1921).

23. Mahajan, Gurpreet, 'Responding to identity conflicts: Multiculturalism and the pursuit of peaceful co-existence', *South Asian Journal of Peace Building*, No 3, Vol. 2, winter.

24. Mahajan, Gurpreet, 'Indian Exceptionalism or Indian model: Negotiating cultural diversity and minority rights in a democratic nation state, In multiculturalism in Asia, ed, Will Kymlicka and Baogang He, Oxford University Press, 2005. *Political Theory*, 1984.

26. Kymlicka, Will and Wayne, Norman ed., *Citizenship in Diverse Societies*, Oxford University Press, 2000.

27. Bloomfield David and Reilly Ben, 'Changing nature and conflict management in democracy and Deep conflict options for negotiators', ed. Peter Harris and Ben Reilly, Stockhome: International institute for electoral assistance, 1998.

28. Ted R Gurr, 'Minorities are at risk: a global view of ethnopolitical conflicts', Washington DC: United States Institute of Peace Studies, 1994.

29. Mahajan, Gurpreet, *Identities and rights: aspects of liberal democracy in India*, OUP,1998.

30. Mahajan, Gurpreet, *The Multicultural Path: Issues of diversity and discrimination in democracy*, Sage 2002.

31. Mahajan, Gurpreet, *Religion, community and development: changing contours of politics and polity in India*, Routledge, 2010.

    The public and the private issues of Democratic citizenship in a comparative framework, (edited), Sage, 2003.

32. Mahajan, Gurpreet, *Accommodating Diversity Ideas and Institutional Practices*. Oxford University Press. Introduction.

33. Emberley, Peter, 'Preserving by Reforming:Diversity at work in Civilizational Adaptation.'edited by Gurpreet Mahajan, *Accomdating Diversity Ideas and Institutional Practices*.

34. Phillips,Anne, 'Cultural Scepticism and 'Group Represtation', edited by Gurpreet Mahajan , *'Accmmodating Diversity Ideas and Institutional Practices.'*

35. Bhatti, Anil, 'Heterogenetics and Homogenetics: On Similarities and Diversities', edited by Gurpreet Mahajan, *Accommodating Diversity Ideas and Institutional Practices.*

36. Joseph, Sarah, 'Multiculturalism and Diversity:Value to be promoted or problem to be Managed? edited by Gurpreet Mahajan, *Accmmodating Diversity Ideas and Institutional Practices.*

37. SriRanjani V, 'Constitution of Religious Identity:Constituent (Assembly) Debates and Beyond, edited by Gurpreet Mahajan, *Accmmodating Diversity Ideas and Institutional Practices.*

38. Sarangi, Asha, 'Linguistic Diversity in a Federal polity:An Indian Experience, edited by Gurpreet Mahajan, *Accmmodating Diversity Ideas and Institutional Practices.*

39. Meetei Bijen, 'Politics of Recognition:Rethinking Existing Institutional Measures in India', edited by Gurpreet Mahajan , *Accmmodating Diversity Ideas and Institutional Practices.*

40. Wanchoo, Rohit, 'Group Rights,Diversity,and Social Justice', edited by Gurpreet Mahajan, *Accmmodating Diversity Ideas and Institutional Practices.*

41. Lamba,Rinku, 'Political Institutions for Remedying Caste and sex-based Hierarchies: A View from colonial India', edited by Gurpreet Mahajan, *Accmmodating Diversity Ideas and Institutional Practices.*

42. Srinivasan,Vasanthi, 'Prudence and statesmanship in Managing Diversity', edited by Gurpreet Mahajan, *Accmmodating Diversity Ideas and Institutional Practices.*

Diversities Unlimited: An Asset

INDIA is home to a variety of people of different communities, religions and ethnic descents, who have fought among themselves from time to time but have after centuries of conflict managed to live in amity and peace by sinking their many basic differences including those of perceptions.

The conflict situations among diverse ethnic groups have been realities in both past and contemporary societies and they have been driven by sharp economic and social inequalities. However, the plurality of India has been maintained and majority of the diverse cultural groups have lived together for over five thousand years. This continuity of coexistence despite conflicts is a typical trait of synthesis of cultures, religions and languages.

In this chapter we will acquaint ourselves with facets of our rich and varied diversity and attempt to examine the reasons why and how this has come about. Though multiculturalism is inherent in its cultural heritage, India has one Constitution guaranteeing rights to people belonging to diverse religious, cultural and linguistic groups and covering all socio-economic strata. After independence, deliberate attempts have been made to promote multiculturalism in India through public policy as part of nation building. Measures like putting multiculturalism in school curriculum, teaching in national language as well as in mother-tongue, exemptions from dress codes in public laws etc. have formed the basis of multicultural society. Efforts have also been made with stress on the need for nation states to move beyond conflict resolution to conflict avoidance.

The ideal of a democratic republic enshrined in the Preamble of India's Constitution can best be explained with reference to the adoption of universal suffrage and the complete equality between the sexes not only before the law but also in the political sphere. The offering of equal opportunity to men and women, regardless of their castes or creeds, in the matter of public employment further implements this democratic ideal. The treatment of the minority, apart from the constitutional safeguards, clearly brings out the fact that the philosophy underlying the Constitution has not been overlooked by those in power. The fact that members of the Muslim and Christian communities are as a practice being included in the Council of Ministers as well as the States, in the Supreme Court and even in Diplomatic Missions without any constitutional reservations amply demonstrates that those who are working within the Constitution have not missed out on its true spirit, namely that every citizen must feel that India is his or her own country. Further, the unity and fraternity of the Indian people, professing numerous faiths has been sought to be achieved by enshrining the ideal of a 'secular state'. This means that the state protects all religions equally and does not itself uphold any religion as the state religion. The question of secularism is not one of sentiment but one of law. Also, the liberty of 'belief, faith and worship' promised in the Preamble is implemented by incorporating the fundamental rights of all citizens relating to 'freedom of religion' in Articles 25-28, which guarantee to each individual freedom to profess, practice and propagate religion and promise strict impartiality on the part of the state and its institutions towards all religions.

Our diverse ethnic groups are our strength as they are engaged in diverse economic activities based on skill of local human resources and their indigenous resource potential like animal husbandry, sericulture, horticulture, weaving and other allied activities. It is economic dependence of one community on the other that binds us.

The idea of a dialogue on conflict-avoidance also emanates from the economic needs of people of different cultures that are evolving as one economic entity.

Followings are some of the diversities which are our strengths and from which we gather different streams of rich cultural heritage which give us the lessons to stand united.

TRIBAL INDIA

India's people are the product of assimilation of countless invasions through its history. Human groups with different racial backgrounds have entered India at different times and intermingled with its local population. India's present day population has acquired its characteristics as a result of this intermixing. The main races that have mingled in various combinations are the Caucasoid, Mongoloid, Australoid and the Negroid.

India has a sizeable tribal population who inhabit three distinct regions of the country. India's north and north-east comprises the States of Assam, Arunachal Pradesh, Meghalaya, Mizoram, Manipur, Nagaland, Tripura, as also parts of eastern Kashmir, Himachal Pradesh, Uttarakhand and Uttar Pradesh. It's central or middle zone consists of the States of Madhya Pradesh, southern Rajasthan, northern Gujarat, Bihar, Jharkhand, Odisha and Andhra Pradesh. Its southern zone comprises the States of Andhra Pradesh, Karnataka and Tamil Nadu. In addition to these three major zones of tribal concentration there is another, smaller, isolated zone comprising the Andaman & Nicobar Islands.

The six main racial groups that are found in India are the Negrito, the Proto-Australoid or Austric, Mongoloid, Mediterranean or Dravidian, the Western Brachycephal and the Nordic Aryan.

Negroids: The Negritos or the Brachycephalic (broad headed) from Africa were the earliest people to have come to India. They have survived in their original habitat in the Andaman and Nicobar Islands. The Jarawas, Onges, Sentinelese and the Great Andamanese are some of their examples. Some hill tribes like the Irulas, the Kodars, Paniyans and Kurumbas are found in South India and middle parts of the Indian mainland.

Proto-Australoids or Austrics: These groups were the next to come to India after the Negritos. They are people with wavy hair lavishly distributed all over their brown bodies, long headed with low foreheads and prominent eye ridges, noses with low and broad roots, thick jaws, large palates and teeth and small chins. The Austrics of India represent a race of medium height, dark complexion with long heads and rather flat noses but otherwise of regular features. Miscegenation with the earlier Negroids may be the reason for the dark or black pigmentation of the skin and flat noses.

The Austrics laid the foundation of the Indian civilization. They cultivated rice and vegetables and made sugar from sugarcane. Now these people are found in some parts of India, Myanmar and the islands of South East Asia. Their languages have survived in Central and Eastern India.

Mongoloids: These people are found in the North-eastern part of India in the States of Assam, Nagaland, Mizoram, Meghalaya, Arunachal Pradesh, Manipur and Tripura. They are also found in the northern parts of West Bengal, Sikkim, and Ladakh. Generally, they are people with yellow complexion and high cheekbones, oblique eyes, sparse hair and small chins. Dravidians: The Dravidians inhabit large parts of South India. They are believed to have come to the Indian mainland much before the Aryans. They have different sub-groups like the Paleo-Mediterranean, the true Mediterranean and the Oriental Mediterranean. They appear to be people of the same stock as the peoples of Asia Minor and Crete or pre-Hellenic Aegean of Greece and neghbouring islands. They are reputed to have built up the city civilisation of the Indus valley, whose remains have been found at Mohenjodaro and Harappa and other Indus cities.

Western Brachycephals: These include the Alpinoids, Dinarics and Armenoids. The Parsis and Kodavas also fall in this category. They are broad-headed people with medium stature, round face, prominent nose, straight long hair and fair complexion, living mainly in the western parts of the country such as the Ganges Valley and the Gangetic delta, parts of Kashmir, Kathiawar, Gujarat, Maharashtra, Karnataka and Tamil Nadu.

Nordics or the Indo-Aryans: This group was among the last to immigrate to India. They came to India somewhere between 2000 and 1500 BC. Their main physical traits are tall stature, long head, long face, blue eyes and blond hair. They are now mainly found in the northern and central part of India.

Important Tribes of India

State and Union Territories	Tribes
Andhra Pradesh	Chenchus, Gonds
Arunachal Pradesh	Abors, Apatanis, Monba, Mishmi, Dafla, Aka, Miri
Assam	Mikirs, Khasis, Kacharis
Bihar	Mundas, Santhals, Oraons, Ho
Chhattisgarh	Bhils, Gonds, Kols, Murias, Baiga, Korkus, Kamars
Dadra and Nagar Haveli	Bhils
Gujarat	Bhils
Jharkhand	Mundas, Santhals, Oraons, Ho
Himachal Pradesh	Gaddis, Gujjars, Bhotias, Kinners, Lahaulis
Madhya Pradesh	Bhils, Gonds, Kols, Murias, Baiga, Korkus, Kamars
Maharashtra	Bhils, Warlis, Kokus, Gonds, Gawaris
Manipur	Kuki, Naga
Meghalaya	Garos, Khasis
Mizoram	Lushous, Ralte, Hmar, Paite, Pawi, Lakher
Nagaland	Angami, Sema, Ao, Tangkul, Lahora
Odisha	Mundas, Chenchus, Gonds, Oraons, Khonds
Rajasthan	Bhils, Meenas, Meos, Banjaras, Rebaris, Grasias
Sikkim	Lepchas
Tamil Nadu	Badagas, Kotas, Todas
Tripura	Chakmas
Uttar Pradesh	Bhotias
Uttarakhand	Bhotias
West Bengal	Mundas, Santhals, Oraons
Andaman and Nicobar Islands	Jarawas, Onges, Shompens, Sentinelese

The People of India project (POI) of the Anthropological Survey of India estimates that there are nearly 4,635 cultural communities in India. The project counts 700 languages and 25 scripts as well as 325 languages spoken at home, with 75 of them identified as major languages in contemporary India. This linguistic diversity is further embedded within the social, cultural and political life of Indian society in numerous ways. For example, 104 languages and dialects are used for broadcasting programmes on the All India Radio, along with 35 languages that are used to print newspapers. Besides, approximately 67 languages are used for imparting primary education and another 47 dialects are used as mediums of instruction. In addition to this, almost 80 languages and dialects are used for literacy work throughout the country while some 13 languages are used for regional cinema and as the administrative language of a particular region, district or sub-division.

Thus, State boundaries in India are almost always drawn along linguistic lines. India has one national language—Hindi in the Devanagari script. It now also recognises English as the language of institutions like High Courts and the Supreme Court, for government work and as the common language of interaction throughout India. The Indian Constitution also officially recognises as many as 22 regional languages. A total of 33 different languages, with 15 of them designated as major languages that are spoken across the length and breadth of India, and 2,000 dialects have been identified in India. This variety in languages has been built up through the ages by various races and ethnic groups that entered India over time. The main ones are Assamese, Bengali, Gujarati, Hindi, Kannada, Kashmiri, Malayalam, Marathi, Oriya, Punjabi, Sanskrit, Sindhi, Tamil, Telugu and Urdu. Some of these are closely allied and may be grouped together. These languages can be further split between four broad families of languages spoken by the majority of the Indian people.

They are the Dravidian and Indo-Aryan family of languages. The other two families are the Austro-Asiatic and the Sino-Tibetan. The Austro-Asiatic language family consisting of the Munda sub-group is confined to central and eastern India. The Sino-Tibetan languages are spoken in the northeastern parts of the country. The Dravidian family of languages—Tamil, Malayalam, Kannada and Telugu—is spoken principally in the southern parts of the country. The Indo-Aryan family comprising Marathi, Gujarati, Punjabi, Sanskrit, Sindhi and Urdu is spoken largely in the northern and western parts of India.

List of languages recognised by the Indian Constitution

Languages	Official Language of
Assamese	Assam
Bengali	Tripura & West Bengal
Bodo	Assam
Dogri	Jammu and Kashmir
Gujarati	Dadra and Nagar Haveli, Daman and Diu & Gujarat
Hindi	Andaman and Nicobar Islands, Bihar, Chandigarh, Chhattisgarh, Delhi, Haryana, Himachal Pradesh, Jharkhand, Madhya Pradesh, Rajasthan, Uttar Pradesh & Uttaranchal
Kannada	Karnataka
Kashmiri	Kashmir
Konkani	Goa
Maithili	Bihar
Malayalam	Kerala & Lakshadweep
Manipuri (Meithei)	Manipur
Marathi	Maharashtra
Nepali	Sikkim
Oriya	Odisha
Punjabi	Punjab
Sanskrit	
Santhali	Parts of West Bengal and Bihar, Jharkhand
Sindhi	Western Punjub
Tamil	Tamil Nadu & Pondicherry
Telugu	Andhra Pradesh
Urdu	Jammu & Kashmir

List of the lesser languages of India

Languages	Language of
Awadhi (sub-variety of Hindi)	Uttar Pradesh
Bhili	Bhil tribals Chhattisgar, Madhya Pradesh
Bhojpuri (sub-variety of Hindi)	Bihar
Bundeli (sub-variety of Hindi)	Madhya Pradesh, uttar Pradesh
Chhattisgarhi (sub-variety of Hindi)	Chhattisgarh
Deccani	Andhra Pradesh
Gondi	Gond tribals, Madhya Pradesh, Andhra Pradesh
Haryanvi (sub-variety of Hindi)	Haryana
Hindustani (mixture of Hindi and Urdu)	Northern part of India
Kanauji (sub-variety of Hindi)	Uttar Pradesh
Kodava	Kodagu (Karnataka)
Kutchi	Kutch (Gujarat)
Magahi (sub-variety of Hindi)	Southern Bihar
Marwari (sub-variety of Hindi)	Rajasthan
Portuguese French	Partly in Goa, Daman and Diu, Dadra and Nagar Haveli Mahe, Pondicherry
Sikkimese	Sikkim
Tibetan	Tibet (Kashmir)
Tulu	Tulu people (Karnataka & Kerala)

FAIRS AND FESTIVALS

There are certain festivals, which we in India, celebrate collectively as a people. Though Diwali, Durga Pooja, Holi are primarily Hindu festivals, celebrated largely by Hindus and Eid-ul-Zuha (Bakr-Eid), Muharram and Eid-ul-Fitr are mostly observed by India's Muslims, the fact is that all Indians, irrespective of the creed to which they subscribe, participate wholeheartedly in celebrating such festivals that also include Christmas of the Christians, Buddha Purnima of the Buddhists, Baisakhi and Guru Parab of the Sikhs and Mahavir Jayanti of the Jains. Participation of India's various communities in festivals that are specific to a particular community is a distinguishing feature of Indian social life.

Similarly, there are pilgrimage centres peculiar to specific communities where the Indian people, putting away their differences of caste, creed and class, get together annually in massive displays of pure unadulterated faith.

January
Lohri

Amidst the freezing cold weather, with the temperature ranging between 0 to 5 degree Celsius and dense fog all around, activities come to a standstill across most of North India. However, below the apparently frozen surface, it is amazing to find a palpable wave of activity. People, especially in the northern India states of Punjab, Haryana and parts of Himachal Pradesh, celebrate Lohri on the 13th of January each year. Lohri is essentially an agrarian festival celebrating the harvesting of the rabi (winter) crop. People gather around a large bonfire to throw sprigs of wheat and mustard into the flames, even as they dance and enjoy themselves by singing traditional folk songs.

Makar Sankranti

Celebrated across South India on 14 January each year, Pongal essentially celebrates the harvesting of new rabbi crops by farmers. Across North India this festival is known as Makar Sankranti. The festival marks the withdrawal of the southeast monsoon as well as the reaping of rabi crops by farmers. Festivities are spread over several days and are marked by general spring-cleaning and the drawing of beautiful kolams (decorative designs) on the floors with moistened rice flour. On this day, newly harvested rice is ritualistically cooked. This day is celebrated in Assam as Magh Bihu.

Moharram

Moharram marks the martyrdom of Imam Hussain, the grandson of Prophet Mohammad who was killed in the battle of Karbala in 680 AD.

Devout Shia Muslims across the country observe a ten-day period of mourning during Moharram. For a month the devout recount the story of Hussain's martyrdom and, on the tenth day, in a grand procession, the tragic tale is re-enacted by the mourners who beat themselves inflicting pain as penance. The mourners in the procession, which is often led by caparisoned elephants, carry beautifully decorated Tazias or floats.

February
Basant Panchmi

Basant Panchami heralds the spring season. The festival celebrates the end of winter and with it, the beginning of the annual agriculture calendar. The festive yellow colour, symbolic of spring, plays an important part on this day. People wear yellow clothes, offer yellow flowers in worship and put a yellow 'tilak' on their forehead. They visit temples and offer prayers to various gods. At home, kesar halva, yellow in colour, is prepared. In Bengal the day is more popularly known as Saraswati Puja. It is believed that on this day Saraswati, the goddess of learning and wisdom (the consort of Brahma, the creator), came down to earth to drive away the pall of ignorance. In a wider sense though, this is the end of winter, symbolic of darkness and ignorance and the beginning of spring, symbolic of knowledge.

March
Shivaratri

Shivaratri, symbolising the wedding day of Shiva and Paravati, is an important day for devotees of Shiva, who stay awake through the night, praying to him. It falls two weeks before Holi. In all major temples of Shiv, Shivaratri also called Maha Shivaratri, is a grand occasion. From very early morning Shiva temples are filled with devotees, who perform the traditional worship of the Shivalinga. All through the day, devotees abstain from eating food and break their fast only the next morning, after the nightlong worship.

Holi

The festival of Holi, which welcomes the agriculturally significant summer season, is celebrated sometime in March. People throng the streets smearing each other with brightly coloured powder (gulal) or squirting coloured water on each other. Originally, a fertility festival, the legend of Prahlad speaks of a king so arrogant that he demanded that his people worship him and him alone. Only his young son, Prahlad refused. Finally, the king's sister Holika, said to be immune to burning, sat with the boy in a huge fire. So potent was Prahlad's devotion to God, that he emerged unscathed while Holika was burnt to death.

Jamshed Navroz

The Zoroastrians, spread in western parts of India, celebrate the Parsi New Year with prayers, giving of alms and donations. There are family gatherings and feast. Some observe it as a day of repentance and making up, putting behind all clashes and ill will.

April

Mahavir Jayanti

Mahavir was the last in the galaxy of twenty-four Teerthankaras (Jain prophets). He was born in the year 599 BC and has been acclaimed as one of the greatest prophets of peace and social reform that India has ever produced. He renounced the pleasures and luxuries of the palace, as also the power and prestige of kingship, and undertook a life of intense penance for more than twelve years. He finally attained enlightenment. But not content with his own personal salvation, he chose to become a great human redeemer. He simplified the religious procedures and concentrated on righteous conduct. Mahivir's message: Do unto others what you would like to be done to you. Injury or violence done by you to any life, in any form, animal or human, is as harmful as it would be if caused to your own self.

Easter

Easter, a Christian festival, embodies many pre-Christian traditions. Scholars believe it probably comes from Easter, the Anglo-Saxon name of a Teutonic goddess of spring and fertility, to whom a month corresponding to April was dedicated. Her festival was celebrated on the day of the vernal equinox; traditions associated with the festival survive in the Easter rabbit, a symbol of fertility, and in coloured Easter eggs, originally painted with bright colours to represent the sunlight of spring. The Christian festival of Easter probably embodies a number of converging traditions; most scholars emphasise the original relation of Easter to the Jewish festival Passover, or Pesach, from which is derived Pasch, another name of Easter. The early Christians, many of whom were of Jewish origin, were brought up in the Hebrew tradition and regarded Easter as a new feature of the Passover festival, a commemoration of the advent of the Messiah as foretold by the prophets.

Ramnavami

The birthday of Lord Rama, the celebrated hero of the famous epic the *Ramayana* is enthusiastically celebrated on the ninth day of the waxing moon in the month of Chaitra, which falls sometime in April. Temples are decorated, religious discourses are held and the Ramayana is recited over a ten day-long period. People gather in their thousands on the banks of the sacred Sarayu river for a dip, believed to absolve one of all sins.

Baisakhi

The Hindu New Year finds expression in this exuberant festival, celebrated throughout India on 14th April. Baisakhi celebrations in Punjab are spectacular, as this is a special day for the Sikhs. It was on this day that Guru Gobind Singh founded the order of the Khalsa. Robust revelry and feasting mark the celebrations and dancers perform the vigorous Bhangra to the rhythmic beat of the drums. In Kerala, the festival is known as Vishu. 'Vishu Kani'—a display of grain, fruits, flowers, gold, new clothes and money, is viewed early in the morning to ensure a prosperous year ahead. Firework display and the buying of new clothes are a part of the festivities. Known as Rangali Bihu in Assam, the festival is celebrated with lively dances, music and feasting.

May

Buddha Purnima

The great celebration of the month of Vaishakh falls on the full moon day on which Gautama, the Buddha, was born. Known as Buddha Purnima, the day falls in the month of May. To Buddhists the world over, the full moon of Vaishakh is the most auspicious. Gautama, the

Buddha, was born in 544 BC in Lumbini, Nepal. Saddened by the realisation that life was a meaningless and hollow passage from one state of being to the next, the prince went into deep meditation under a Bodhi tree near Gaya, until he finally attained enlightenment, once again on a full moon day of Vaishakh. He was then 35 years of age, and thereafter came to be known as Gautama, the Buddha. He gave his first sermon in Sarnath, near the holy city of Varanasi, to his followers who formed a Sangha or order, also on the Vaishakh Purnima. The Buddha, considered the ninth avatar of Vishnu, reached Nirvana or the extinction of self and freedom from the cycle of rebirth, also on the full moon day of Vaishakh. Therefore, Buddha Purnima marks the three major events in the life of this great apostle of peace.

Thrissur Pooram

This festival is held in the month of April/May in honour of Lord Vadakkunnathan (Shiva) in Thrissur. The presiding deities of the temple are honoured with processions of caparisoned elephants carrying the temple images, accompanied by temple drums and fireworks.

Eid-i-Milad (Barah-Wafat)

The Prophet was born on the twelfth day of Rabi-ul-Awwal, the third month of the Muslim year. His death anniversary also falls on the same day, the word 'barah' standing for the twelve days of the Prophet's sickness. During these days sermons are delivered in mosques by learned men, focusing on the life and noble deeds of the Prophet. In some parts of the country, a ceremony known as the 'Sandal' rite is performed over the symbolic footprints of the Prophet engraved in stone. A representation of 'buraq', a horse on which the Prophet is believed to have ascended to heaven, is kept near the footprints and anointed with sandalwood paste or scented powder, and the house and casket containing these are elaborately decorated. Elegies or 'marsiyas' are sung in memory of the last days of the Prophet. The twelfth day or the Urs is observed quietly, in prayers and alms giving.

June

Hemis Mela

Buddhist festivals provide an opportunity for the faithful to meet and meditate in the local temple or monastery. In the true essence of Buddhism, the Hemis festival of Ladakh is dedicated to Lord Padmasambhava, venerated as the reincarnation of Buddha. He is believed to have been born on the 10th day of the fifth month of the Monkey year as predicted by the Shakya Muni Buddha. It is also believed that his life's mission was, and remains, the improvement of the spiritual condition of all living beings. And so on this day, which comes once in a cycle of 12 years, a major extravaganza is observed in his memory. The observance of these sacred rituals is believed to give spiritual strength and good health.

The Hemis festival takes place in the rectangular courtyard in front of the main door of the Hemis monastery. The space is wide and open save two raised square platforms, three feet high, with a sacred pole in the centre. A raised dais with a richly cushioned seat and a finely painted small Tibetan table is placed along with the ceremonial cups full of holy water, uncooked rice tormas made of dough and butter and incense sticks. A number of musicians play the traditional music with four pairs of cymbals—large-pan drums—small trumpets and large sized wind instruments. Next to them, a small space is assigned for the Lamas to sit. The ceremonies begin with an early morning ritual atop the Gompa where, to the beat of drums, the resounding clash of cymbals and the spiritual wail of pipes, the portrait of 'Dadmokarpo' or 'Rygyalsras Rimpoche' is ceremoniously put on display for all to admire and worship. The most esoteric of festivities are the mystic mask dances. The Mask Dances of Ladakh are referred collectively as a Chams performance. Chams performance is essentially a part of tantric tradition, performed only in those Gompas that follow the Tantric Vajrayana teachings and where the monks perform tantric worship. Around the Hemis monastery a fair is also held during the festival where local handicrafts are sold.

July

Teej

Right in the middle of the verdant monsoon, in the month of Shravan, or July, occurs the royal festival of Teej. Dedicated to Parvati this celebration is special to Rajasthan and is observed with pomp and pageantry in Jaipur. Teej is marked by a splendid procession of decorated elephants, horses and camels. The idol of Parvati is set atop a caparisoned elephant and taken around the streets of the Pink City. From far and near men and women come to see the procession, dressed in tie-and-dye turbans and ghagra cholis to match the gaiety of the procession. During the monsoon season, the environs of Jaipur turn lush and green and women worship the mother Goddess and distribute Ghevar, Churma Ladoos and other traditional sweets.

Rath Yatra

This spectacular chariot festival is held at the famous Jagannath temple of Puri. Images of Lord Jagannath, his sister Subhadra and brother Balbhadra are taken out in a procession in three chariots to their summer temple for a week. The main chariot is 14 meters high and 10 meters wide with 16 wheels. The ropes of the huge chariots are pulled by hundreds and thousands of devotees who believe the act bestows salvation upon them.

Naag Panchami

This festival, mainly celebrated in Jodhpur, Rajasthan and Maharashtra, is dedicated to the thousand-headed mythical serpent called Sheshnaag, the seat of Lord Vishnu. The ritual consists of feeding milk to the snakes. The day is also observed in many other parts of Western and Eastern India.

Guru Purnima

A special worship is performed on 16th July to all teachers and is called Guru Purnima. Worship of the great Vyasa, author of the great epic Mahabharata, is a part of the celebration. On this day students visit their elders, teachers and guides in order to show respect to them with gifts of coconuts, clothes and sweets. These gifts are called Guru Dakshina. Discourses are held in community gatherings wherein the audience gets to hear readings from the holy Gita.

August
Independence Day
August 15 commemorates the National Independence Day. It is India's biggest secular celebration, on the anniversary of her independence from the British in 1947. It is celebrated all over the country with meetings and flag hoisting ceremonies. The Prime Minister addresses the nation from the ramparts of Delhi's Red Fort.

Raksha Bandhan
This festival is mainly celebrated in Northern and Western India. Brothers and sisters exchange gifts, as sisters tie rachis, or beautifully decorated threads, on their brother's wrists. It signifies the brother's responsibility of protecting his sister all her life. This festival, celebrated in the month of August, also heralds the monsoon in these parts.

Janamashtami
Lord Krishna was born on the eighth day of the dark fortnight of the month of Bhadon, eight days after Raksha Bandhan. People keep a fast on this day. The celebrations begin in the evening and culminate at the stroke of midnight, when Krishna was born. The fast is then broken and people eat sweets and savouries made of Kotu (a black coloured seed) flour. The festival is celebrated with great pomp and show in temples where incidents from Krishna's life are displayed.

September
Onam
Essentially a harvest festival, Onam, which falls towards the end of the monsoon season, celebrates the homecoming of Mahabali, the demon king who ruled over Kerala and was ousted by Lord Vishnu. His return once a year to his kingdom is marked by floral courtyard decorations, feasts and snake boat races at Alappuzha, Champakulam, Aranmula

and Kottayam. In the coconut tree-lined backwaters of Kerala, these boat races are an event of great pageantry. Onam falls two days before the immersion ceremony of Lord Ganesha.

Ganesh Chaturthi

Ganesha, son of Shiva-Parvati, is the ever-present deity of India. His blessing is invariably invoked at the beginning of any task; he is seen on wedding invitations, at shop entrances, at street-corner shrines, on doorways of most Hindu houses and in every temple. On the fourth day of the bright half of Bhadrapad, sometime in September, the festival of Ganesha Chaturthi is celebrated all over India. In the western state of Maharashtra, Ganesha Chaturthi is a magnificent event. Numerous community celebrations are centered around huge Ganesh idols, which are taken for ceremonial immersions after ten days of music, dance, theatre, feasts and fun.

Tarnetar Mela

An exciting and a unique fair is held annually at Tarnetar in Saurashtra. The fair coincides with the festival at the Trineteshwar temple, celebrating the wedding of the legendary Mahabharat hero, Arjuna with Draupadi. The fair is a kind of a marriage market for the local tribals—the Kolis, Bharwads and Rabaris. Traditional costumes, exquisite jewelry and wonderful Tarnetar Chhatris (umbrellas) with intricate embroidery and mirror work are sold. An added attraction are the lively folk dance performances.

October

Durga Puja

Durga is the most benign face of the mother goddess Shakti, a synthesis of the combined powers of Brahma, Vishnu and Mahesh. Durga Puja is performed twice a year, for nine days known as Navratri, once in the beginning of summer and the other in the beginning of winter. The first one is mostly a private affair culminating in Ramanavami. The second one is celebrated with great pomp and show, especially in Bengal. Huge tents are put up displaying Durga in different moods. There is much festivity for nine days. Pujas are organized on a mass scale at the tents or pandals. Songs are sung narrating the story of Durga, who was created by the gods to fight demons. The last or the tenth day, on which Durga kills the demon Mahishasur, coincides with Dussehra. On this day Durga idols are taken in large processions for immersion.

Dussehra

Dussehra is one of the greatest festivals of India, and comes sometime in October heralding the winter season. It celebrates the victory of Rama, the hero of the epic *Ramayana*, over Ravana, the demon king of Lanka. In vast open spaces, effigies of Ravana, his son Meghnad and brother Kumbhakarna are erected. Stuffed with firecrackers, they are burnt in the evening. People decorate the entrances of their homes with torans, flower studded strings and worship the tools of their trades. In Bengal it is celebrated as Vijayadashami, the day on which Durga killed the terrible demon Mahishasur. The celebrations begin ten days earlier, from the first day of Durga Puja.

November

Diwali

Diwali is one of the biggest and grandest celebrations in India, coming twenty days after Dussehra. It is also known as Deepawali, or a festival of lights, celebrating Rama and Sita's homecoming in the Ramayana. It signifies the victory of good over evil. Streets are illuminated with rows of clay lamps and homes are decorated with rangoli (coloured powder designs) and candles. Diwali is celebrated with new clothes, spectacular firecrackers and a variety of sweets, in the company of family and friends. In South India and parts of North India, Lakshmi, the goddess of wealth, is supposed to visit every home on Diwali, so Lakshmi Puja is also done on this day.

Sharad Purnima

It is a harvest festival and in Eastern India it is believed that the deity Lakshmi, the goddess of prosperity, brings fortune and good luck to all. Kojagiri, the special night, is celebrated with ice-cold, saffron-flavoured sweet milk, shared in the cool moonlight. The full moon night is called Navanna Purnima or the moonlit night of new food. The newly-harvested rice is offered to the gods and lamps are lit before the full moon.

Guru Purab
The birth anniversary of Guru Nanak, the first guru of the Sikhs, is celebrated with great fervour. The 'Akhand Path' or recitation of the Sikh holy book, the Guru Granth Sahib, is held in gurduwaras all over the country. Taking the holy book out in procession is also an integral part of the celebrations. Langars (community feasts) are organized where people sit together to eat and sing hymns from the Guru Granth Sahib. The celebrations at Amritsar are especially impressive.

December
Christmas
Christmas is celebrated on 25th December, as the birthday of Christ. As elsewhere in the world, in India also the celebration of Christmas has always been, and continues to be, a time to spend with family and friends, to make new resolutions and exchange gifts. As Christmas comes around, the spirit of gaiety is reborn with people getting busy with the cards carrying combined greetings for Christmas and the coming New Year. Churches are given a new look with paint and colour wash as a prelude to the great celebration. Christian homes too are spruced up.

India is fairly familiar with the Christmas tree and its star and lights as well as the jovial figure of Santa Claus bringing presents to good children., People are also familiar with Christmas crackers, cakes, and turkey. The major cities of India witness the festive celebration into the wee hours of the morning, the moment of Christ's birth having been celebrated at midnight. Christmas is most exuberantly celebrated in Goa. The important part of the festival is the midnight service or the mass given in the church, which lasts for three to four hours. Tribal Christians in the northeast and the western parts of the country go out at night for about a week prior to Christmas Eve where choruses sing their equivalents of Christmas carols. Christians in southern India light clay oil lamps in the evening, giving the houses a twinkling look.

DIFFERENT PEOPLE, DIFFERENT STATES DIFFERENT CULTURES

Andaman and Nicobar Island

People

The tribal population of the Andaman and Nicobar Islands comprises the Great Andamanese, Jarawas, Onges and Sentinelese in the Andaman Islands and the Nicobarese and the Shompens in the Nicobar Islands. The Andaman tribes belong to what is known as the Negrito stock that is distantly related to Africa's Negroids. These are the representatives of the once Negrito race which dominated the Southeast Asian region. The other surviving representatives of this race are the Semand tribe of Malaysia and the Aeta of Phillippines. The Nicobar tribes are a mixture of the Malay and Myanmar strains and live in twelve island communities in the Nicobar Islands. The Shompen is the other tribe that lives in the valleys of the Great Nicobar.

These tribesmen are believed to have been living on this archipelago for nearly 60,000 years but they are still confined to their geographical limits. The area inhabited by the primitive tribes has been declared as tribal reserve area to prevent them from the exploitation by the outsiders. Any person entering into the reserve area without permission is liable for punishment with imprisonment and fine. The Andaman Adim Janjati Vikas Samiti is an autonomous body which looks after the welfare of these primitive tribes.

The Great Andamanese inhabiting the Strait Island are the only tribe which has been affected by the modern outside world. They came in contact with the modern world after the 'Battle of Aberdeen' in which thousands of the tribesmen were killed. It is due to the outside influence that Hindi films and movie starts are quite popular among the Great Andamanese. The new generation is sent to school and a few of the local youth have been absorbed into government jobs.

However, they have still retained much of their traditional cultures and customs. They are superstitious and believe that they can keep the sea storms away if they flow chopped palm leaves into the sea water.

They are good artisans and comfortable with both traditional and modern tools. They prepare their own ornaments, baskets, tools and earthen pots. The ornaments they wear is made up of leaves, barks, and shells which is worn during traditional functions and dances. They have their own system and practice of medicine. For instance, to treat the chronic back aches they pierce their body with a small piece of glass in a belief that it will drain off the bad blood from the person and thus relieve him or her from the pain. Before the advent of glass, pointed stones were used for the purpose of piercing.

They speak the 'Jero' language, which is mix of some words from the languages of the other tribes, completely assimilated into it. Their numbers have also increased as a result of mixed marriages, since these people are free to mix with the people of the mainland, and have adapted to their way of life, speak Port Blair Hindi, dress like them, eat their kind of food, some of them have contractual jobs with the Andaman and Nicobar administration.

The Jarawa tribes were the most feared among all the aborigines until 1995-96. The short-height and dark skin Jarawas live in protected areas in Middle Andaman, South Andaman and Interview Island. The Jarawas are excellent craftsmen as evidenced by the skill of making various metal tools and arrows. They are fond of red clothes, though majority of them are found nude. They are non-vegetarians and mostly eat pork. It is known that the Jarawas do not kill deer for food.

They were very hostile in the past and were known to attack intruders with poisonous arrows till as late as the eighties. Several human expeditions by contact teams consisting of officials were undertaken in the past near the Interview island, where the teams left eatables, red cloth, coconuts and plastic goods as gifts for the Jarawas. It helped to bring them closer to the outside world and today they have become sympathetic towards other fair skinned humans.

As per government policies, entry into their area is forbidden to save them from modern diseases, from which they don't have natural immunity, and other exploitations. Isolation will also help to retain their ancient culture. Photography inside the Jarawa reserve area is forbidden by law.

The Onge's of Little Andaman are of Negrito racial stock with features such as dark skin and woolly hair. These tribes are semi-nomadic and continue to live in remote seclusion and official permission is required to visit their habitation.

The Onge men go out to the forest for hunting while the women stay back at home and search the local area for roots and tubers under the soil. Originally, they found their sustenance from the forest, living mainly on fish, turtles, and other aquatic animals, as well as roots and jackfruits. Cultivation was unknown to them before contact with the modern world. The government has helped them to raise local crops and coconut plantations.

Few years ago they did not even boil their food because the concept of cooking was again unknown to them. They use bows and arrows to catch fish along the shallow sea coasts. The fishing line and fishing net is still not popular among them. The local delicacy is honey. They rub some special herbs to avoid the bee stings while they collect honey from the hives.

Tobacco and alcohol have become very popular among the Onges after their contact with the outside world. Hair dressing is done with the help of sea shells as razors. The Onge children now go to school and they speak Hindi.

The Onges are good artisans and experts at fashioning sturdy canoes but contact with the modern world is causing them to slowly forget these indigenous skills. However, the future of the tribe is threatened by very low reproduction rate among them.

The Shompens living in the interiors of Great Nicobar Island are of medium height with Mongoloid features. They were believed to be hostile earlier but in recent decades they have not shown any hostility and now have established trade relations with Nicobarese. The main activities of Shompens are hunting, food-gathering and fishing. They collect wild yams, roots, fruit, honey and insect larvae. They love to hunt pigs with their spears and they take help of pet dogs while hunting.

They are nomads and wander from place to place within the jungles and live in self-made huts. Their settlements are generally irregular in shape, and they prefer to build these either on the slopes of the hill or at the bottom of a valley near some water source. The houses are normally rectangular or square with a gabled roof.

The Sentinelese tribe inhabits the small North Sentinel Island and because of its geographical separation from other islands they have maintained strict isolation from rest of the world. In fact, they are currently the only known primitive tribe known in the world to live in complete isolation and are very hostile to outsiders. They do not allow anybody to enter the North Sentinel Island and attack with their self-made bows and spears, which they otherwise use for fishing and hunting the wild pigs.

Their population is still not known but attempts have been made to figure out their numbers on the basis of the photographs and assessment of the contact teams sent periodically by Andaman and Nicobar administration.

The Sentinelese fish in the coastal waters with bows and arrows and hunt wild pigs available on North Sentinel Island. They use small canoes made of wooden logs but do not know the use of oars and only use long poles to propel the canoes. The Sentinelese men and women are naked.

The Nicobarese belong to Mongloid stock and are horticulturist and pig-herders inhabiting large permanent villages mostly close to the sea shore. They have territorial distinctions such as people of Car Nicobar, Chowra, Teressa with Bompoka, the Central Group, the Southern Group and the single inland tribe of the Shompen on Great Nicobar. Nicobari families are patriarchal and called as Tuhet. They do not have individual ownership but the Tuhet owns land, coconut and pigs. Love marriage is very common and the age of marriage is sufficiently high. The staple food is coconut, fish and rice.

Andhra Pradesh
People
The people of Andhra Pradesh are a result of the inter-mixing that has taken place over centuries. There is a sizeable tribal population in the State: these include the Koyas, the Chenchus in the dense forests west of Rajamundhary, the Savaras in the northern hills of Srikakulam and Vishakhapatnam, and the Yerkulas in the southern districts. A

large part of the population is Hindu; other religious groups include Muslims and Christians. The two main languages in the State are Telugu and Urdu.

Kuchipudi is Andhra's traditional narrative dance form and is an offshoot of the classical Bharat Natyam of Tamil Nadu. A popular craft, Bidri, is specialised woodcarving, where skilled artisans fashion toys and figures, which are lacquered or painted. Bidri workers from Bidar create delicate designs, inlaid in silver or gold on gunmetal hookahs, vases, boxes and jewelry.

Festivals and Fairs

Important national festivals celebrated in Andhra Pradesh include Moharram, Bakr-Eid, Pongal or Sankranti, Dussehra and Diwali. Some other festivals specific to the state included the following:

The Golconda Festival: The festival is celebrated amidst the grandeur of the Golconda Fort with cultural events that include mushairas, which are typical of the city. A handicrafts and food fair with the celebrated Hyderabadi cuisine are the other highlights of the festival.

Samakka Festival: It is celebrated every two years in February at Medaram by the Koya and Waddar tribes. Held in memory of the Koya queen Samakka who died fighting the Kakatiyas of Warangal, the festival is an opportunity for the tribes of the states of Andhra Pradesh, Orissa, Madhya Pradesh and Maharashtra to gather together. Samakka is worshipped with offerings of coconut and jaggery. The festival relives an important chapter in the history of the tribes and provides an opportunity for the Koya oracle to foretell the future.

Brahmotsav Festival: Held in August-September in the honour of the presiding deity Lord Venkateshwara (Vishnu), this is a grand celebration in Tirupati. According to the Puranas, when Lord Vishnu reincarnated as the white boar (Varah) to save Mother Earth (Bhu Devi) from the demon Hiranyakashyap, he bathed at the Pushkarni tank at Tirupati after emerging from the underworld. On the final day of the festival, the image of Lord Venkateshwara is taken to the tank in a grand procession and bathed there.

Arunachal Pradesh

People

The State is home to over 20 major tribes and their sub-tribes. The communities in the state can be classified under three broad categories of the Kameng, Subansiri and Siang districts. The Monpa, Sherdukpen and the Aka tribes inhabit the Kameng district. The Subansiri district is home to the Dafla, Apatani, Tagin, and the Hill Miri tribes. The Siang district is inhabited by a group of tribes which, are collectively referred to as the Adi. The other tribes include the cluster of communities known as the Mishmis and the Kampti and Singpho tribes in the Lohit district. The Thangsa, Nocte and the Wanchoo tribes are located in the Tirap district. The main languages are Monpa, Aka, Miji, Sherdukpen, Nishi, Wancho and Shingpo.

The tribes do not intermarry and each follows distinct social, cultural, and religious practices such as animism, in which deities of nature and various spirits are worshiped. Ritual sacrifice is also common, and the Mithun (a domesticated gaur or wild ox) is especially revered as a sacrificial animal. Hindu beliefs and practices have penetrated the region, especially among populations near the Assam lowlands. Tibetan Buddhism is practiced by tribal groups living in and around the Tibetan border. Some tribes along the Myanmar border practice the Hinayana form of Buddhism.

Christians continue to stand strong in a deeply fractured society. Christianity still carries the image of the colonial rulers. However, Christians are considered to be kind towards women, children and animals. Cleanliness is typically a feature of most of Christian homes.

They are accomplished craftsmen and experts in mat weaving, handloom textile weaving, hyacinth grass weaving and jewellery. Their skill in weaving is apparent in the precise rendition of designs and textile patterns.

Festivals and Fairs

The people of Arunachal Pradesh celebrate a number of annual and seasonal festivals. Some of the important festivals include Moyoko, Bori Boot, Duba and Mopin.

Moyoko: This festival is celebrated in the month of March each year by groups of villages in rotation. The villages that celebrate are the host villages and the other villages are the guests of the Moyoko. During the festival, 'Suki' a god of the Apatani, is worshipped and offered food, drinks and meat. The festival continues for three days and is marked by lavish eating and drinking.

Bori Boat: Held in the month of February, this festival of the Hill Miris signifies unity, with no division of caste or community.

Duba: Dube means the destruction of evil spirits. This is the religious festival of the Membas, a Buddhist tribe that inhabits the northwestern areas of the Sing district. Held for a week, people visit the monastery in Tuting to receive blessings from the Lama of the Tuting monastery.

Mopin: This is the annual festival of the Adis and is celebrated during March-April. A community festival, Mopin is celebrated by people in all villages. Prayers are offered to the god and goddess of wealth for good harvest, health of the domestic animals and the well being of human beings.

Assam
People
The people of Assam are a broad racial intermixture of Mongolian, Indo-Burmese, Indo-Iranian and Aryan origin. The important tribes of Assam include the following: the Miris who inhabit the plains of Lakhimpur, the Abors and Bon-Abors who occupy the mountainous region of the Assam Himalayas, the Akas and Kapachors who occupy the area between Bhutan and Darrango, and the Singphos, the biggest and most powerful tribe who occupy the north-eastern districts of the State. Assamese and Bangla are the two most important languages spoken. Cultural institutions and religious centers like Satra (seat of a religious head, the Satradhikari) and Namghar (prayer hall) established at different places in Assam have been looking after the religious and social well being of the villagers as well as urban dwellers for the last 400 years. Weaving of fine silks and cotton cloths with floral and other decorative designs is practiced by women and is an important aspect of the cultural life of Assam.

Most Assam households have at least one loom, and each woman is required to know the art of weaving.

Festivals and Fairs

The Assamese observe pan-Indian religious festivals such as Holi (known as Dol-Jatra or Fakuwa), Janamashtami, the Eid and Durga Puja. Bihu is the most important festival celebrated in Assam. Originally an agricultural festival, it is celebrated by villagers at different seasons of the year. Rangali Bihu or Bohag Bihu celebrated in mid-April marks the start of the cropping season and also the start of the Assamese New Year. Bhogali Bihu or Magh Bihu is the harvest festival celebrated in mid-January. And Kati or Kangali Bihu marks the coming of autumn. It is known as Kangali (meaning poor) because by this time of the year the houses of the common people are without food grains, as the stock is usually consumed before the next harvest.

Assam became the settling ground for many civilisations like Negritos, Dravidians, Alpines, Tibeto Burmese and Aryans. The largest population in Assam is of the Tibeto Burmese origin like the Bodo tribe and Mishing tribe. Major tribes of Assam earn their livelihood through agriculture and by selling their handicrafts. Different types of tribes are famous for variety of handicrafts. While some are famous for handloom, others have mastered in pottery works. Their languages too differ according to their place of origin.

Bodo tribes constitute a large part of Assam population accounting to around 5.3% and spread over almost all parts of Assam. They speak Bodo language that is derived Tibeto Burmese family of language and most of them are engaged in rice cultivation, tea plantation and poultry farming. Bodo Women engage themselves in weaving which has become a known culture of Bodo Tribe. Bodos were earlier known to worship their forefathers, however in recent times they have started practicing Hinduism and Bathouism.

Karbi tribesmen generally reside in hilly areas of Assam and form the major portion of population of Karbi Anglong district. They also inhabit places in North Cachar Hills, Nagaon and Sonitpur districts of Assam. They are mentioned as Mikir in the constitution of India.

The Mishing tribesmen belonging to Tibeto Burmese group have agriculture as their occupation. They inhabit districts of Tinsukia, Sibsagar, Sonitpur, Jorhat and Golaghat. Mishing people found the most fertile land on the banks of River Brahmaputra and settled on sides of the river. Though their production was great, frequent floods prevented them from climbing the economic ladder. The main festival of Mishing tribe is Ali-Lye-Ligangin the month of February which is the harvest festival. They speak language known as Mishing language.

Residing in Dirugarh and Tinsukia district of Assam, along river Dihing, they are said to have come here from Thailand in the late 18th century. They speak Assamese language as well as Phake language. They are also known as Phakial and are a follower of Theravada Buddhism.

The Assamese tribesmen have a rich tradition of performing arts and traditional folk music. Folk songs and music related to different festivals dates back to time-immemorial. The Mishings musicians use a large numbers of traditional musical instruments including several types of drums, string instruments, flutes, cymbals, pipes, etc. They have made good use of bamboo and there are some of the most exquisite types of flutes made from bamboo. The musical instruments are made by local artisans using the locally available raw materials like bamboo, wood, gourds, hides etc.

Bihar

People

The people in Bihar are an amalgamation of the various races and racial strains. Until the creation of Jharkhand, Bihar had a sizeable tribal population accounting for about 9 per cent of the total population. Most of the tribal population is concentrated in the district of Rohtas. Hindus constitute more than 82 per cent and Muslims some 12 per cent of the population. The major languages spoken in the state are Hindi and Urdu and the dialects of Bhojpuri, Magahi and Maithili.

Festivals and Fairs

Kartik Purnima: This festival is celebrated by millions of people in north Bihar by bathing at the confluence of the Ganga and Gandak.

Sonepur Cattle Fair: It is the largest cattle fair in Asia held on the banks of the Ganga at Sonepur, located 22 kilometres from Patna.

Chatth Puja: is the only occasion when people of Bihar worship the rising as well as the setting sun. They have immense faith in this festival, which is celebrated twice a year, once in Chaitra (according to the Hindu calendar) which falls in March; and again in Kartik, which falls in November. It is a four-day festival with people worshipping the Surya Dev or Sun god and Chatthi Maiyya and singing folk songs eulogizing them. Although a festival of the Hindus, some Muslims also participate actively in the Puja.

Sama Chakeva: The celebration of this unusual festival commences with the flight of birds from the Himalayas that migrate towards the plains. This is a festival especially celebrated in Mithila. Girls make clay idols of various birds and decorate them in their own traditional way. Various rituals are performed and the festival ends joyously with the 'bidai' or farewell to the bride with the wish that she returns the next year.

Bihula: is a prominent festival of eastern Bihar, especially popular in the Bhagalpur district. People pray to goddess 'Mansa' for the welfare of their families.

Chandigarh

Chandigarh, a Union territory of India, is post-Independence India's first planned modern city. It also has the unique distinction of being the joint capital of the two states of Punjab and Haryana. Spread over 144 km sq, the Union Territory was constituted in 1966. The territory consists of the capital Chandigarh city and 22 surrounding villages. As both Punjab and Haryana laid claim on Chandigarh, it was decided that it be the capital of both the states under the Central government's administration as a Union Territory.

People

The people of Chandigarh belong to the same racial stock as the neighbouring States of Punjab and Haryana. They are descendants of the Aryan tribes that entered India from the north-west around 1500 BC. Hindus and Sikhs constitute the dominant section of the population. The people are hardy and boisterous and enjoy food. *Sarson ka saag* or mustard greens, eaten with *makki ki roti* or maize bread and lassi or sweetened yoghurt shake, are a particular favourite in Chandigarh and a staple of Punjabis everywhere. Punjabi and Hindi are the important spoken languages. The use of Urdu, which was widely spoken in the State earlier, has declined over the years.

Festivals and Fairs

The major festivals and fairs celebrated in Chandigarh are the same as the ones celebrated in Punjab and Haryana, like Ram Navami, Janamashtami, Buddha Purnima, Christmas, Guru Nanak Dev Jayanti, Diwali and others.

Guru Nanak Dev Jayanti: The birthday of Guru Nanak, founder of the Sikh faith is celebrated in October-November. The anniversaries of Guru Nanak and other Sikh Gurus are known as Gurupurab (festivals); they mark the culmination of prabhat pheris, the early morning processions that start from Gurudwaras (Sikh temples) and then go around localities singing Shabads (hymns). The celebrations also include the three-day Akhand paath, during which holy book, the Guru Granth sahib, is read continuously, from beginning to end without a break. On the day of the festival, the Granth Sahib is also carried in a procession on a float decorated with flowers throughout the village or the city. Five armed guards, who represent the Panj Pyare or the five disciples deeply loved by the gurus, head the procession carrying the Nishan Sahib (the Sikh flag). Local bands playing religious music form a special part of the procession. Free sweets and langar or community lunches are also offered to everyone. Sikhs also visit Gurudwaras where special programmes are held.

Chhattisgarh

People

One third of Chhattisgarh's population is of tribal stock, settled mostly in the thickly forested areas in the state's north and southern parts. The tribals here are mostly of Gond and Dravidian stock. The Mudia, Maria, Parja and Mathara tribes inhabit the Bastar district. The Pandos and Korbas live in Sarguja. Chhattisgarh has a rich cultural heritage.

Folk songs are sung on every occasion. Sohar songs are related to child birth, Bihav songs are related to marriage celebrations while Pathoni songs are related to the 'gauna' or the departure of the bride to the home of the bridegroom. Raigarh district is well-known for the art of Dhokra casting. Toy animals and other objects are moulded in clay, coated with wax and are encased in more clay. The molten metal is poured in through a small hole in the outer layer, melting the wax that runs out with the metal and taking its place and hardening in the process. The clay coating is removed and the object is polished, chased and finished on a lathe.

Gonds are a very large tribe of Central India with a population of around 12.7 million. Traditionally they have been cultivating land, producing crops, and raising livestock. They grow rice, wheat, and different types of lentils, sesame, millet and cotton.

A diverse society, the Gond demonstrates a range of cultural variations which extend from the most primitive to progressive. The Gonds from the northern region appear to have been influenced by neighboring communities.

The people speak Gondi, which belongs to the Dravidian family of languages and is similar to Tamil and Kannada. The literacy levels of the Gond are below average.

Their social divisions are based on groupings of two or more clans who claim descent from a common patriarchal ancestor, either mythological or real. They do not marry from within their clan but marriage among cousins and polygamy is socially acceptable. Marriages are arranged for them either as adults or children. A partner may also be acquired by mutual exchange (two families give brides to each other in marriage), by working to obtain a partner, or by forcing themselves into the home of their intended partner. This is a custom where a prospective bride intrudes on the household of an unmarried man who she fancies and stays on even if she is unwelcome, abused and refused food and shelter. After some time, she is accepted as a member of the family. Running away to get married and simply by gaining possession of a mate by capturing them is not unusual. A vermilion mark is the marital symbol for married women. Bride-price in cash and goods is paid to the bride's father. The practice of dowry is less common but is becoming popular among some groups.

Families live as smaller unit with parents and children and also in extended families with other relatives. Gond society is male dominated and the sons inherit parental property equally. The eldest son succeeds to the late father's authority in addition to receiving extra land and kitchen ware.

The Gond folk tradition is rich in art and craft and they are very fond of music and dance. Both men and women sing and dance to the energetic sound of instruments like the dholak, a double-sided drum. The Pardhan tribe is the official narrators of traditional folk stories for this community. They tattoo their bodies with stars, scorpions, flower, bird and animal patterns. The walls of their homes are painted with scenes inspired by nature – animals, birds, people and trees. These are drawn in red and black on a white background. They make colorful floor designs called rangoli and beautiful pottery, baskets and other crafts. Woodcarving is another talent.

Each subgroup of the Gond tribe is governed by a council known as the panchayat. The primary purpose of these councils is to maintain peace and harmony in their villages and to safeguard and uphold Gond customs.

Some social reform movements appear from time to time, encouraging the Gond to protect the uniqueness of their traditional Gond culture and customs. There are those that believe that the religion of the Gond is different from mainline Hinduism and have called on people to continue to eat beef (which is not permitted to a Hindu) to prove that they are different.

The majority are Hindu. Some are animists, who believe that things in nature—trees, mountains, and the sky, have souls or consciousness and that a supernatural force animates the universe. They believe that their gods inhabit the forest. Ancestor worship is an integral part of their religion. Village gods are worshipped by the villagers as a group and a priest conducts the rites. Idols of gods are often spear shaped, made of iron and are smeared with vermillion powder and kept at a special place called Deo-Khulla, the threshing floor of the gods.

Festivals and Fairs

While the traditional festivals of Hindus, Muslims and other communities are celebrated in Chhattisgrah as enthusiastically as in the rest of India, it is the tribal fairs and festivals which celebrate the ethnic lifestyles of the colourful tribes of the land. The tribal festivals in Jhabua and Bastar are marked by carefree revelry, drinking bouts and exotic entertainment like cockfighting and rounds of uninhibited dancing.

Bhagoria Haat: The colourful festival of the Bhil and Bilala tribes, particularly in the district of West Nimar and Jhabua, is actually of the nature of a mass *swayamvara*(a pre-marriage market) usually held on the various market days falling before the Holi festival in March. As the name of the festival indicates, (bhag to run and haat, a market to choose from), after choosing partners, the young couples elope and are subsequently accepted as man and wife by society, through predetermined customs and traditions. Earlier, the Bhagoria Haat was also a place where old disputes were settled through the intervention of the village elders. The Bhagoria Haat also coincides with the completion of the harvest season and is thus an agrarian festival as well.

Dussehra: The Dussehra celebration at Jagdalpur is a mixture of Hindu and tribal beliefs. An important feature of this festival is that an underlying spirit of inclusion, cutting across caste and creed, prevails. During the celebrations, along with Danteshwari Mai, which represents the Hindu Goddess Durga or Kali, a number of lesser powers and tribal deities, some indigenous and some borrowed from Hinduism are also worshipped. Dussehra starts with the worship at the temple of Kachhingudi, a local goddess. A seven year-old girl of the weaver caste is chosen and ceremonially married to the priest of the shrine. The girl symbolises the goddess. On the tenth day of the celebration the chief of Bastar is symbolically kidnapped while asleep, by Murias and is taken to the Muria settlement of the village Kunharbokra. In the evening the kidnapped chief is slowly brought back to the town, seated on a huge rath (chariot).

An annual fair is held every year in the month of Magh (January-February) in Raipur district's Champaran village. A Follow-up to the fair is the birth anniversary of Mahaprabhu Vallabhacharya that is celebrated every year in the month of Baisakh (April-May) and a large number of followers of the sect assemble to pay homage.

Dadra & Nagar Haveli
People

Nearly eighty percent of Dadra & Nagar Haveli's population is tribal. The territory has no original tribe of its own but tribes of neighbouring States such as the Koli, the Dhodia and the Warli are widely found here. The main language of the people is Bhili or Bhilodi. The various tribes here follow their own peculiar traditions and customs.

The Dadra & Nagar Haveli region is blessed with heavenly natural beauty. The union territory has emerged as a popular tourist hub. Agriculture is the main occupation of the state. The Adivasis mainly produce rice, wheat, sugarcane, paddy, pulses, and fruits. Dadra and Nagar Haveli came under Portuguese control between 1783 and 1785 and Portuguese ruled over this land for more than 150 years, till 1954. Portuguese introduced potatoes, tomatoes, cashews, squash, and various other fruits and vegetables in Indian food.

Festivals and Fairs

Although all festivals are celebrated, the tribals also celebrate their own festivals. Some of the tribal festivals include Diwaso, which is celebrated by the Dhoda and the Warli tribes and Bhawada, which the Warli and Koli tribes celebrate particularly exuberantly. The Bhawada dance during the Bhawada festival which is performed by masked dancers is particularly fascinating. All the tribes in the area celebrate the sowing festival of Gram Devi and the harvest festival of Khali Puja.

Daman and Diu
People

The people of the Union Territory are representative of the waves of conquering races from the plains of North India and West India. The people of the Union Territory are no different from the people of adjoining Gujarat. The population of Daman and Diu consists of people belonging to several religions, numerically, the majority are the Hindus followed by Muslims, Sikhs and the Jains. The spoken language in Daman is mainly Gujarati. In Diu, it is mainly Marathi.

Daman was a Portuguese enclave for four centuries and a half till 1961. The first Portuguese Captain Diogo de Mello, while on his way to Ormuz, met with a violent cyclone and when all hopes were lost, suddenly found himself at the Daman coast. This land with its coastline about 12.5 km along the Arabian sea was once known as Kalana Pavri or Lotus of Marshlands.

The entire region comprising union territories of Daman, Diu Dadra & Nagar Haveli has a distinct Portuguese heritage. The most persistent evidences of Portuguese presence in India are the monuments (edifices of archives) and the distinct Indo-Portuguese people, a product of cross fertilisation of European, African and Asian sources The Great Gate and doorways at St Paul's Cathedral at Diu, Bom Jesus Church at Daman, words in stone Indo-Portuguese creoles currently spoken in Diu and Daman, the religious and the musical culture of this coastal region are some of the examples of the Portuguese influence. In Daman and Diu, Gujarati food and traditional Portuguese food are common.

Festival and Fairs

Two fairs are held which are actively participated in; one on Mahashivaratri day at Palsana and one on Chaitra Punrnima at Mahalaxmi. The Gangaji fair is held every year in the village of Dabhel near the Somnath Mahadev temple in Daman. Large numbers of people, both from within the district as well as outside, gather at the temple to take ritual baths in the tank and worship Lord Shiva. The most important fair in Diu is held in Kalagrimata at Bucharvada. Hindu festivals such as Holi, Dussehra, Diwali are also celebrated in the district of Daman. Christians celebrate Christmas and New Year day. Muslims celebrate the festival Eid.

Delhi
People

The people of Delhi represent a cross section of the people of India. Over time, people from across the country have made Delhi their home. The majority of the population belongs to the Hindu faith; Sikhism and Islam are the other important religions. Hindi is spoken by a majority of the population and the other languages include Punjabi and Urdu.

The people of Delhi are known to be food-lovers and the city is home to many restaurants offering cuisines from all over the country as well as the world. The influence of the Mughals is evident in the Mughlai cuisine as well as the Tandoor, a conical earthen oven from which emerge a delectable array of kebabs and rotis. Also typical of Delhi and north India are the Barfis or milk cakes and crisp golden jalebis dripping with sugar syrup.

Festivals and Fairs

Since Delhi is a cosmopolitan city, all the important festivals in the country from Holi and Diwali to Muharram and Christmas are celebrated here. Specific to Delhi are the Republic Day and Independence Day celebrations, due to its status as the capital of India. The Republic Day which falls on 26 January commemorates the country becoming a republic and is celebrated with a spectacular parade in New Delhi.

Independence Day which falls on 15 August, marks the independence of India from the rule of the British Empire and is celebrated with parades as well as an address to the nation by the prime minister.

Goa

People

The people of Goa comprise of Christians and Hindus. The principal languages are Konkani, Marathi and English. The Christians spoke Portuguese in the past. However, its use has declined over the years. An idyllic day in the life of a Goan might include stopping at a small taverna (bar) for a drink of feni (a local brew made from cashew or coconut), listening to the sounds of a Mando (love song) and the strains of a guitar, and then basking on the golden sands of the beaches or fish for mackerel, crab and lobster. Meat dishes cooked with vinegar are a specialty of Goanese cuisine. The pork sorpotel, vindaloo, Goan sausages and the chicken shakuti or cafreal are famous.

Festivals and Fairs

Given the exuberant and colourful nature of the people of Goa, it is natural that they enjoy fairs and festivals. Music and dance is integral to a Goan's concept of a good life and thus during festivals much merriment takes place.

Jatra: This fair is held in the temple of Goddess Lairai, located in the village of Sirigao. A special feature of this festival is the walk over burning coals, performed by devotees of the goddess known as 'dhonds'.

Feast of St Francis Xavier: This is held on the 3rd of December each year at Vela Goa or Old Goa, 10 kms away from Panaji. The mummified body of St. Francis is brought for public viewing every ten years.

Zatra at Consaulim: The Zatra celebrates the arrival of the three kings at Bethlehem and is held on 6th January each year at Consaulim near Margao and is marked for its widespread merriment.

The Carnival: The Carnival in Goa is a colourful festival. Celebrated for three days preceding Lent, this annual festival is marked by singing and dancing on the streets, with the mythical King Momus, Lord of the festival, presiding over the festivities.

Since Goa was a Portuguese colony for centuries, from about 1510 until 1961, it has different culture and traces of foreign cultural influence. It is a melting pot of people, happenings, events, that draw visitors to this city from all over the world. The region, due to its proximity to rivers and the sea, was the principal port of entry for the Portuguese, who used it to access even other parts of India. It has a mix of beaches, carnivals, forts, temples, rivers, churches, chapels, museums and Portuguese villas.

There are possibly more than 400 churches in Goa, and about 800-900 chapels and 600-700 temples.

Some of these temples almost look like a combination of a temple, mosque and church and have distinctive impact of Portuguese architectural workmanship.

The culture of Goa, including its language, has been influenced by different cultures during its long history. The history of Goa has been marked by periods of Hindu, Muslim, and Christian rule. That's why the language of this state of India has also been exposed to all these religions and cultures.

The native language of most Goa people, which is also the official language of Goa, is Konkani. This name the language received from the similarly-named region of Konkan which covers the whole western coast of India. The language currently uses scripts of other languages like Marathi. The Konkani language underwent changes due to Portuguese colonization, facing the gradual lack of usage and support. However it has recently revived due to the efforts of dedicated traditionalists.

Approximately one-third of Goa population recognises the language of Marathi as their mother-tongue. This language has a special stature in Goa. It sounds very similar with Konkani. Both these languages belong to the Indo-Aryan group of the Indo-European family of languages and have numerous dialects of common origin (probably from Sanskrit) and script — Devanagari. Many Goa people speak both, Konkani and Marathi well enough.

The citizens of Goa, like the rest of people in India, are mostly bi-or multilingual. All educated people of the State speak fluent English, and many people, especially teenagers and adults, prefer this language even in communication at home. English is one of two official languages of Goa and is the only common language for all Indians. Even Hindi—the second official language of the State has no stature ofbeing the obligate language at the State level. Each State has its own official language. Generally, there are 22 languages in India.

The generation of Goans that were born and grew up in the period of Portuguese rule also speak the Portuguese language. At schools it is studied at will as the third language and its use is limited and gradually dying. However, many Portuguese words have entered the local languages firmly, especially among the Christian population of the State. Besides, as a result of the influence of the Portuguese and English languages the Latin alphabet is often used in written communication even in local languages.

Gujarat

People

Gujarat, located on India's western coast, on the Arabian Sea encompasses Kathiawar Peninsula , Kuchh as well as the surrounding area on the mainland. Gujarat draws its name from the Gurjara, a subtribe of the Huns, who ruled the area during the 8th and 9th centuries. The state assumed its present form in 1960, when the former Bombay state was divided between Maharashtra and Gujarat on the basis of language.

Gujarat has the greatest number of sub-divisions of communities in the country. The State also has a tribal population represented by the aboriginal Bhil and the Koli, Naikda, Dubla, Bhangi and the Macchi-Kharwa tribes. There is one entire tribal district of Dangs.

Gujarati, the principal language, belongs to the Indo-Aryan family of languages. Most of the population is Hindu with Jains and Muslims constituting the rest. The people of Gujarat are proficient in the arts and crafts. Every village surface, utensil and garment is vibrantly alive with colour and ornamentation spontaneously created for their own pleasure. Gujarati woven fabrics are famous throughout India. The tie-and-dye Bandhini saris and scarves, in which fine cotton or silk is knotted into minute patterns with waxed string and dyed in successive deepening shades of different colours, is particularly enchanting. The knots are untied later to produce delicate spotted designs, each dot often no bigger than a match head, all over the body of the fabric. In the case of the Patola and Pochampalli weaves, the warp and weft threads are separately tie-dyed before being woven into intricate, stylized designs of flowering shrubs, birds, elephants and fish set in geometric squares and stripes.

Gujaratis make delicious vegetarian food without using onion or garlic, but with stimulating spices.

Festivals and Fairs

Akin to other states, festivals and fairs in Gujarat, are mostly organised during the change of season, usually after one crop has been harvested and preparations are being made for the sowing of the next one. These are also held during religious occasions. Fairs are usually held in the open and coincide with the full moon day.

Bhavnath Festival: This five-day festival is held at the foot of Mount Girnar in Junagadh. The festival is dedicated to Lord Shiva and the highlight of the festival is the Mahapuja on the Shivaratri day.

Madhavpur Fair: This fair is held at Madhavpur village, about 60 km from Porbandar. This fair celebrates the marriage of Lord Krishna and Rukmini. A large number of marriage processions are taken out to commemorate this event and both men and women sing and dance in the honour of Lord Krishna.

Sarkhej Fair: This fair is held in the memory of Shah Ahmed Khattu Gunj Baksh, a Muslim saint. The fair is held at the saint's mausoleum at Sarkhej, on the outskirts of Ahmedabad.

Tarnetar Fair: Tarnetar is a small village is located about 75 km from Rajkot in Saurashtra. It is in this village that the temple of 'Triniteshwar' or Lord Shiva is located. The fair is held during the 4th, 5th and 6th days of the bright half of the month of Bhadrapada (August/September).

Chitra-Vichitra Fair: This is a tribal fair that takes place 14 days after Holi at Gunbhakheri village near Khedbrahma, and is associated with the curative powers of this place.

Dangs Durbar: Dangs is Gujarat's southern-most district inhabited by tribals. Dangs Durbar begins a week before Holi and is attended by tribal chieftains. Dancing, playing of tribal musical instruments, especially the Kahalia and Tadpur and eating and drinking mark the week-long festivities.

Haryana

People

Haryana is predominantly a Hindi speaking State and Hindus constitute more than 90 per cent of the population with the rest of the population comprises Sikhs, Muslims and Jains. Other than Hindi, the other languages spoken in the state are Punjabi and Urdu.

A large part of Haryana being rural, farmers known as Jaats, constitute a significant number of the population. Folk theatre and folk dancing, especially Saang, are popular. Saang is the most popular variety of performances with the participants' females dressed as male singing and dancing continuously for five to six hours. The themes are mostly drawn from mythology. At times, the love lore of Punjab forms the central theme of these performances.

Festivals and Fairs

Besides the festivals of Holi, Dussehra, Diwali and Raksha Bandhan, the people of Haryana hold fairs very enthusiastically. Located 18 kms from Delhi, Surajkund is the site of an annual crafts festival in the month of February. Held in a specially created village setting, the fair attracts craftsmen and artisans from all over the country. The Janamashtami fair at Bhiwani, on the occasion of Lord Krishna's birthday and the Masani fair at Gurgaon are the other important fairs in Haryana.

Himachal Pradesh

People

The state consists of both tribal and non-tribal populations. The earliest inhabitants of the region, it is believed, were tribals called 'Dasas' who were later assimilated by the incoming Aryans. Historically the earliest hill aborigines are found among the scheduled castes in the state. The Brahmins and the Rajputs belong to the oldest Aryans or to the mixed stock that evolved over a long period of time. The tribal population in the state is found in the Kinnaur, Lahaul-Spiti and Chamba areas. Tribal groups like the Kinnauras, Lahaulis, Pangwals and Gaddis are called after the geographical region they belong to. The majority of Himachalis are Hindus but Buddhism is also a dominant influence. Hindi and Pahari are the main languages spoken.

Polyandry marriage system is prevalent among the Kinnaure tribe of Himachal Pradesh. They inhabit the border of Kinnaur district and earn their livelihood by rearing farm animals. Kinnaures consider themselves as the ancestral link of the Kinnaurs of Mahabharata and believe in the custom of Pandava marriage codes. Accordingly, one girl gets married to different brothers of a family. Heavy-price is paid for a bride, who is granted freedom to participate in any of the cultural occasion in the parental home even after marriage. These tribal folk believe that Polyandry is the best way to creating a joint-family system and a smart way to safeguard inherent property from division. One inspiring point lies in the system of re-marriage in their society. Women, after the death of the husband, are allowed to marry again without any social stigma.

The people of Himachal Pradesh enjoy folk songs and dances. The most popular folk dance is Naati. Naati is performed in a chain formation with hands linked by dancers wearing appropriate masks. In Kinnaur and Lahaul-Spiti, the dances depict the perpetual strife between gods and demons. Life is mainly rural, with people living in traditional village houses. Traditional village houses are generally three storied; the household cattle occupy the lowest storey, the middle storey provides space for storing grain and for sleeping in winter, while the top floor provides the living space for the family.

Festivals and Fairs

The fairs and festivals of the hill people are occasions for joyful singing and dancing. The Lavi fair held at Rampur in the Shimla district is the most important fair of Himachal Pradesh. Held on the 25th of November each year, its origin dates goes back to the signing of the trade treaty between the erstwhile Bushahr state and Tibet. The Naati dances and cultural shows are some of the highlights of the fair. The Shivaratri festival is held in Mandi during February and March to celebrate the wedding of Lord Shiva and his wife Parvati. Devotees shoulder the palanquins of their village as well as family gods and goddesses and march in a procession to Mandi where they later pay homage to Shiva.

The Dussehra festival is celebrated with great pomp and show at Kullu. The statue of the presiding deity Raghunathji is brought down from the local Raghunathpur temple to join a procession with two hundred other deities.

Jammu and Kashmir
People

Diverse and different races inhabit Jammu and Kashmir. Most of the people are descendents of the Indo-Aryan stock. However, in the Ladakh region, people have mongoloid features and in the State's Kishtwar region, the people have typical Dravidian features. The Gujjars or the hill people of Kashmir have migrated from Rajasthan. The region has both Hindus and Muslims, with the former mostly concentrated in Jammu and the latter in Kashmir. Kashmiri is the language spoken in Kashmir while Dogri is spoken in the Jammu region.

Pahari painting, literally meaning a painting from the mountainous regions, is an umbrella term used for a form of Indian painting, done mostly in miniature forms. It originated from Basholi State, hence it is also called Basholi painting. Basholi is a town in Kathua district in the state of Jammu and Kashmir, India. It is situated on the right bank of River Ravi at an altitude of 1876 ft. From Basholi the style spread to the Hill States of Mankot, Nurpur, Kulu, Mandi, Suket, Bilaspur, Nalagarh, Chamba, Guleand Kangra. Basholi style of painting is characterised by vigorous use of primary colours and a peculiar facial formula and is considered as the first school of Pahari paintings or Miniatures paintings. It is considered as prototype of the Kangra school of art, which became famous for its exquisite colours and styles.

The people are charming and hospitable and are well versed in creating beautiful shawls as well as delightful cuisine. Kashmiri meats prepared in a peculiarly distinctive way, include Gustaba, Rista and Yakhni. Feasts are celebrated with a banquet called Wazwan, featuring meat delicacies served with rice.

Festivals and Fairs

Hindu festivals like Diwali, Dussehra and Holi and Muslim festivals like Eid-ul-Fitr and Eid-ul-Zuha, are celebrated. Buddhists celebrate the Hemis festival.

Eid-ul-Fitr is celebrated in the months of August-September and means the 'Festival of breaking the fast'. The fast of Ramadan is broken with special prayers and festivities. 'Fitr' is derived from the word 'fatar' meaning breaking. The fast is broken on Eid-ul-Fitr with sumptuous feasts. The festival originated when after proclaiming Ramadan as the period of fasting and austerity, Prophet Muhammad announced a day for celebrations to reaffirm the feeling of brotherhood. Vermicelli cooked in sweetened milk, is a popular dish on this day.

Eid-ul-Zuha: The feast of sacrifice popularly known as Baqra-Eid is celebrated on the tenth day of the Zilhijja, which falls in April/May. The sacrifice of an animal like the goat offered on the day symbolically suggests the commemoration of Abraham's or Hazrat Ibrahim's willingness to sacrifice his only son Ishmael to god or Allah.

Hemis Festival: The Hemis Gompa or monastery located 45 kilometres from Leh is one of the largest monasteries in Ladakh. While most of the Gompas have festivals during winter, the one at Hemis is the only one held during summer.

Jharkhand

People

Jharkhand is home to several tribes. The most ancient among them are the Mundas while the Santhals were the last of the tribes to settle in the state. Other tribes include Hos, Oraon, Karias, Birhors, Sauria Paharias, Mal Paharias, Birjas, Asurs and the Bhumijs. Most of the tribal population is found in the districts of Santhal Parganas, Hazaribagh, Singhbhum and Ranchi.

Festivals and Fairs

Besides festivals like Christmas, Holi and Dussehra, festivals peculiar to Jharkhand include Sarhul and Mukka Sendra.

Sarhul is the most important festival of all the tribes in Jharkhand though each tribe has its own way of celebrating the festival. During Sarhul, which also means the blossoming of the Sal tree, tribal communities worship the Sal tree to seek the blessings of its spirits. The festival is marked by dance and music and uninhibited drinking of Handia (a local brew made of rice).

Mukka Sendra is another festival that is celebrated once every twelve years by the women of the Oran tribe. During this festival, the women of the tribe wear male clothes and gear and explore the region to hunt animals for an entire day.

Karma (Karam) *festival* is celebrated by the Oraon, Baiga, Binjhwari and Majhwar tribes of Jharkhand. This festival is falls in the

Hindu month of Bhadrapada. Karma Festival is a religious festival. On this day people go in the forest to collect fruits and flowers, and they worship Karma Devta, a goddess who is represented with a branch of karam tree. Karam Devi is believed to be the goddess of wealth and children. People sing and dance whole night. Branches are worshipped and their blessings sought.

The *Sohrai festival* is a popular festival of the tribes of Jharkhand. It is associated with the cattle and is celebrated during the festival of Diwali, which falls in the month of November. During the festive celebrations the cattle are washed and worshipped. This is a time for great amusement and performances of cattle such as bullfights are organized to multiply the fun and excitement.

Traditionally, tribal artists and householders in Jharkhand have been using natural colours to make Sohrai and Khovar paintings on walls, caves but in recent times they have taken to paper.

Karnataka
People
The population of Karnataka is ethnologically Dravidian, signifying that they are the original inhabitants of India. However, similar to the rest of the country, intermingling with other races has taken place over time. The predominant religion is Hinduism. Buddhism, Jainism, Christianity and Islam are the other religions that are practiced. Kannada is the language spoken by more than 70 per cent of the population. Along its borders Tamil, Telugu, Marathi and Konkani are also spoken. A school of music is centered in Dharwad for the training of Yakshagana dance drama artists. These artists perform in the folk theatre, called Bayalata. Traditional crafts include silk-weaving, sandalwood and ivory carving, and Bidriwork in the state's Bidar region.

Festivals and Fairs
Besides popular celebrations of Dussehra and Diwali, Karnataka celebrates festivals like Hoysala Mahotsava, Pattadakal Dance Festival, the Karaga Festival and the Hampi Festival.

Hoysala Mahotsava: Held in Belur and Halebid this dance festival is held amidst the surroundings of the ancient Hoysala temples.

The splendidly sculpted Hoysala temples of Belur and Halebid in Karnataka, a UNESCO World Heritage site, are the venue for the Hoysala dance festival. Hoysala dynasty ruled parts of South India from 1000 A.D. to 1346 A.D and during that period only these temples were constructed. The splendid Hoysala temples with their sculptural extravaganza, make the perfect venue for this cultural feast.

Hampi Festival: Held at Hampi, the capital city of the erstwhile Vijayanagar Empire, this festival recreates the glory of its royal past.

Pattadal Dance Festival: Pattadakal, the ancient capital of the Chalukyas, celebrates a dance festival against the backdrop of temples in January.

Pattadakal is a small town located on the banks of the Malaprabha River in the state of Karnataka, popular for its historic temples. It is 22 km away from Badami which was the capital of Chalukya dynasty. Kings of Chalukya dynasty constructed the temples in Pattadakal in 7th and 8th century. The extraordinary aspect of these ancient temples is the excellent amalgam of Dravidian and Indo-Aryan architecture that makes the site a perfect example of India's diversity. Every year in the month of January/ February, a famous cultural dance event is held here that is known as Pattadakal Dance Festival. The festival is conducted against the backdrop of the famous Pattadakal Temples, dedicated to Lord Shiva. The temples, having been declared as World Heritage Sites by UNESCO, are famous for their unique blend of north and south architectural styles. The festival is also known by the name Chalukya Dance Festival, and attracts thousands of tourists from all over the country and the world at large. Famous dancers from all over India come here to participate in this festival. It provides a musical treat to all admirers of dance and music.

Karaga Festival: This festival is celebrated in the Dharmaraya temple in Nagarathapet, in the month of April. Karaga is an earthen pot covered with flowers, which is carried on the head by a priest dressed like a woman. Sword brandishing devotees known as Veera Kumars follow the priest in a procession on a moonlit night.

Kerala

People

As is the case with the rest of the southern States, the bulk of the population is of Dravidian stock. However, Kerala also has considerable ethnic diversity; some of the hill tribes exhibit Negroid features while others seem to be related to the Veddas, the forest nomads of Sri Lanka. There is also a small population of the descendants of Indo-European migrants from the north. Although it occupies just 1 percent of India's land area, Kerala supports almost 4 percent of the nation's population. Most Keralites are Hindus, but there is also a large Christian, Islamic and lesser Jain and Jewish populations of minorities. The official language of Kerala is Malayalam.

Kerala has its own distinctive cuisine using the ingredients locally available. The local Kerala food includes a lot of coconut as that is grown aplenty in the coastal areas. Grated coconut is included in virtually every dish. Coconut milk is used to make the gravies and lends a sweet tinge to the cooking. The oil used for cooking also is mainly coconut or vegetable oil. Rice that grows well in this fertile soil is the staple food. Sea food such as fish, crabs, shellfish, lobsters are included in everyday cooking especially in the coastal regions. The commonly used spices are green chillies, cumin, coriander, clove, cinnamon, cardamom, dried red chillies; and curry and coriander leaves added fresh provide a subtle yet irresistible flavor. The food in Kerala is generally steamed. A traditional festival meal, Sadya or Saddya as it is called, is served on a plantain leaf end with the narrow end to the left.

Matrilineal form of society is considered to be one of the significant features of Kerala. It is also known as Marumakkathayam. Marumakkathayam or matrilineal system was followed by Kshatriya, Nayars (Nairs), Moplahs or Muslims of Malayali race, and Ambalavasis and to some extent by the Ezhavas and the outcaste groups. Under the Marumakkathayam system of inheritance, descent and the inheritance of property was traced through females. Marumakkathayam literally meant inheritance by sisters' children as opposed to sons and daughters. The word 'marumakkal' in Malayalam means nephews and nieces. The joint family under the matrilineal system is known as Tharavad and it formed the nucleus of the society in Malabar.

The people of Kerala practice different types of performing arts. Kathakali is the most scientific and elaborately defined dance form of Kerala. The dancers, all male, depict characters from the Puranas and the Mahabharata. They wrap themselves up in huge skirts and head-dresses and also wear green makeup and check extensions. Dialogue is combined with dance to bring myth and legend vividly to life. Kalaripayattu is the traditional 11th century martial art form of Kerala. Said to be the forerunner of oriental martial arts like Kung-fu and Karate, it follows a system as specialized and intricate as the Jujitsu of Japan.

Kerala is home to a number of dance and art forms. Several dance forms which originated in Kerala are today popular worldwide especially the Kathakali dance form. Originated over 500 years ago, Kathakali is a spectacular classical dance form of Kerala. It is a combination of drama, dance, music and ritual. Kathakali is one of the oldest theatre forms in the world. The word 'Katha' in Malayalam means Story and 'kali' means Play. Thus Kathakali literally means 'Story-Play'. Mohiniattam dance form is a beautiful feminine style with surging flow of body movements.It focuses mainly on feminine moods and emotions. Usually, the theme of Mohiniattam dance is 'sringara' or dressing up for a love tryst and is closely related to Bharathanatyam of Tamil Nadu.

Festivals and Fairs

Kerala celebrates many festivals. It is only during the monsoon months of June to August that a ritual, ceremony or festival does not take place in Kerala. Notable festivals include the Onam, Thrissur Pooram and the Nishgandhi Dance festival.

Onam:Essentially a harvest festival, Onam celebrates the home coming of Mahabali, the demon king who ruled over Kerala and was ousted by Lord Vishnu. His return, once a year, to his kingdom is marked by floral courtyard decorations, feasts and the famous snake boat race in the state's backwaters at Alapuzha, Champakulam, Aranmula and Kottayam.

Thrissur Pooram: This festival is held in the month of April/May in the honour of Lord Vatakunnanthan (Shiva) in Thrissur. The presiding deities of the temple are honoured with processions of caparisoned elephants carrying the temple images accompanied by temple drums and fireworks.

Nishagandhi Dance Festival: This dance festival is held each year at the Nishagandhi open-air auditorium in Thiruvanthapuram. Leading exponents of almost all classical dance forms including Bharatanatyam, Odissi, Mohiniyattam and Kathak perform at this dance festival.

Lakshadweep

The Indian Ocean island of Lakshadweep was constituted into a Union Territory of India in 1956. Known earlier as the Laccadive, Minicoy and Amindivi Islands, the name of this Union Territory was changed to Lakshadweep in 1973. The five northern islands of Amini, Kadamat, Kittan, Chetlat and Bitra constitute the Amindivi group of islands. Andrott, Kavaratti, Agatti and Kalpeni are known as the Laccadive group and Minicoy is the southern-most island. The administrative center for this Union Territory is Kozhikode, in mainland, in the west coast of Kerala.

People

From the earliest times, people from the mainland of India had settled the Lakshadweep group of islands. The early settlers were people from Tamil Nadu, Kerala and Gujarat. It is believed that around the 14th or 15th century, people from Kerala migrated to these islands. Most of them were Muslims and are today the majority community in the islands. Among them, a majority of the people belong to the Shafi School of the Sunni sect. Malayalam is the common language spoken. The matriarchal system survives and flourishes in Lakshadweep; it is the only island where the husband visits his wife only in the night. Women are present everywhere, in the fields, on the roads and in offices and mosques. Communal feasts are lavish and expensive affairs with the cost of the feasts being shared by the community in a unique system called Bir. Rice, tender coconut, fish and jaggery made from toddy tapped from coconut are the ingredients with which hundreds of dishes are made in Lakshadweep.

Coconut fibre extraction and production of fibre products is Lakshadweep's main industry. There are five coir fibre factories, five production demonstration centres and seven fibre curling units run by the government of India. These units produce coir fibre, coir yarn, curled fibre and corridor mattings.

Festivals and Fairs

The important events are the annual death commemorations of Rifai Sheikh and Sayed Mohammad Qasim. They are held each year at the Ujra mosque.

In Lakshadweep, the Sunni branch of Islam is the predominant faith and Eid-Ul-Fitr, Muharram, Bakra Eid and Milad-Un-Nabi are the prominent festivals.

Madhya Pradesh
People

The southern and the southeastern districts of Madhya Pradesh have a high proportion of tribal population. The Chaons live in Jashpur, the Mundas and Korbas in Betul, the Gonds and Baigas in Mandla and the Bhils dominate the state's western region.

Madhya Pradesh is known for its rich cuisine and the innate artistry of its people. The region of Bhimbetka around the river Narmada in Madhya Pradesh boasts of the largest concentration of rock art sites of the Stone Age period in India. The images, show a distinct Indian character and are mainly of large animals such as the bull or the bison. They are similar to those created by the European cave-dwellers during the Paleolithic Age. In style, they tend towards naturalism. The tribal tradition is still vital and strong, with the tribal mythology and folklore of the State still being preserved.

Festivals and Fairs

All the national festivals are celebrated in the State. Important tribal festivals include the celebration of Dussehra by the tribal people of Bastar and Bhagoriya in Jhabua. Shivaratri is celebrated in Kahajuraho,

Panchmarhi, Bhojpur and Ujjain. The highlights of the Dussehra celebrated by the tribal people of Bastar and Bhagoriaya include quantities of local brew being consumed and feasting followed by dancing.

Shivaratri is the night of Shiva, which occurs on a moonless night in February or March. This is the night when Shiva performed his Tandava or the dance of primordial creation, preservation and destruction. A fast and a nightlong vigil are considered particularly auspecious on Shivaratri. Shiva temples all over the state attract devotees and large fairs spring up near the temple sites.

Cultural festivals include the Khajuraho Dance Festival, the Tansen Music Festival in Gwalior, Kalidas Samaroh in Ujjain and the Ustad Alauddin Khan Music Festival at Maihar.

Maharashtra
People
Ethnically the people of Maharashtra are a mixture of races which are both indigenous and immigrant. The indigenous people, the Australoid aboriginals, are found in the higher reaches of the Sahyadri and Satpura ranges. Dark and short statured with long heads and flat noses these indigenous people consist of the Bhil, Warli, Koku, Gowari and Gond tribes. The majority of the population consists of the descendants of people from the north who had settled in this region.

Marathi is the State language and is spoken by over 90 per cent of the people. Along the border with other States, Telugu, Gujarati, Hindi, Kannada and Sindhi are also spoken. Hinduism is the dominant religion followed by Islam and Buddhism. Parsis or people following the Zoroastrian faith are mainly confined to the city of Mumbai and its environs.

Maharashtra has a distinct cultural life with folk art forms like the Tamasha or folk theatre, which is very popular in the rural regions. A peculiar feature of the life of the Maharashtrian, especially the Mumbaikar, is the home-cooked lunch delivered by the city-wide organization of Dabbawallas or Tiffin carriers. Of the many dishes produced in Maharashtra, Parsi cuisine is quite popular.

Festivals and Fairs

Maharashtra celebrates many festivals throughout the year. Besides Holi, Dussehra and Diwali, fairs and festivals include Ganesha Chaturhthi, Gudhi Padwa, Pola, the Pune Festival, Govinda and the Hurda party.

Ganesha Chaturthi: Lord Ganesha is the patron deity of Maharashtra. Ganesha Chaturthi or the auspicious day when Lord Ganesha was born is celebrated throughout the state in August-September. The 11 day festival is the most important festival in the state.

Gudhi Padwa: 'Gudhi' is the bamboo staff with coloured silk cloth and a garlanded goblet atop which symbolises victory or achievement. Maharashtrians erect Gudhis on Padwa or the first day of the Hindu New Year. People welcome the New Year with Gudhi worship and distribute 'Prasad' comprising tender Neem leaves, gram pulse and jaggery.

Pola: This is a harvest festival celebrated by farmers all over Maharashtra. On this day, bullocks which are an integral part of the agricultural chores and consequently the village economy are honoured. They are bathed, colorfully decorated and taken out in processions across the village, accompanied by the music of drumbeats and the Lezhim which is a musical instrument made of a wooden rod and an iron chain full of metallic pieces.

Pune Festival: Held during Ganesha Chaturthi, the Pune Festival is a cultural festival held each year. During this festival one can participate and revel in traditional and modern sports events, shop for exquisite textiles and handicrafts, relish the delectable cuisine and rejoice in the colourful customs of Maharashtra.

Govinda:Janamasthmi or the anniversary of Krishna's birth is celebrated as Govinda in Maharashtra. Devotion is expressed in exuberant enactments of Krishna's childhood attempts to reach pots of curd and butter placed out of his reach. Matkas or earthern pots containing his favourite foods are suspended between buildings high above the street. Groups of young men form human pyramids till one is able to reach and break the Matka.

Hurda party: This celebration occurs in rural Maharashtra wherein the farmer invites village folk to partake of fresh ears of jowar (sorghum) in the celebration. Folk songs and traditional dances accompany all these celebrations.

Manipur
People
Over two-third of the population of Manipur are Meiteis who are largely Hindu and occupy the Manipur Valley. The rest of the population consists of indigenous hill tribes divided further into clans. The Nagas and the Kukis are the important tribes in the State. Manipur is the language spoken by over 60 per cent of the people. The Manipuris excel in such martial arts as the spear dance (Takhousarol), the sword fight (Thanghaicol) and wrestling (Mukna). The typical Manipuri culture of expression is seen in every man, woman and child of Manipur. The musical form of this culture is reflected in the worship of Vishnu and it is around episodes from his life that the faith of people is entwined. The Sankirtans and Raas are revered musical traditions. The dance form illustrates a tender yet vigorous style, a continuity of movement and a restraint of power.

Manipur is home of several tribal communities who live together in mutual harmony. The Meities and Tangkhuls are the principal tribes that reside in the hilly state. Other tribes include the Kukis, the Anals and the Monsangs. The Meiteis, one of the most eminent ethnic groups of Manipur hail from the Manipur Valley and are an industrious lot. The Mongol features and the jet black hair are distinctive characteristics of the Meitei men. The people of Manipur are natural craftsmen and their skilled hands are the creators of some of the most exquisite handicrafts of Manipur. Textile Weaving, Wood Carving, Block Printing, Kauna Mat or Water Reed Mat are the popular and unique handicraft of Manipur.

Manipuri is one of the six major classical dances of India. Manipuri dance is indigenous to Manipur, e is entirely religious and aims at gaining spiritual experience. Manipuri Dance is a common name and envelopes all the dance-forms of Manipur. Thus, Manipuri dance can be called a basket of various dances. The true culture of Manipur livens up in its dance and drama. The Raas Lila (love story of Radha and Krishna) dominates the state's performing arts. The 29 tribes of Manipur have their different dances to present, such as, Lai Haroba (representing celebration of Gods), Pung Cholem (Mridang dance), Mao Naga, the priestess dance of Malbe Jagoi, Thangal Surang dance, etc.

Festivals and Fairs

A year in Manipur represents a cycle of festivals. Some of the important festivals in the State include Gang-Ngai, Lui-Naig-Ni, Yaoshang, Cheiorba, Lai-Hairoba, Ratha Jatra, Heikru Hitongba, Kwak Yatra, Ningol Chakkouba and Kut.

Gang-Ngai: This festival is celebrated for five days in the month of Wakching (December/January). The Gang-Ngai is a festival of the Kabui Nagas.

Lui-Naig-Ni: This is a festival of the Nagas and is observed on the fifteenth day of February. It celebrates the start of the seed sowing period after which tribes belonging to the Nagas group begin the cultivation of their fields.

Yaoshang:The Yaoshang is celebrated during the month of Phalgun (February/March). One of the major festivals of the State, it is associated with the Thabal Chongb, a Manipuri folk dance.

Cheioraba:This Festival is celebrated during the month of April. People clean and decorate their houses and prepare special dishes which are offered to the deities.

Lai-Hairoba: The Lai-Hairoba is held during the month of May. This festival represents the worship of traditional deities and ancestors. Both men and women perform a number of dances, the most famous of which is the Lai-Hairoba of Thanjing, who is the ruling deity of the Moirang.

Ratha Jatra:This is one of Manipur Hindus' biggest festivals and is celebrated for ten days in the month of Ingel (June/July). It is dedicated to Lord Jagannath.

Heikru Hitongba: The festival of Heikru Hitongba is celebrated in the month of September and is a festival of joy with little religious significance.

Kwak Yatra: Kwak Yatra is dedicated to Goddess Durga and is celebrated in the month of October. It represents the victory of righteousness of good over evil.

Ningol Chakouba: This is a festival of the Meiteis and celebrates the revival of familial ties. During this festival married women come to the houses of their brothers. It is celebrated on the second day of the new moon in the month of Hiyanggei (October/November).

Kut: This is an autumn festival is celebrated by the different tribes of the Kuki,Chin andMizo groups. Observed on the first of November, Kut is a harvest festival and is held in the honor of the giver of bountiful harvests.

Meghalaya
People
The Khasi, Jaintia and Bhoi people predominantly inhabit the districts of eastern Meghalaya and belong to the Proto-Australoid Mon-Khmer race. The Garo Hills are inhabited by the Garos who belong to the Bodo family of the Tibeto-Burman race. They are believed to have migrated from Tibet.

The most commonly spoken languages are Khasi and Garo followed by Pnar-Synteng, Jaintia, Haijong and Nepali. Bengali, Hindi and Assamese are also spoken. Christianity, Hinduism and Animism are among the major religions in the area; small populations of Muslims and Buddhists are also present.

The women weave Dakmandes, a kind of women's wear, which is well decorated with depictions of beautiful flowers and butterflies in various colour combinations. Baskets, sleeping mats, winnowing fans, rain shields manufactured out of plaited bamboo and cane are found in the rural areas. Jaintia fishing traps made of bamboo splices are noted for their functional beauty. The cane bridges hanging over quick-flowing steams testify to the superb craftsmanship of the Khasi and Jaintia people.

Festivals and Fairs
The festivals of Meghalaya include Ka Pomblang Nongrem, Shad Sukmynsiem, Behdeinkhlam and Wangala.

Ka Pomblang Nongrem: This is also known as the Shad Nongrem and is one of the most important festivals of the Khasis. Essentially a harvest festival, this five-day festival of dances is held each year at Smit village near Shillong.

Shad Sukmynsien: Shad Sukmynsien literally means 'the dance of the joyful heart'. It is another important Khasi festival. Both men and women dressed in traditional finery participate in the dance.

Behdeinkhlam: An important festival of the Jaintais, it is held in the month of July after the sowing of crops. Men of all ages participate in the dance festival. Women, as a rule, do not dance in the celebrations.

Wangala: Wangala is a festival celebrated by the Garos. Held in October-November, the week-long harvest festival is held in honour of their God called Saljong.

Mizoram
People
The term 'Mizo' meaning hill-men or highlanders is a generic word and includes a number of tribes that reside in Mizoram. They include the major tribes such as the Lushai, Ralte, Hmar, Paite, Pawi, and Lakher and the smaller tribes such as the Khiangte, Chawngthu, Fanai, Ngente Pang and Pattu. The other tribes in the State are the Reang and the Chakma. All the tribes excluding the Reang and the Chakma speak Lushai. A Lushai dialect called Duhlian is a part of the spoken language. However, a number of the tribes are bilingual and speak in their own dialect and Duhlian.

The popular traditional dances of Mizoram are many and include Cheraw or the bamboo dance and Khuallam and Chheillam to honour the guests.

Festivals and Fairs
The people of Mizoram have kept alive their rich cultural heritage, colourful customs and lively traditions. The Festivals and dances of the Mizos have a unique tribal flavour. Apart from Christmas and New Year's Day, the Mizos also celebrate a number of traditional festivals called Kut. These include Chapchar Kut, Mim Kut and Pawl Kut.

Chapchar Kut: This is a popular spring festival and is celebrated after the completion of the arduous task of clearing the jungle for 'jhum' cultivation. On this day, people of all ages, young and old, men and women, dressed in their respective colourful costumes and head gears assemble and perform various folk dances, sing traditional songs which are accompanied by the beating of drums, gongs and cymbals.

Mim Kut: The Mim Kut or the Maize Festival is usually celebrated during the month of August and September after the harvesting of the maize crop. Mim Kut is celebrated with great fanfare by drinking rice-beer, singing, dancing and feasting. Samples of the year's harvests are consecrated to mark the departed souls of the community.

Pawl Kut: This is also known as the harvest festival and is celebrated sometime in between December and January, after the harvesting of crops is over. It is perhaps the greatest festival of all Mizo festivals. With plenty of grains in the barn after a year-long labour in raising crops, it is an appropriate time have a grand festival.

Nagaland
People

The Nagas belong to the Indo-Mongoloid ethnic group. The word 'Naga' is used to designate many tribes and sub-tribes. However, its origin is debatable. The term 'Naga' was most probably given to the hill tribes by the people from the plains. There are more than 14 major tribes and several sub-tribes that differ in dialect and customs. The important tribes include the Angami, Ao, Chakhesang, Chang, Khemungan, Konyak, Lotha, Phom, Pochury, Rengma, Sangtaqm, Sema, Vimchunger and Zeliang. Some of these tribes are of recent origin;the Chakesangs, for example, were earlier known as the Eastern Angamis and are a combination of Chakru, Khezha, Sangtams and a few Rengmas. Languages spoken include English, Ao, Konyak, Seema and Lotha.

The Nagas are an artistic, social people whose passion for beauty, colour and fondness for intermingling are expressed in their crafts and dances. Nagas carve beautiful designs with their simple equipment like the Dao. They use homemade colours and pieces of bamboo to make beautiful decorative materials. Unique to Nagaland, is the village institution of Morung, meaning communal houses or dormitories, for young unmarried men. Skulls and other trophies of war are hung in the morungs. The pillars are carved with striking images of tigers, hornbills and human and other figures. War dances and dances belonging to distinctive tribes form the major art form in Nagaland. Wearing colourful costumes and jewelry, the dancers enact mock war motions.

Folk dance of Nagaland forms the main component of the traditional culture of the people of Nagaland. Folk dances of Nagaland are generally performed in religious and festive occasions. Mainly the Naga men perform war dances. This dance is martial and athletic in style. All the folk dances of Nagaland are performed along with war cries and songs by the dancers. There are several folk dances in Nagaland which are generally performed at the time of harvest. Each Naga tribe has its own dance, but they have a common feature. All the folk dances of Nagaland require the use of legs while keeping the body in an upright position.

Festivals and Fairs

Some of the important festivals are Sekrenyi, Moatsu and Sankarni Puja. Festivals in Nagaland are mostly related to agricultural operations. The important thing about a Naga festival is that it has the community as a whole participating in the celebrations. The tribes also celebrate their seasonal district festivals.

The Kohima Summer Festival: This is a North East Regional cultural meet. The high points are rock music, a flower show, archery and traditional Naga wrestling.

Moatsu: This is an important festival of the Moatsu and is celebrated once the sowing of the rice crop is over. The festival lasts for six days.

Sekrenyi: The Sekrenyi festival is possibly the most important festival of the Angamis. Sekrenyi is celebrated in February by the Western Angamis and in December by the Southern Angamis. The festival is celebrated to ensure the health and well being of the community during the coming year. It is an occasion of great merry-making with enormous quantities of rice-beer, beef and pork being consumed.

Sankarni Puja: This is a major festival of the Zemis and coincides with Shivaratri. Single boys and girls join in in the Sankarni Puja festivities, which lasts over a week. Chanting songs, they smoke, eat and drink to their hearts content. Contribution, in money and kind, is welcome from both the participant families as well as the visitors.

Odisha
People

The population belongs to the Australoid, Mediterranean and Alpinoid racial groups. The Savara, Khond, Gond, Munda, Juang, Ho, Santhal, Gadaba, Oraon, Koya and Bhuina tribes represent the Australoid stock. Most of the tribal population lives in the hilly areas of the State. Out of all the tribes the Bondos are the least acculturated. Women wear a stack of nine metal rings around their neck and men get drunk on toddy. The Alpinoid and Mediterranean races constitute the rest of the population. Oriya is the language spoken in the State. The tribal population speaks their own language and Oriya. All Oriyas look to Lord Jagannath (one of the forms of Hindu god Vishnu) and consider him to be the center of their religious faith.

The Oriyas have a rich artistic heritage and have produced some of the best examples of Indian art and architecture. Mural paintings, stone carving, wood carving, icon painting (also known as patta paintings) and paintings on palm leaves reflect the artistic traditions of Odisha. Handicraft workers are famous for their exquisite silver filigree ornamentation and decorative work. Odissi is the classical dance of Orissa and is a 700 year-old dance form. Originally a temple dancer performed this dance before gods; its modes, movements, gestures and poses are depicted on the walls of the great temples, especially at Konarak in the form of sculpture and relief carvings. Odissi dance festivals are held at Konarak each January. Chhau is a dance performed by groups of masked dancers from the Mayurbhanj and the Seraikela region.

Festivals and Fairs

Orissa celebrates important festivals like Holi, Diwali, Dussehra as well as festivals specific to the State, like the Puri Festival and the Boita Bandana ceremony.

Puri Festival: Located 60 kms to the south of Bhubaneshwar, Puri is the site of the Jagannath Temple which dates back to the 12th century AD. Every June, on the day of the 'Ratha Yatra' or the chariot festival, thousands of pilgrims pull the chariots of the deities Lord Jagannath, Subhadra and Balbhadra to the Gundiacha Temple about 1.5 kms away.

Boita-Bandana festival: In October-November, for five consecutive days before the full moon, people gather near river banks or the seashore and float miniature boats as a symbolic gesture that they will leave for faraway lands, once visited by their ancestors. This is the ceremony of Boita-Bandana or the worship of boats.

Puducherry

People

The people of the Union Territory of Puducherry are no different from the people of the adjoining States, which includes Tamil Nadu, Andhra Pradesh and Kerala. There is a small population of the Irula tribals in the Puducherry region. The spoken languages in the Union Territory include Tamil, and French. Hindus and Christians constitute the majority in Puducherry with Muslims forming an important minority.

In 1674, Pondicherry became a French colonial possession., it was transferred to India de facto on 1 November 1954, legally on 16 August 1962. The uniqueness of this town invariably lies in skillful town planning and Franco Tamil architecture. The town is built on the model of 'bastide', a fortified French coastal town of the late 18th Century.

The plan of the city of Puducherry is based on the French grid pattern and features perpendicular streets. The town is divided into two sections: the French Quarter (*Ville Blanche* or 'White Town') and the Indian quarter (*Ville Noire* or 'Black Town'). Many streets retain French names, and villas in French architectural styles are a common sight. In the French quarter, the buildings are typically in colonial style, with long compounds and stately walls

Several monuments in the city pertain to the French period. A French Consulate is in Puducherry, along with cultural organisations. Another important building is Le Foyer du Soldat, a veterans legion hall for soldiers who served in French wars. Among the French cultural organisations, the French Institute of Pondicherry, the Puducherry Centre of the École française d'Extrême-Orient and a branch of theAlliance Française are noteworthy.

Influenced by East and West, Pondicherry has unique handicrafts in leatherware, pottery, hand made paper, incense and antique colonial furniture. Crops like coconut, areca nut, condiments and spices are grown here. Paddy crop is a major crop and pulses, groundnut and chillies are the other rain-fed crops grown in Yanam. Pondicherry boasts of a sumptuous cuisine that shows strong French and Tamil influences.

Festivals and Fairs

Mahashivaratri, Ramanavami, Janamasthami, Vijayadashami, Navaratri and Diwali are the important festivals celebrated in Pondicherry. The Masimagam Festival, Villanur Temple Car Festival, Bastille Day and the birth anniversary of Shri Aurobindo are peculiar to Pondicherry.

Masimagam Festival: This festival is celebrated during the full moon around mid-March. On this day, the deities of the sixty-four temples from in and around Pondicherry are brought to the beach for a sea bath. Thousands come to witness and participate in this festival.

Villanur Temple Car Festival: This festival is held around mid-May and features a procession where the ornately decorated car of the Thirukameswarara Kukilambal temple is pulled by thousands of devotees.

Bastille Day: The Bastille day is observed on July 14 and Pondicherry witnesses a Indo-French pageantry. Donning their uniforms, war veterans march through the streets singing the Marseillaise. The French and Indian flags are flown together.

Birth Anniversary of Shri Aurobindo: Celebrated on August 15, the birth anniversary of Shri Aurobindo is a holy day in the Sri Aurobindo Ashram, which is located in Pondicherry. On this day, thousands of people from all over the world come to the ashram to pay homage to the great sage, poet and philosopher of the twentieth century. *Christmas*: Due to the historical background and also since Pondichery has a large population of Christians, hence Christmas is celebrated here with a lot of enthusiasm and vigour.

Punjab

People

The people of Punjab are predominantly Sikhs who trace their religion to Guru Nanak, the first Sikh Guru. Other than the Sikhs, a large part of the population consists of Hindus, Muslims and Christians. Punjabi is the spoken language; other languages spoken in the State include Urdu, the usage of which has declined over the years. Folklore and ballads comprising of old romances such as Heer-Ranjha, Sassi-Punnun and Mirza-Sahiban including the mystical and religious verses of the 13th century Muslim Sufi Shaikh Farid and of Guru Nanak, who used the Punjabi language as a medium of poetic expression are illustrious examples of the versatility of the Punjabi language.

Dances include the vigorous and colourful Bhangra, Jhumar and Sammi, where people dance with great abandon. The Giddha, a native Punjabi dance, is a boisterous song and dance performed by women. The Phulkari or flower-craft technique with its bold surface satin stitch in vivid orange, pinks and flame reflects vigour and energy, which is typical of the Punjabi people.

Festivals and Fairs

Punjab celebrates a host of festivals and fairs. Baisakhi and Basant Panchami are witness to the Punjabi's love of a good time, with much fun and frolic and of course, dancing in these fairs. Apart from the festivals of Dussehra, Diwali and Holi, the other festivals celebrated in Punjab include Niman Kasti, Teeyan and Rakhi.

Basant Panchami: This is the most famous of the seasonal festivals in Punjab. It heralds the advent of spring and fairs are held in many villages, with people putting on yellow clothes appropriate to the season. Kite-flying is a popular entertainment of the people on this occasion.

Baisakhi: Baisakhi is a harvest festival celebrated during the month of April. When the harvest is gathered, the farmers join in the merry-making with full gusto. Since this fair is also an expression of prosperity, singing and dancing constitute its most enchanting features. Punjab's universally famed dances such as the Bhangra and Giddha are linked to this festival.

Nimani Kasti: The festival of Nimani Kasti is celebrated in May-June. Hindu women observe a fast on this day, one that is very hard to keep because they have to abstain from water for the whole day. Charitably inclined people put up stalls to distribute sweetened and chilled water. The stalls, known as Chhabils, are a common sight on this day.

Teeyan: A festival of the rainy season, Teeyan is celebrated in July-August. One day before Teeyan, girls apply henna to their hands and feet and on the day of the festival, put on their best clothes and go out to the fairs. The Giddha dance is a regular and enchanting feature of this festival. At home, women make kheer or rice-pudding.

The Rakhi festival: This festival celebrates the bond between sisters and brother. On this day, sisters tie a multi-coloured thread on the right wrists of their brothers. The Brothers give gifts to the sisters and affirm their bond as well as make a vow to protect them all their lives.

Rajasthan
People
A majority of the States' population are adherents of the Hindu faith with small populations of Jains, Muslims and Sikhs. There is also a large population of Bhil tribals inhabiting Rajasthan with a sprinkling of other tribes such as the Meenas, Damor, Dhanka, Garasia, Kathodi, Patelia and Seharia who share the state. The main languages spoken are Rajasthani and Hindi.

The typical folk dance of Rajasthan is the Ghoomar, which is performed on festive occasions by women. The Geer dance is performed by men and women. The Penahari dance is a graceful dance performed by women and the Kacchi Ghori, in which male dancers ride dummy horses, is also popular.

The engraved and enameled Meenakari brassware of Rajasthan has designs chased on tinned brass, which is then filled in with black or coloured lacquer applied with a hot tool and finally polished. The coloured patterns which are generally flowing arabesques of flowers and foliage, stand out in the glittering metal. Jaipur and Udaipur are also known for exquisitely enameled silver and gold ornaments and fanciful artistic works that are adorned with precious stones. Also famous is the moulded blue pottery of Jaipur made of ground feldspar mixed with gum and painted a pure opaque white with turquoise and cobalt blue floral and a figurative design.

Festivals and Fairs

Besides Holi, Dussehra and Diwali, Rajasthan has many local fairs and festivals of its own.

The Urs at Ajmer: Ajmer has the unique distinction of having the most important Muslim shrine in the country;the Dargah of Moinuddin Chisti, a Persian saint who came to India and established the Sufi order of Chistiya. People of all religions visit the Dargah Sharif or his tomb during the Urs or commemoration of his death.

Pushkar Fair: Pushkar, located northwest of Ajmer, is the site of a temple believed to be the only Brahma temple in the country. Pushkar is also famous for the annual cattle fair. Held during October or November, it is the venue for villagers from all over the State, who bring cattle, camels and horses for sale.

Gangaur: Clay images of Mahadevi and Parvati, representing the benevolent aspects of the Hindu mother goddess, are worshipped by all women for fifteen days and thereafter taken out to be immersed in water. Their procession is joined by a priest, who is led to the water by trumpeters and drummers. Hindus and Muslims both celebrate the festival.

Teej: Teej is celebrated during the July or August months, to welcome the monsoon.

Sikkim

People

Sikkim is home to the Lepchas, who are the original inhabitants of the State. However, migration over the years has led to an influx of other tribes and people who have settled in Sikkim. Prominent among these are the Bhutias from Tibet and the Nepali people from Nepal. Almost all of the State's people follow either the Buddhist or the Hindu religion.

Unique to the people are the thangka paintings preserved in monasteries across Sikkim. Thangka paintings are traditional paintings of a religious nature which are mounted on brocade. Celebrations translate into folk dances and the drinking of Chang or millet beer, popular amongst the Himalayan north-easterners. Poured into tall bamboo containers, the drink is sipped through a bamboo pipe.

Festivals and Fairs

The festivals of Sikkim are related to Tibetan and Hindu religious and aesthetic traditions but retain a unique character due to the infusion of pro-Buddhist customs from the various tribes.

Phang Lhabsol: This is the most important cultural festival in Sikkim, the two day festival is held in honor of the Himalayan mountain peak Kanchenjunga, the guardian deity of Sikkim. Masked dances performed by Lamas are the highlight of this festival.

Saga Dawa: This is a very auspicious day for Buddhist adherents of the Mahayana sect. People go to monasteries on this day to offer butter lamps and pray. A huge procession of monks carrying the Buddhist Holy Scriptures goes around Gangtok.

Dasain: The biggest and most important festival of the Hindu-Nepali population, Dasain or Dussehra is celebrated in September-October and symbolizes the victory of good over evil.

Tamil Nadu

People

The population of Tamil Nadu belongs to the Dravidian race. The people are of short to medium stature with a complexion ranging from brown to dark as well as wavy hair. There are a few tribes that live in the hilly regions of the State.

Tamil is the official State language. Along the State's border, Telugu, Kannada and Malayalam are also spoken. Hindus constitute a majority with Christians, Muslims and Jains also residing in the State.

Whether it is Bharatnatyam, Tamil Nadu's most celebrated art form, metal work and fabrics, or the cuisine, the people of Tamil Nadu have been demonstrating their creativity in myriad ways. Classical South Indian or Carnatic music as it is called differs from the Hindustani in its stricter adherence to structure. Bhakti or devotion is its mainstay.

Metal work includes Cire-Perdue or the lost-wax technique of casting bronze objects, especially the life size bronze statues of Hindu deities made at Swaimalai. Kalamkari meaning literally 'the art of the pen,' is a wax-resistive technique taking its name from the bunch of steel wires attached to a wooden handle with which the melted beeswax is painted on to cloth before it is dyed.

Bharatanatyam is the officially recognised classical dance form of Tamil Nadu. The dance requires intense training to master its gentle movements, subtle poses and flexible gestures of senses and body. Rich in diversity, the states boasts of a variety of folk dances like Parai, Karakaatam, Villupaatu and Koothu that add spice to the life of local inhabitants including tribes in hill areas.

Both vegetarian and non-vegetarian dishes are common in the menu of a Tamil's family with rice being the main course. Usually, food is served in a long, broad plantain leaf that has medicinal properties. The vegetables have plenty of fibres, protein and vitamin that nourish the body. On the selection of rice, a household prefers raw rice (Ponni variety) for daily consumption.

Festivals and Fairs

Among Tamil Nadu's important festivals are Pongal, Adiperukku, the Thyagaraja festival, the Floating Festival and Chithirai.

Pongal: Pongal is celebrated in Tamil Nadu around the middle of January. The three-day festival is a celebration of a good harvest and a thanksgiving to Surya, the Sun God.

Bull racing or Jallikattu is a bull's game day event celebrated in Tamil Nadu as a part of Pongal celebrations. Jallikattu has been known to be practised during the Tamil classical period and It was common among the ancient tribes also. Bulls are bred specifically by private landlords of the village for the event and attended mainly by many villages' temple bulls (kovil kaalai). A temple bull is like the head of all cattle in a village. Special rituals are performed for this temple bull during important days. It is considered as proof for knowing Tamil civilisation that they were highly civilised to make a festival game day even for their bulls and cattles which help very much in their agriculture. The event often results in major injuries and deaths. Animal activists also protests against the practice over the years. In fact apart from human injuries and fatalities, the bulls also sustain serious injuries.

Adiperukku: Adiperukku is commonly known as the Aadi monsoon festival. It is a Hindu Tamil celebration on the 18th day of the Tamil month of Adi (mid-July to mid-August). The festival pays tribute to water, which is necessary to sustain life. For the blessing of mankind with peace, prosperity and happiness, nature worship in the form of Amman deities are organized to shower Nature's bountiful grace on human beings. Adi is held along the banks of rivers to welcome the water brought by the monsoon.

Thyagraraja Festival: An annual musical event, this is a unique festival of Carnatic music held in early January at Thiruvariyar, the birthplace of the famous singer poet Thyagaraja.

The Float Festival: The Float Festival commemorates the birth of Tirumala Nayak, a 17th century king. Elaborately decked images are taken out in a procession outside the city of Madurai and installed there in an ornamented barge which is illuminated by thousands of lamps.

Chithirai: Chithirai is celebrated in the State's temple town of Madurai during the month of April-May, in symbolic remembrance of the celestial wedding of Goddess Meenakshi and Lord Sundareshwar.

Tripura

People

Of the total population, more than 50 per cent belong to the Scheduled Castes and 19 Scheduled Tribes. Half the population speaks Bengali; the other languages spoken in the State are Tripuri and Manipuri. Most of the population is Hindu, with Muslims and Buddhists also accounting for a good number.

Tripura, is a storehouse of tribal crafts and culture. Most tribals live in elevated bamboo houses called Tongs, which are superb works of craftsmanship. Tribal dances reflect the emotions of these people.

The Cheraw dance is associated with the confinement of Lusai women before their child's birth. Basata Rass is the dance of the Hindu Manipuris in Tripura while the Halam community of Muslims celebrates the Hak Hak dance.

Festivals and Fairs

Besides all-India festivals like Holi, Dussehra, Diwali and Eid, a couple of fairs specific to Tripura include Ashokastami Mela and Pous Sankranti Mela.

Ashokastami Mela: This fair is held in the month of April at Unakoti and is visited by thousands of pilgrims.

The Pous Sankranti Mela: The Pous Sankranti Mela is held on the 14th of January of each year at Tirthamukh, which is located near the Dumboor Lake, about 110 kms from Agartala. Tirthamukh marks the origin of the River Gumti.

Uttar Pradesh

People

The people of the State are predominantly of Aryo-Dravidian stock. Hindi is the official language of the State and is spoken widely throughout; Urdu is the next important language. Hindus are, by far, the dominant religious community and comprise almost 85 per cent of the population. Muslims are the next important religious community followed by Buddhists, Sikhs, Jains and Christians.

The people of Uttar Pradesh are an accomplished lot whose creativity is attested to by the musical styles, dances and food of the region. The Chikan work of UP consists of delicate white embroidery on white floral net and the shadow embroidery work shows the subtlety and refinement of the Mughal court. Legend says that Noorjahan, the Queen of Jahangir, devised the craft. What is known as North Indian music has essentially originated from UP. The forms of music include Dhrupada, Khayal, Thumri, Tappa and Ghazal, each having a specific history of development. The Kathak (storyteller) of yore was a versatile actor-musician-dancer who addressed himself directly to his audience. Involved and complicated footwork and rapid pirouettes are the dominant features of this dance style.

Festivals and Fairs

Uttar Pradesh celebrates important national festivals like Muharram, Holi, Dussehra, Diwali and Janamashtami.

Kumbh Mela: Perhaps the largest fair in the world, the Kumbh Mela is the most important Hindu fair held at Prayag (Allhabad) every sixth and 12th year. Held in the month of January, this bathing festival draws millions of people from all over the country.

Holi: This festival is celebrated in early March. People throng the streets smearing each other with brightly hued powder (gulal) or squiring coloured water on each other. Bhang (Hemp) or Thandai adds to the relaxed mood of the revelers and an atmosphere of hilarity prevails.

Originally, a fertility festival, the legend of Prahlad speaks of a king so arrogant that he demanded his people worship him. Only his young son Prahlad refused. Finally, the king's sister Holika, said to be immune to burning, sat with the boy in a huge fire. So potent was Prahlad's devotion that he emerged unscathed while Holika burnt to death.

Uttarakhand

People

The population of the State belongs to a distinct ethnographic group, with people in the plains exhibiting Aryan features and giving way to distinct Mongoloid features in the bordering areas with Tibet.

Many tribes inhabit the region with the Kol tribe dominating the Kumaon region. The Bhotia tribe is spread over Almora, Chamoli, Uttarkashi and Pithoragarh. The Buxa tribe is concentrated in the Nainital district. Tharus are tribal people from the Thar Desert region of Rajasthan with their own distinct lifestyle. Jaunsari is a mixed tribe and the largest group to inhabit the peaks in Kalsi, Chakarata, Lakha Mandal and Jaunsar Bhabar.

The main languages spoken include Hindi and Pahari, with the most common dialects among the latter being Kumaoni and Garhwali. The artistic ability of the people is revealed in the woodcarving, painting styles, ornaments and folk songs and dances. The folk songs of the State capture the spirit, heritage and lifestyle of the people. There are songs for religious rites and ceremonies with every festival being an occasion for musical expression. Among folk dances, Chaufulla is the popular dance form of the Garhwal region with men and women gyrating to the rhythmic beats in pairs. Tharya is a dance performed on the occasion of the bride's first visit to the parental home after marriage while Jaagar is performed to invoke the blessings of the local deities.

When Mughal prince Suleman Shikoh took refuge in Garhwal he brought along artists well versed in the Mughal style of miniature painting. These court painters stayed back and developed the Garhwal School of Painting. Other styles of painting in the region include the Aipan, Peeth, Patas and Rangwali.

Festivals and Fairs

A strong awareness of their roots is evident in the people of Uttaranchal and is shown through the fairs and festivals which are celebrated with traditional gaiety and fervour.

Makar Sankranti: On Makar Sankranti, people give Khichdi in charity, take ceremonial dips in holy rivers, participate in the Uttarayani fairs and celebrate the festival of Ghughutia or Kala Kauva. During the festival of Kala Kauva (literal translation: black crow), people make sweetmeats out of sweetened flour, shape them like drums, pomegrantes, knives and swords and offer them to the crows as a token of welcome for all migratory birds who are now coming back after their winter sojourn in the plains.

Phool Devi: This festival is celebrated in mid-March. On this day, young girls conduct most of the ceremonies. In some places, this festival is celebrated throughout the month with the advent of spring. During this festival, young girls go to all the houses of the mohalla or the village with plates full of rice, jaggery, coconut and flowers. They offer their good wishes for the prosperity of the household and are given blessings and presents in return.

Ganga Dussehra: Ganga Dussehra is celebrated sometime during the moths of May and June. The goddess Ganga is worshipped on this day and Dussehra posters (known as Dwarpatras or Dasars), which have various geometric designs (Yantras) on them, are put up on the doors of houses and temples.

The Nandadevi Fair: This fair is held at Almora, Nainital, Kot, Ranikhet, Bhowali and also in the far-flung villages of Johar and Pindar valleys. People come from far and wide to Danadhar, Suring, Milam and Martoli in order to worship the goddess. In Nainital and Almora, thousands take part in the procession carrying the Doli or palanquin of Nanda Devi.

Diversities of Dharma and it's Philosophy

We need to understand the basic philosophy and meaning of Religion, derived from the Latin religare. Religion in short means 'to serve humanity' and to follow the principles of dharma, truth, non-violence. To know yourself and above all it's a way of life. Religion doesn't mean creed, dogmas and fanaticism. Religion gives us lessons to stand unitedly. Truth is one and we call it by different names. The morality of every religion is one. We all are children of one supremebeing.

According to 2011 census, 79.8% of the population of country are designated 'Hindu'. It is one of the most ancient religions of the world, which began about 6000 years ago. Besides Hindus, Muslims are the most prominent religious group and are an integral part of Indian society. There are approximately 14.2% Muslims (over 172 Million), 2.3% Christians (over 27 Million), 1.7% Sikhs (20 Million) and others including Buddhists (8 Million), Jains, Parsis (Zorastrians), Jews and Bahais, less than 2%. Hindus and muslims are spread throughout the country. Muslims are found mostly in the states of Uttar Pradesh, Bihar, Maharastra, West Bengal, Andhra Pradesh and Kerala. They represent a majority in Jammu & Kasmir and Lakshadweep. High Christian concentration is found in North eastern states like Nagaland, Mizoram and Meghalaya and the Southern states of Kerala, Tamil nadu and Goa. Sikhs are a majority in Punjab whereas Buddhists are found in large numbers in Arunachal Pradesh, Laddakh, Bengal and Sikkim. Though a tiny minority, jains are found all over India. Most Jains are found in the states of Maharastra, Rajasthan, Karnataka and Gujarat.

Sanatan Dharma: Basic philosophy and expression

Sanatan dharma can be described as the 'museum' of religion. No other religious tradition is so eclectic and so diversified in its theoretical premises as well as its practical expression. Hinduism can be called as Sanatana dharma or the religion Perenis. As the name ananta implies (without a beginning), it is eternal and ever-lasting (Shashvata). It is the only major religion which has not been traced to a specific founder and the only one which does not have a holy book as the one and only scriptural authority. Sacred texts of Hindu religion consists of Vedas, Upanishads Bhagavad Gita etc. Hinduism always absorbs anything that is good and valuable and at the same time, shares its wisdom with whomever earnestly seeks it. Its doors are open to all.

Dharma is derived from the Sanskrit root *dhric* (to hold), dharma stands for that which holds up the existence of a thing. Sanatan dharma have a much deeper and wider and inner meaning. It has nothing to do with any dogmas and creed. It is free from religious fanaticism. Sanatan dharma means eternal religion. It is basically a 'culture' or 'a way of life'. It allows for absolute freedom. It teaches us how to lead a perfect life. This perfect life makes us divine. It is not a fixed code but a response to the changing demands of society. But its goal is to reach god through purifying our mind. It trains us for spiritual discipline and moral assets.

The Vedic sage says that 'Vedas love him who is awake'; they come to meet him. It means that Jnana and bhakti come to him who is awake. Bhakti and jnana are not different from the effort. They, in fact, make the effort interesting and add flavour to it. This is what Vinoba Bhave says, that Karma, Jnana and Bhakti appear disconnected from each other but are really not so. Jnana, bhakti and karma that is ceaseless effort, are three legs of the tripod of life. Life should be built on these three pillars. Logically, we may take jnana bhakti and karma as different things, but they cannot be separated from each other in practice. These three together make one great entity.

Sanatan dharma stands for truth purity, cleanliness of mind, spiritual awakening and moral values. In one sentence it is way of life. It's an art of living. It asks us to know about self and to unite oneself with God, even in the midst of activity with equanimity. Sanatan dharma teaches us to destroy, to kill Rajas and Tamas and nourish and develop Sattva, asceticism within you.

There are three brothers in the Ramayana, Ravana, Kumbhakarana and Bibhishana. Kumbhakarna is the embodiment of Tamas, Ravana that of Rajas and Bibhishana that of Sattva. The drama of the Ramayana with these three characters, is being continuously enacted inside our body. In this drama, Ravana and Kumbhakarna ought to be killed and only the Bibhishana principle, provided it takes refuge at the feet of the Lord, may be nurtured, as it can help our progress. The Gita is thus placing before us the ideal of the lotus flower.

In the Indian culture, the highest and the noblest things of life are described using the smile of the lotus. The lotus is the symbol of Indian culture. It expresses the most elevated thoughts. It is clean and pure and remains unsoiled by the mud around. Sanctity and detachment are its distinguishing characteristics. Different organs of the Lord are described employing the smile of the Lotus. He has lotus eyes, lotus feet, lotus heart and so on. It is means to show and impress upon us that everywhere there is beauty, holiness and detachment.

Sanatan dharma teaches us that the lord is everywhere in the universe. Tukaram has said, 'The Lord is everywhere, but to the wretched, He is elusive'. For the saints there is prosperity everywhere, while for us there is famine. Holy rivers, high mountains, serene oceans, tender hearted cows, noble horses, majestic lions, sweet-voiced cuckoos, beautiful peacocks, clean and solitude loving snakes, crows flapping their wings, the upward rising flames, the still stars – He pervades the whole creation in different forms. We should train our eyes to see him everywhere, first in simple and then in complex phenomena. We should first understand simple letters and then strive to make sense of the the complex 'joint letters' or words.

Our life should be full of Yajna or moral virtues. Only then can we realize God. Vinobha very beautifully described how to become nearer to God. He reflected that The Lord had said to Arjuna, 'All these warriors are going to die. Be only an occasion, an instrument. I have already slain them'.

Vinobha concluded that he who is free from enmity to all creatures, who is every engrossed in serving the world impartially without any expectations, who dedicates all his actions to the Lord, who is full of devotion who forgives all and is detached and full of love becomes an instrument of the Lord. He reflected that this was the essence of the Gita's teaching.

The Hindu religion believes in the theory of incarnation. In fact it is deemed necessary for protection of dharma against *adharma*. According to Hindu theology, from time to time, evil overpowers good and the earth comes to be ruled by wicked kings and demons who deny the rule of dharma, which is the cosmic law of righteousness. They suppress virtue and morality till life on earth becomes unbearable. Only the true devouts survive and they put their faith in their god. In response to their prayers, Vishnu incarnates himself again and again as an avatara, to put an end to adharma or unrighteousness and restore order on earth. It is believed that he has manifested himself nine times, with the tenth or final incarnation yet to come. Some texts enumerate more incarnations; with the Bhagavata Purana mentioning twenty two incarnations, but ten is the most popular number.

Swami Vivekanda, in his 1893 paper on Hindusim, said, 'To the Hindu, man is not traveling from error to truth, but from truth to truth, from lower to higher truth. To him all the religious, from the lowest fetishism to the highest absolutism mean so many attempts of the human soul to grasp and realise the infinite. Every soul is a young eagle soaring higher and higher,gathering more and more strength, till it reaches glorious sun... to the Hindu, then, the whole world of religions is only a travelling, a coming up, of different men and women, through various conditions and circumstances, to the same goal. Every religion is only evolving a God out of the material man, and the same God is the inspirer of all of them. Why then, are there so many contradictions? They are only apparent, says the Hindu. The contradictions come from the same truth adapting itself to the varying circumstances of different natures. Thus the whole object of their system is by constant struggle to become perfect, to become divine, to reach God and see God, and this constitutes the religion of Hindus'.

Thus, Sanatana dharma stands for peace and harmony and its motto is to wipe the tears of helpless eyes and not to create unnecessary rituals, dogmas and creeds which destroy the purity of any religion.

Baudh Dharma

Buddhism stands on three pillars: the Buddha (its founder), the Dhamma (his teachings) and the Sangha, the order of Buddhist monks and nuns.

Siddhartha, who was later known as the 'Buddha' meaning the enlightened one, was the son of king Shuddhodana of Kapilavastu and his queen, Maya. He was born in 563 BC on the Vaisakha Purnima day in the royal grove at Lumbini near Kapilavastu, the Capital of the Sakyan republic. His family name was Gautama and he belonged to the Shakya clan. Hence he is sometimes called Shakyamuni (Shakya sage) or Shakyasimha (Shakya lion). Among his other names are Amitabha (infinite light) and Thathagata (he who has arrived at perfection).

Queen Maya died a week after delivering the prince. So the child was brought up by his step mother Gautami. At Siddhart has birth, the royal astrologer prophesied that he would one day become disillusioned with worldly pleasures and go forth as a mendicant in search of the wisdom that could overcome suffering.

The king, remembering the astrologer's prophecy, tried to save his son from unpleasant sights. The king found for him a lovely wife, Yashodhara. Yashodhara bore him a son. He named his son Rahula (impediment). But the seeds of disenchantment had already sprouted in Siddhartha's heart. As prophesied, Siddhartha saw the three signs of suffering; sickness, old age and death. These sufferings touched his heart and he left his palace on the night of the full moon in the month of Vaisakha, at the age of twenty-nine, to seek mental peace in the homeless life of an ascetic.

With a view to finding a true solution, the Buddha endeavored for full six years. During this period, he searched, scrutinized and examined in detail the prevalent schools of thought. He realised that wisdom could not be attained through self-mortification. At last, meditating under a tree near Gaya, he attained Bodhi (Illumination). Prince Siddhartha became the 'Buddha', the fully awakened one and the tree which had sheltered him came to be known as the Bodhi tree.

After becoming enlightened, Gautama the Buddha could have immediately realised himself from the cycle of rebirths and attained

'Nirvana' ie supreme liberation. But he decided to share his wisdom with others. His first sermon was preached in the Deer park at Saranath, near the ancient holy city of Varanasi. The five ascetics who had been his earlier colleagues became his first audience. Thereafter, for 45 years, the Buddha went about the country, from town to town, from village to village, disseminating spiritual illumination for the benefit of suffering humanity. He attained 'Maha-Parinirvana' at Kusinara in 483 BC at the age of eighty. Just before his death, when his favourite disciple Ananda started weeping, Buddha said 'All component things must dissolve. Buddha can only point the way. Become a lamp unto yourself and work out your own salvation diligently.' Besides being a great spiritual teacher and preacher, Buddha was also a great social reformer. The Buddha revolted against oppressive social laws and proclaimed his new philosophy of liberty, equality and fraternity for the common welfare of all. Lord Buddha was considered as the creator of the virtues like individual liberty, tolerance, fellow-feeling, compassion, non-violence (Ahimsa), moral character, benevolence as well as service and sacrifice.

In the life of the Buddha, there are two sides, the individual and the social, The familiar Buddha-image is of a meditating sage who is absorbed and withdrawn and lost in the joy of his inner meditation. This is the tradition associated with Theravada Buddhism and Asoka's missions. For these the Buddha is a man, not God and a teacher and not a saviour. There is the other side of the Buddha's life, when he is concerned with the sorrows of men, eager to enter their lives, heal their troubles and spread his message for the good of the many : *bahu-jana-sukha bahu-jana-hitaya*. Based on this compassion for humanity, a second tradition matured in North India under the Kusanas (70-480 AD) and the Guptas(320-650 AD) It developed the ideal of salvation for all, the discipline of devotion and the way of universal service. While the former tradition prevails in Ceylon, Burma and Thailand, the latter is found in Nepal, Tibet, Korea, China and Japan.

Christianity

The followers of Jesus Christ are called Christians. Christianity has the largest number of followers in the world. Jerusalem, the place where Christ lived and preached, is considered to be the most sacred for Christians all over the world.

Jesus Christ was born in Bethlehem of Judea in 4 BC Until he was 30, Jesus lived in Nazareth as an ordinary carpenter. Then he plunged into a very active public life for about three years. During these years he preached that God is a loving and merciful Father. Jesus insisted only on the necessity of showing our love towards God through loving our fellowmen without any distinction or reservation. He was the sitting example for his own preaching. He treated both the sinner and the saint with the utmost love and respect. Jesus became a revolutionary figure among the Jewish religious leaders who presented Gods as being always demanding, angry and ready to punish. They forced the ruling Roman Governor, Pontius Pilate to crucify and kill Jesus.

But the life of Jesus did not end with his death on the cross. He rose from the tomb on the third day, thus proclaiming to the world the hope of universal resurrection after death. His disciples realised that Jesus was not an ordinary man but the 'Son of God' who really became man in order to announce to the world God's love and concern for the human race. He wanted to bring peace on earth. He strengthened his Apostles with the help of the Holy spirit, to preach his teachings and spread the good news about God being a loving father to the entire human race.

The Bible

Bible, the holy book of the Christians has two parts, namely *The Old Testament* and *The New Testament*. The Old Testament presents God dealing with man before Christ and gives the history of the Jewish people for a period of roughly 2000 years before Christ. The New Testament records the life and preaching of Jesus, his death and resurrection and the growth of Christianity in its early years as well as the message of the Apostles sent to various churches. The Bible is considered as the holy book of Christians because it is believed that the Bible was written under the guidance and inspiration of God. The Bible comprises a collection of 73 books. The 'Old Testament' consists of 46 books and in the 'New Testament' of 27 books.

When seen in the India context, the thoughtful among the younger generation of Indian Christians believe that God works in all men and in the whole world, although Jesus so perfected his nature that he manifested the god in himself in a more marked degree than other men. They think that the life of Jesus which brought out the aspect of redeeming love in the nature of God, which was practically ignored by the old Testament writers although some of their great prophets like Isaiah were not unaware of it, has the highest ethical significance for us in the present condition of the world. They confidently anticipate the coming of the kingdom of God by the gradual growth of goodness and the spread of Christian love though not of Christian doctrine. They are deeply concerned when vital doctrines of Hinduism such as the unity and omnipresence of God, Ahimsa, karma and rebirth are misrepresented and caricatured. Christianity in India hears the call of Hinduism today. She may pay heed to it and follow or she may be deaf to it and refrain. But all signs indicate that she is choosing wisely. She is attempting to combine the best elements of Hinduism with the good points of Christianity and if she succeeds, it is not India alone that will be better of with this syncretism. The quality of the spiritual life of the world will be better.

Islam

Islam is an Arabic word meaning both 'Submission to God' and 'peace'. The followers of Islam, who are called Muslims, are found all over the world. There are over 100 crores Muslims all over the world and out of this around one-tenth live in India.

Islam is not only a religion but also a way of life. Muhammad, the prophet of Islam, was born in Mecca about 570 AD. In Around 610 AD, god sent his first message to Muhammad. Messages came to him from god till his death in 632 AD. These messages were recorded by the companions of Muhammad. The collection containing these messages is called the 'Quran', which is the holy book of Muslims. The teachings of Muhammad which were distinguished from the words of god, were collected and are known as 'Hadith', the second most important source of Islam.

The Arabs called Muhammad, 'Al-Amin' or 'The trustworthy man' and respected him greatly. But when god sent through him the first message of Islam, there was stiff opposition against Muhammad from all sides. The opposition kept mounting and Muhammad was forced to leave Mecca in 622 AD. It is from this year that the Muslim calendar starts. Muhammad arrived in Medina where people listened to Muhammad and accepted him as a true prophet. The people in other towns challenged those who had already become Muslims and war became inevitable. However, when Muhammad died in 632 AD, not only had the whole of Arabia embraced Islam but also his religion was being called the Perfect Religion and was fast spreading in many lands.

The death of the Prophet of Islam posed the problem of succession. One group of Muslims wanted a person from the family of the Prophet to be his successor. This group was known as the 'Shias'. The other group, the 'Sunnis', wanted the successor to be chosen by majority opinion. The majority went in favour of Abu Bakr, who was chosen as Caliph. The Sunnis won, but this brought about two broad divisions in Islam. After Abu Bakr, two more caliphs,'Umar and Uthaman',were chosen. Then Ali, the son-in-law of Prophet Muhammad and a candidate chosen by the Shias from the very beginning, became the fourth Caliph of Islam. These four Caliphs are known in Islamic history as the Pious Caliphs.

Islam was revealed by God to the Prophet of Islam at a time when Arabia was witnessing a period of ignorance and tribal warfare. A common cause of wars was the dispute over which god was superior since each Arab tribe had its own god. Islam substituted one god in place of many and brought the Arab tribes together under the supreme Islamic belief that there is only one god. From the belief in the unity of god, Islam went on to preach the unity of mankind. The great force with which the message of the 'Quran' spread from Arabia to the whole of Middle Asia and other far-off lands, gives proof that it had a unique appeal for human beings.

It was the Arabs who went to trade with various countries and carried the message of Islam forward along with their merchandise. The great increase in knowledge in all fields that followed the birth of

Islam was a result of the great emphasis laid by the 'Quran' and by the Prophet, on the acquisition of knowledge, from whatever source available. The contribution of Muslims to literature can be seen in books like the 'Arabian Nights' and their contribution to art and architecture is evident in many thousands of buildings, from the giant and majestic palace of Al-Hamra in Spain to the Taj Mahal in India.

The mystics of Islam, known as 'Sufis', played an important part in spreading the message of universal love and toning down the aggressive trends in Islam. Islam's spirit of brotherhood helped in loosening the rigidity of the caste system. It is observed that the local cultures of Muslims in various parts of the world have remained unchanged. On the other hand, it has allowed them to nurture their culture within the broad framework of the basic beliefs and practices.

With a rich spiritual background, it is the privilege of the Indian Muslims to interpret the faith of Islam in its truest, highest and noblest sense, so as to distinguish it from the creed professed today by the ignorant bigot, the political intriguer and the religious fanatic. If the Indian Muslim combines his inherited tradition with his acquired faith and in effect creates a synthesis of the old and the new, he will be led to emphasise those neglected aspects of the truth of Islam which really promoted culture and civilisation and brought to life a dying world. He will also tend to discard those unimportant details which happened to be exaggerated out of all proportion on account of historical accidents. He will break the yoke of the crystallised religion which pervades and blindly influences the life of the people, and will give the world of Islam an interpretation of the message of Mohammad, which will be more in accord with the spirit of the Prophet than with the dogmatic developments of his later followers. Ameer Ali in his book, *The Spirit of Islam* (on which I have drawn freely in this paper), and Sir Ahmed Hussain in his *Notes on Islam* give us a foretaste of the wonderful flowers which will grow out of the soil of India's past.

In the Quran, there are ever so many things of strictly local and temporary interest, which are not all relevant to religion *qua* religion. The conservatives of all creeds forget that 'the dry bones of a religion are nothing, the spirit that quickens the bones is all. Sir

Ahmed Hussain distinguishes the spirit of Islam from the dogmatic Mohammadanism of some of our Maulvis. He goes on to say 'I make a difference between Islam and Mohammadanism. The latter is not pure Islam. It has forgotten the spirit of Islam and remembers only the letter of its law.'

When we take our stand on the experiential side of religion, we realize that the truly religious men of all faiths are nearer each other than they imagine. In the broad spirit of Hinduism, the author recognises that the truth conveyed by all religions is the same and quotes with approval Jalal-ud-din Rumi's saying that 'All religions are in substance one and the same.' It is impossible for the Indian Muslim to accept whole-heartedly the spirit of exclusiveness which is a marked feature of Semitic religions. India has stood for religious freedom and harmony from the beginning of her history. In accordance with this spirit, the great Akbar tried to fuse India into a homogeneous nation by promoting the unifying bond of a common religion in the practice of which, both Mohammadans and Hindus would join hands. Although he failed in his attempt as the conditions were not in his favour, it was a noble endeavour in the right direction.

Considerably influenced by the idealism of the *Upanisads,* which steer clear of all images and dogmas and thus have universal value, Dara Shikoh(the great grandson of Akbar), wrote the *Majma'e Bahreen* or the union of the two oceans (of Hinduism and Islam). He recognized that the two religions were equally efficient in helping us live a meaningful life. Sir Ahmed Hussain holds that though different ways of striving, we may reach the same goal of salvation. The erroneous belief that there is no true religion besides Islam breeds bigotry, intolerance and fanaticism and is contrary to the teachings of the Quran. The first verse of the second Sura commands us to believe in not only what was revealed to Mohammad but also in what was revealed to those who went before him. It clearly indicates that there are, and will ever be, many true religions, of which Islam is one.

Jainism

Principles of Jainism

Jainism is primarily an Indian religion with more than 4.5 million Jains in India. In spite of its small number, the Jain community has a strong influence in Indian life. Jains belong chiefly to the mercantile class and are spread mainly over central, northern and southern India. Splendid Jain temples and statues can be found in almost all parts of the country. The Jains have also set up many trusts and charitable institutions in the country.

The theme of self-conquest, common to all religions, is supremely important to the Jains. The very word Jaina is derived from 'Jina' meaning conqueror. Carrying the idea of self-conquest to its extreme, Jainism has become the world's most rigorously ascetic faith. God has no place in this system. The popular gods of Hinduism are accepted, but they are placed lower than the Jains who are regarded as the true recipients of worship.

Mahavira is called 'the jina', ie. 'the conqueror'. He did not conquer kingdoms but he conquered his own self. He is called Mahavira, the great hero not of the battles of the world that he fought but due to the battles of inward life. By a steady process of austerity, discipline, self purification and understanding, he raised himself to the position of a man who attained divine status. His example is an incentive to others to pursue the same ideal of self-conquest.

Mahavira had 11 disciples and each was entrusted with a band of about 300 to 500 monks to preach the religion. Bhadrabahu, a contemporary of the great Mauryan king Chandragupta, was the greatest propagator of the faith. After Bhadrabahu's death, serious differences began to arise among the Jain community. The group led by him migrated towards the west coast and the Deccan, while others remained in the north.

The group which remained in the north were chiefly led by Sthulabhadra, the last of the omniscient. The final break between the two groups came around AD 79. Jains divided into Digambaras (sky /air as their cloth) ie. naked who follow Mahavira and

Swetambaras (wearers of white clothes), who follow Parshvanatha. Most famous among the disciples were Gautama, Indrabhuti and Sudharman and they are said to have attained omniscience (knowing everything). Mahavira is said to have preached in Ardhamagadhi language. A fixed form was given to the Jain Canon in the 5th century AD, which consists of 45 works of varied content, at Valabhi. Digambaras did not accept this canon. They believed mostly in the oral teachings of the monks and that liberation was impossible unless one renounced clothes and followed in the footsteps of Mahavira. They contested that Mahavira was married. They do not believe women can attain liberation and the omniscients can take ordinary nourishment. The Digambara tradition believes that the ancient texts have definitely been lost and do not believe in the authenticity of the scriptures which constitute the canon of Swetambaras. The Swetambara canon is called 'Agama' or 'Sidhanta' or even 'Gampidaha'. The other important Jain religious texts are 'Devadashangas', 'Upangas' and the 'Mulashatras'.

Jains have made valuable contributions in many areas of Indian culture: philosophy, literature, painting, sculpture and architecture. Their poetry is often excessively didactic. Their sculpture is of a high quality and some of the images of Tirthankaras are technically perfect. Their faces are however devoid of any expression, as they are supposed to have transcended all human emotions. The greatest glory of Jaina religious art lies in temple architecture, particularly at Ginar, Palitana and Mount Abu. These temples reveal a breadth of aesthetic sensitivity and a feeling for ornamentation reminiscent of the finest specimen of classical Hindu and Buddhist architecture.

Judaism

Judaism is the religion of the Hebrews. It is a religion older than Christianity. Moses was the first prophet and law giver of the Hebrews. In order to save the Hebrews from the cruel Pharaohs of Egypt, Moses led them to the promised land of God. On the way, at Mount Sinai, Moses received the 'Ten Commandments' from

Jehovah, the Supreme God. Thus around 1000BC the Hebrews established themselves in Israel.

Holy Books of the Law, the Prophets and the Psalms were put together and came to be known as the 'Hebrew Bible' or 'The Old Testament'. The term Hebrew Bible can be understood as an attempt to provide specificity with respect to contents, while avoiding allusion to any particular interpretative tradition or theological school of thought. It is widely used in academic writing and interfaith discussion in relatively neutral contexts meant to include dialogue among all religious traditions. The 'Talmud' is the collection of detailed laws for the guidance of civil, domestic and social life of the Hebrews. According to Judaism right conduct is more important than right belief. Judaism does not believe in self imposed suffering or asceticism.

In India there are two ancient indigenous Jewish communities-Malayalam speaking Cochinites and the Marathi speaking Bene Israel (children of Israel). Ancestry of Cochin Jews dates back to the period when King Solomon's merchant fleet began their trade. As per scholars, the Jewish people settled along Kerala's Malabar coast soon after the Babylonian conquest of Judea in 586BC. They were well received by the rulers and a small Principality was granted to Joseph Rabban, a Jewish leader. Their Synagogue at Cochin is one of the oldest in India and its interior is worth visiting. Today emmigration to Israel and other countries has considerably reduced the Indian Jewish population. Now, only a few of them remain in Cochin.

Sikhism

The word 'Sikh' goes back to the Sanskrit word 'Shishya', meaning disciple or leader.

Sikhism had its birth in Punjab. The founder of the Sikh faith, Guru Nanak belonged to Punjab, a region where Hindus and Muslims had been in closer contact than in any other part of India.

The Sikhs are recognised by their beards and turbans. They value these as signs of their religious faith. These symbols are an essential part of the Sikh way of life. The men grow beards and wear turbans over their long hair which is never cut. Every Sikh considers it an obligation to wear a Kara (steel bangle). There are other religious injunctions, like abstaining from tobacco, which are obeyed rigorously.

The 'Guru Granth', meaning the Holy scripture, is the spiritual authority and is venerated as the living presence of the Gurus. It gives form and meaning to the Sikh's religious traditions and social customs. Their faith has a broad humanitarian base. Singly and in groups, in their homes and in congregations at their places of wor ship, the Sikhs conclude their morning and evening prayers with the words : 'Nanak nam Charhdi Kala, tere bhane Sarbatt Ka Bhala' meaning May Thy Name, Thy Glory, forever be triumphant, Nanak and in Thy will, may peace and prosperity come to one and all.

Zoroastrianism

Zoroastrianism is one of the oldest religions. It explains man's duties in this life and the high destiny which he can achieve by establishing his conduct in accordance with the eternal and immutable law of nature. Zarathushtra, the founder of Zoroastrianism, called it the law of Asha. Zoroastrianism is based upon knowledge and illumination and its emblems are the Fire and the Sun.

Zarathushtra is said to have been born around 6th century BC in the town of Amui near Rae, on the salt lake Urumiah later renamed Razsieh, in the Azarbaijan province. He went up the mountains of that province for meditation and preached his faith for many years among hostile tribes. As a young boy, he was placed under able teachers but they soon found that he was more knowledgable. Zarathushtra spent several years in meditation and study, pondering over the fundamentals of life and existence and trying to find a rational explanation based upon the Law of nature, Asha. He discovered the perfection which lies in the absolute, as possessing perfect power or energy and perfect wisdom, which he called 'Ahura Mazda', ie the Lord of Life and Wisdom.

The religion of the Iranian people of his time was a primitive form of polytheism of Indo-Aryan origin. It is partly based on the

Rig-Veda. There were many deities and each family had sacred idols. Each tribe had different rituals, sacred obligations and customs. To this Eastern world, Zarathushtra brought a new universal concept of religion. His religion was not a set of superstitious rituals based on fears, but a universal call for a better life to be achieved with the aid of an invisible god of wisdom, truth, light and goodness.

Zarathushtra was the first man who gave a definitely moral character and direction to religion and at the same time, preached the doctrine of monotheism which offered an eternal foundation of reality to goodness, an ideal of perfection. Zarathushtra showed the path of freedom to man, and on that path the freedom of moral choice and freedom from blind obedience to meaningless injunctions were present. He preached that the moral worth of a deed comes from the goodness of intention and the value of religion was upholding a man in his life of good thoughts, good words and good deeds. Zarathushtra was the first prophet who emancipated religion from the exclusive narrowness of the tribal god.

At the age of seventy-seven, Zarathushtra was killed by a Turanian soldier during an attack on the city of Bulkh.

The active and heroic aspects of the Zoroastrian religion reflect the character of the people. They had zest in life and confidence in their own strength. By force of will and deeds of sacrifice, they tried to achieve Haurvatat, wholeness, well-being, in this world and Ameretatat, immortality.

Unlike the West, religion in India is not synonymous with creeds or dogmas. Here religion has a wider perspective, being closely associated with 'dharma'. The classical Sanskrit noun 'dharma' is a deviation from the root 'dhri' meaning to hold or to sustain. Diversity of religion is not the nation's Achille's heel but an asset which strengthens and sustains multiculturalism.

India is the birthplace of several religions of the world like Hinduism, Sikhism, Jainism, Buddhism etc. Basic thoughts, behaviour and character of a person is greatly influenced by the teachings and philosophy of one's religion. A child learns 'how to live' from the social environment in which he is born and brought up. He becomes liberal and accommodative from the beginning itself as he finds a lot of diversities in society. He learns to live with the diversities. It is similar to the concept of joint family system, where a child learns from his childhood only, how to care for others and how to co-exist with others peacefully. He learns about the power of tolerance and develops the ability to accommodate diverse views and opinion. This is the beauty of India that it is like a garden where a large number of f flowers with different colours and different fragrance are blooming together. Accomodating all the diversities in the form of caste, creed, religion, value, ethnic group, language, food habit etc, the Indian society has become progressive, tolerant and accommodative. This is the beautiful, multicultural India.

Multiculturalism can be a guiding philosophy to respond to cultural and religious diversity only through recognition and positive accommodation of group differences. It cannot be achieved by mere toleration of differences of diverse religions and ethnic groups but through group rights and linking it with nationalism.

In Indian context, our cultural heritage rooted in our combined spiritual treasure is the foundation of a multicultural and cohesive society. The country's plurality and diversity are strongly reflected in the multiplicity of the experiences. But we need to address the diversity in state-sponsored policies and programmes with an objective to prevent conflicts.

One way to attain multiculturalism is formulating policies based on an assimilationist model which envisages that cultural and ethnic groups are incorporated fully into the society. But the role of government in this model is limited since cohesion is viewed as the individual's responsibility and it cannot be forced. People of different religious and cultural background can be bound only by territorial identity and nationalist philosophy.

Another model is based on policies that tend to avoid conflict among the diverse communities. It is the core essence of a free society to accommodate a wide variety of beliefs, diversity of customs, tastes and code of conduct. A free society is one that aims at equality with respect to enjoyment of fundamental freedoms and regards the inherent dignity and the inviolable rights of other communities.

However, for mitigating cultural conflicts and strengthening social integration among different cultures, India has initiated its own multicultural policies. Traditionally, these state oriented multicultural policies maintain reservation treatment for the socially unprivileged or discriminated communities.

Such attempts have borne fruits and brought the hitherto sidelined communities into the social mainstream. The promotion of economic opportunities and unique education system can lead different races to a common goal, and thus racial and cultural differences can be mitigated.

For instance, new settlements for tribes of Andaman and Nicobar have opened up the aboriginals to the outside world and adapt modern ways of living without any resistance. However, a section of intelligentsia and policy makers argue that such attempts have worked only with extremely backward communities like aboriginals but not with the minority communities with literacy and substantial numerical presence.

Despite being a multi-ethnic country in terms of religion, language, community, caste and tribe, India has successfully addressed its multicultural concerns and survived as a state in conditions of extreme regional disparities, underdevelopment, mass poverty and illiteracy. Compared with many less diverse and plural countries, India's record of relative political unity and stability has indeed been quite remarkable.

Thus, in the Indian context, the concept of multiculturalism envisages the rationale behind the institutional measures for the political accommodation of identity, difference and community, which has been responsible for India's survival as a state.

References

1. The Wordworth, *Dictionary of beliefs and religions.*
2. Radhakrishnan, S, *Eastern Religions and western thoughts.*
3. Aurobindo, Sri, *The secret of Veda The foundations of Indian culture.*

4. Veerdar van, Peter, *Religious nationalism Hindus and Muslims in India.*

5. Moore, Christopher, *Hinduism reviving spiritual awareness.*

6. Hasnain, Nadeem, *Tribal India.*

7. *The laws of Manu*, Penguin books.

8. Diwan, Paras, *Modern Hindu Law.*

9. Diwan, Paras, *Muslim Law in India.*

10. Kothari, Rajni, *Caste in Indian Politics*, Revised by Monor James.

11. Kymlicka, W. (2002), *Western Political theory and ethnic relations in eastern Europe.*

12. Dirks, Nicholas (2001), *Castes of mind: colonialism and the making of modern India,* Permanent Black.

13. Dalmia, Vasudha and Heinrich Von Stietencron (eds) (1995) *Representating Hinduism: The construction of religious traditions and national identity,* Sage publications.

14. Bayly, Susan (1999), *Caste, society and politics in India from the eighteenth century to the modern age: The new Cambridge history of India*, vol. 4, No. 3, Cambridge University Press.

15. Kaviraj, Sudipto (1992), ' The imaginary institutions of India, In Partha Chatterjee and Gyanendra Pandey (eds), *Subaltern studies VII: Writings on South Asian History and society*, Oxford University Press.

16. Kymlicka, Will (2001), Politics in the vernacular: Nationalism, multiculturalism and citizenship , Oxford, Oxford University Press.

17. Nehru, Jawaharlal, *The discovery of India*, Oxford University Press.

18. Austin, Granville, *The Indian constitution cornerstone of a nation*, Oxford India paperback.

19. Husnain, Hadeem, *Indian Anthropology*, Palaka Prakashan, Delhi.

2. Joshi A P, Srinivas, M D, Bajaj, JK, 'Religious demography of India', updated upto 2001, Centre of Policy studies.

21. Basu, Durga Das, *Constitutional law of India*, Prentice Hall of India, New Delhi.

22. Savarkar, VD, *'Hindutwa*, Hindi Sahitya Sadan.

23. *Holy Quran*

24. *Bible*

25. Bansal, Sunita Pant, *Encyclopaedia of India.*

26. 'The Holy Geeta', Commentary by Swami Chinmayananda.

27. Swami Nirvedananda, 'Hinduism at a Glance'

28. Radhakrishnan, S. *Indian Religions.*

29. Swami Vivekananda, *Bhakti yoga'.*

30. *The Bhagavadgita.*

31. Swami Nikhilananda, *The Bhagavadgita.*

32. Krishna, Nandita, 'Vishnu'.

33. Bhave, Vinoba, 'Talks on the Gita'.

34. Goyandka, Jayadayal, 'The Bhagavadgita or the song Divine'.

Genesis of Sustaining Multiculturalism in India

WE, on earth, have been blessed with an enormous quantity of natural resources and an even greater amount of natural diversity. Undoubtedly, we have the undeniable right to use these for the welfare of humanity but we must remain wary of taking it for granted. So it becomes our duty to ensure that we utilise our fair share but do not meddle with the rest. As Mahatma Gandhi put it, 'There is enough for everybody's need but not for anybody's greed'.

Innumerable stalwarts, cutting across the boundaries of countries and continents, class and religion have been reiterating the need for a symbiotic relationship between nature and humanity through ethical, normative and scientific means. This is where the concept of sustainable development, introduced in 1984 by the Brundtland Commission Report, starts taking shape.

If we extend this analogy to multiculturalism, we get a very clear picture. For a multicultural nation like India, sustaining the existent diversity through harmony, mutual cooperation and widespread peace is of utmost importance. It is very easy to create a cacophonous situation in a weak, loosely bound, diverse society. Therefore, it becomes imperative for us to bind each and every component of diverse

India with an unbreakable bond of harmony and mutual trust. This is why, the spirit of tolerance is inculcated in every single Indian child. What this means is that every child is taught to be accommodative and adaptive. We, in India, are preservers of the SALAD BOWL CULTURE and not the Melting Pot Culture.

The genesis of this innate bond needs a multifaceted and holistic analysis because Multiculturalism is part and parcel of India's cultural heritage. There are basically two strong bonds which bind the different sections of a diverse India. First is the ineffable greatness of our cultural heritage which inspires us to rise above petty divisions and embrace ethereal beauty. Second is the legal legitimacy granted by our Constitution.

Cultural Heritage as the Sustainer of Multiculturaism

Our cultural heritage lays a lot of emphasis on virtues like truth, compassion, tolerance, accommodation, non-violence etc and completely abjures all vices. Spiritualism, the most invaluable treasure of our cultural heritage, is the doorway to an ocean of virtues. It ensures equanimity in society and inculcates tranquillity in the mind and in the soul. A nation is as good as its citizens. Therefore, if the individuals are virtuous, definitely the nation will reach its pinnacle of success. The opposite also holds true. Therefore, spirituality is the foundation on which a nation and its unity rests.

It is clear that Multiculturalism and Spirituality are intertwined aspects. Spirituality bestows the spirit of accommodation due to the sole reason that religion in India is not associated with creeds and dogmas. Rather, it stands for dharma, which means to hold or to sustain. Religion's first priority is sustaining diversity by serving humanity. Thus, religion is a way of life and if we comprehend this wider perspective, there is no question of any rift due to religion. Instead it strengthens multiculturalism by continuously reminding us that we are headed towards a common goal, through different paths. Different religions may have different customs and may prescribe different ways to reach the same common goal, ie. the light of truth.

Our cultural heritage lays a lot of emphasis on communitarianism which further strengthens multiculturalism. Our values propagate the principle of *Vasudhaiv Kutumbakam*, meaning that the whole world is our kindred and *Sarve bhavantu sukhinah sarve santu niramayaha*, rather than promoting the ideals of Jeremy Bentham, ie. Greatest Good of the Greatest Number or Spencer's concept of Survival of the Fittest. Our cultural heritage aspires for the happiness, prosperity and contentment of each and every citizen of the Earth.

Communitarianism is the preserver of a multicultural India. It widens the thoughts of humanity and ensures that more emphasis is laid on the collective good of the community rather than being obsessed with individual good. It bears a discernible *contrast* with neoliberalism which quite wrongly hypothesises that a welfare state is inimical to an *individual's* liberty and revives the principle of *Laissez-faire*, ie. noninterference of the state in social, political and economic spheres. In a nutshell, the exponents of neoliberalism like FA Hayek, Milton Friedman and Robert Nozic uphold full autonomy and freedom of the individual, while laying no emphasis on the collective welfare of the society. Neoliberalism believes in the primacy of the 'spontaneous order' of human relationships which is exemplified in the free market system.

The growing threat to multiculturalism in other nations is due the obsession of the neoliberals with unlimited individual liberty, lambasting the interests of the society. In India, much more weightage is given to communitarianism which enables innumerable cultures and traditions to flourish under the same roof, side by side.

In addition to it, the spirit of Integral Humanism, coursing through our veins acts as yet another pillar of multiculturalism. The concept of Integral Humanism, given by Deen Dayal Upadhyay, renders an integrated view of individual and society. Therefore, it paves the way for peace and unity—the necessary ingredients of multiculturalism.

Countless Indian philosophers have tried their level best to spread the message of unity amongst different cultures and their efforts have not gone in vain. Aurobindo's concept of mass spiritualism seeks to spiritualise the individual as a whole to inculcate equanimity in the society. Mahatma Gandhi's philosophy of *Sarvoday*a or the rise of all was another such concept. Numerous others—Vivekananda,

Bipin Chandra Pal, Rabindranath Tagore, Lala Lajpat Rai, Sarvepalli Radhakrishnan etc have had their own impact and made contributions to multiculturalism.

When Lord Macaulay toured the length and breadth of India, he made one apt observation: *This country is so rich that I couldn't find even a single beggar or a sick person. The cultural heritage of this country is so strong that you cannot rule it unless you destroy its spiritual heritage.* This shows that the cultural heritage of our nation is its life and breath, the most powerful force sustaining and preserving multiculturalism.

In the era of globalisation, the world today has become a platform of many clashes between differeing socio-cultural groups in the form of terrorism and ethnic violence. At the same time, it is also a platform for healthy cultural interaction among different cultures. It is only because multiculturalism has been the essence of Indian culture since antiquity and is becoming the pivot of a globalising world with attendant consequences, that India is what it is today. The need of the hour in this globalised world, where every culture is encountering one another, is to make the foundational structure of multiculturalism strong and powerful so that it may be capable of sustaining its existence and overcome all the clashes and turmoil among different cultures and civilisations.

Some of the broad foundational structures of multiculturalism are assimilation of people of different cultures and race, respect to values and beliefs of different cultures by eachother, tolerance of stray incidents of attack on eachother's culture and traditions and state-sponsored initiatives to tie people with one thread of nationalism.

The liberal ideology holds that when people differ on what is right or wrong, the dominant view should either be ignored or settled with consensus. The minority view too should be taken into consideration rationally and it should not be forced on society. What is required essentially is that each respects freedom of others, tolerates and conforms to eachother's beliefs.

Indian culture is so spiritually woven that it can fight any hurdle thrown up from time to time by multiculturalism. The interaction of several spiritual qualities such as faith, creativity, patience, humour, flexibility and the ability to detach from or let go one's point of view, even momentarily, will assist the process of multiculturalism. The feeling of love and compassion among people increases the chances of working through difficult cultural variations. The qualities of being multicultural and spiritual are almost similar as goals are important and transcend across spiritual traditions and across social group identities.

It is only necessary to awaken the sleeping wisdom of the Indians, which has disappeared over the years because of greed for political power and use faith to achieve the socio-political goals of divisive forces driving wedges among different social groups in the name of ethnicity and caste. This sleeping wisdom is nothing but spiritual awakening in the form of peace, non-violence (*ahimsa*), self-knowledge, creativity and, above all, attitudinal changes towards accommodating all faiths. Our cultural heritage has spiritual treasures that provide breathing space for the existence of the majority and various minority communities. In our scriptures and mythology, there have been references which intellectually justify diversity and there are social practices that explicitly accommodate other cultures. The Vedic treatises in India are the saga of the Aryan migration from north-west to east and their assimilation with the different local racial stocks. Unlike some Western countries, which have witnessed decline in social values, India still stands on a much better stead.

In the previous chapter we have seen how diverse our culture is. We have considerable religious and ethnic diversity as well as diversity of customs, traditions, festivals and languages. But a question arises regarding the maintenance of this diversity. The connecting link which joins this diversity is our rich cultural heritage, which is the foundation of our multicultural India.

The basis of multiculturalism is an ideal socio-political setting in which all communities feel equally part of the country and fearlessly pursue their economic, social and religious activities. Under such situation, every community, whether migrants or indigenous ones, will identify with the country they live in and then nationalism can coexist and even foster multiculturalism.

The second half of the 19th century witnessed the emergence of national political consciousness in India and growth of an organised national movement in India. The most striking feature of the Hindu culture (Sanatan dharma values) is its flexibility and assimilative character. By virtue of this quality, it has been able to assimilate traits of different cultures since ages and impact people practicing other faiths. Therefore, it will not be wide off the mark to assert that Hindu culture was the essence of nationalism when leaders during freedom struggle espoused nationalism to unite different parts of the Indian subcontinent.

In the post-independence era, the hurdles in the geographical unification of the country continue and the majority community has been guided by a section of political outfits to usurp nationalism to attack the minorities.

The fundamentalists in majority and minority communities make frequent attempts to divide society on the Kashmir issue, on Ram temple-Babri mosque structure at Ayodhya and other such unimportant matters but they have not succeeded in breaking the secular fabric of the Indian society. Their edge gets blunted with majority among them vowing for social justice and religious freedom of Muslims, Buddhists, Jains and other minorities.

The foundation of Indian nationalism is embedded in its historical and geographical identity, its religious and cultural heritage and economic backwardness during the British rule. The large part of the Indian peninsula was ruled by emperors in the Mauryan and Gupta period and had several big and small princely States in different phases of history. But the people had common religious beliefs.

During the British period, a large number of Indians imbibed modern rational, secular, democratic and nationalist political outlook due to spread of modern Western education and thought. This English-educated intelligentsia provided the leadership to common masses during the national movement, leading to independence in 1947.

In Europe, however, nationalism is based on the Westphalian doctrine of 1648, when it was agreed upon that major continental European states like the Holy Roman Empire, Spain, France, Sweden and the Dutch Republic, each will have sovereignty over its territory and domestic affairs. It was based on equality in terms of international law, no matter how big or small the state was. In the late 18th century, the French Revolution based on the principles of 'liberty, equality and brotherhood' paved the way for modern nation-states in Europe. In later stages, these nation states spread their rule in Asian and African continents mainly to control the natural resources and economy of the colonised territory. In its history, Europe has witnessed several wars of division of landmass and for redrawing the territorial boundaries on the basis of racial purity, religious considerations, cultural identity, language and petty political aspirations.

Following are the Indian stalwarts who nurtured multiculturalism through their thoughts and ideals, which are highly important in today's globalised world. They have the potential to make India a shining example for the whole world, in this respect.

Bipin Chandra Pal

Bipin Chandra Pal (1858-1935) in his book, *Nationality and Empire: A running study of some current Indian problems,* explains the inner nature and the spiritual and cultural ethos of nationalism in India. Pal defined nationality as the 'Personality' of people rather than the 'Individuality' of a people as defined by Mazzini. Personality is derived from Latin world 'Persona', meaning a mask. 'Personality implies, therefore, not isolation but only differentiation and the difference that the concept personality implies, is a difference which only breaks up uniformity in appearance or organisation but it in no way destroys, or even disturbs the fundamental unity of being', Pal opined.

Pal explained the cultural basis of Indian nationalism, which clearly demarcates our nationalism from European nationalism. According to him, National differentiations among us (for example, that all of us are Indians but we are at same time Gujaratis, Maharatis or Tamils or Telugus) have not been based upon territorial demarcations only, or upon political or economic competitions and conflicts, but upon differences of culture.

Pal said, 'Even under the Muslims and the British rule, we never lost the integrity of Hindu culture. We took many things from our Mohammedan neighbours, and gave them also something of our own, but this interchange of ideas and institutions did not destroy our special character or our special culture. And that special character and culture is the very soul and essence of "nationalism". This is by no means a mere political idea or ideal. It is something that touches every area of our collective life and activity. It is organised in our domestic, communal, social and social-economic institutions. In fact, politics remains, from some points of view, the least important factor of this "nation" idea among us. Institutions like the so-called free political institutions of Europe might, indeed, hinder, instead of help the growth of our real national life: while under conceivable conditions, mere political subjection might not be able to touch even the outermost fringes of this life'.

Pal explained the real value of nationalism in which he considered the nation as superior to family and race or tribe. He said: Indeed, the real value of the ideal of nationality consists in the fact that it offers a much larger and broader formula of human associations than the idea of either the tribe or the race. As the family is larger than the individual, and the tribe is larger than the family, and the race is larger than the tribe, so is the nation much larger than the race. And in this ascending series, each subsequent term represents a higher category of social life and evolution than the antecedent term. And consequently, family life offers a much narrower field for the development of the human faculties than the life and activities of the tribe and the comparatively simpler and more limited needs of the tribal life, offer a much narrower scope to our powers and possibilities than the larger and more complex life of the nation. And it is just here that the higher value of the nation-idea truly lies.

Pal distinguished between European concepts of freedom from our concept of *swadheenta*. He said that freedom or independence or liberty was a negative concept. But *swadheenta* was a positive concept because it laid emphasis on complete identification of individual with the land he lives in. For him, the word swadheen means 'self-governance' within the limit of one's territorial boundary.

Pal saw positive value in nationalism and warned us not to adopt imported culture because it gave preference to material over the moral and the spiritual. Thus, we should be loyal to our national ideals. The real conflict between ours and the Europeans' is on idealism vs materialism, he said.

Pal's opinion was that for the preservation of our cultural heritage, it is necessary that autonomy should be distinguished from independence. Thus, autonomy meant living according to one's will or law and where our culture flourishes freely. Pal very clearly expressed the fundamental ideas of Indian nationalism. He said: Association not isolation, cooperation not competition, socialism in the highest and truest sense of the term and not merely what is understood by the followers of Marx, this socialism and not individualism, duty and not right were the rudimentary concepts of our social and political philosophy. These were the fundamental ideas of Indian nationalism some eighty years ago. Our 'individuality' as a people is based upon these distinctive notes or marks of our thought and evolution. These are the primary factors of our differentiation from other nations of the world.

Humanity needs these larger social concepts to be able to create the next higher social synthesis. They are our moral title to live as a nation. Europe is growing after these. For us to seek isolation in the name of independence, to seek selfish competition with other nations under the pretence of furthering our national interests, to set up individualism in place of collectivism as the true social goal or give preference to a narrow, selfish and competing and quarrelling nationalism over the broader, altruistic, humanitarian ideal of cooperative internationalism and universal federation, is really to strangle with our hands that very nationalism to which so many of us are ever ready to swear deathless allegiance. If we are to preserve the distinctive character of our thought and culture, we must perpetually keep autonomy distinguished from independence as our ideal political end.

In the words of Pal, 'Swaraj, the accepted political ideal of the Indian nationalists, does not connote the same thing as what is called "Independence" in English. The correct rendering of Swaraj is autonomy and not independence. Autonomy is positive while independence is a negative concept. Independence means isolation. Autonomy implies no necessary severance of outside connections or associations. Nationalism implies that collectively, we the composite Indian community, are a distinct and individual social organism, and as such we have a distinct end unto ourselves and a specific law of our own national being through which we must seek to reach and realise that end. Because autonomy means the act and the power of living according to one's own law, it is a legitimate nationalistic ideal. For nationality implies that we have a special character, a distinct individuality of our own, a law of our being and by submitting to which alone we can perfect and realise our collective life. It is for this reason that national autonomy is an absolute condition, the pursuit and realisation of which is the nationalist ideal'.

Pal said that autonomy, meaning the right or act of living according to one's own will, bases itself, therefore, upon one's own inner nature and constitution, upon one's on individuality or personality and upon one's own being. National autonomy, the declared ideal of Indian nationalism meant much more than the attainment either of colonial self-rule under the aegis of Great Britain, or of absolute political independence. We might gain these and yet lose our national autonomy. We might not gain either colonial self-government, or absolute independence, and yet attain true and substantial national autonomy. Nationalism, therefore, neither demanded the import of parliamentary form of government like that of England or her colonies into India, nor the absolute severance of Great Britain's political connection with her. Its only demand was to live and grow as an individual social organism according to its own special law, engraved upon its own nature and constitution and revealed through its historic evolution. It was the demand of self-India, which in her spirit, her soul, her being is to be fulfilled and realised.

Pal wanted that people should deeply realise the inner nature of Indian culture. He said our highest conception of salvation was 'Brahma Nirvana' which means not the annihilation of self-consciousness but only the conscious identification of the individual with the universal through transcending all the carnal limitations of human personality.

Pal had deeper appreciation of the cultural, social and political aspirations of the Muslims in India. He always took a balanced view on this question. During the heyday of the *Swadeshi* movement, he delivered a speech, the 'Contribution of Islam to Indian Nationality' at Young Men's Mohammedan Association in Madras in 1907, where he explained the multinational character of the Indian nation. He said, 'The Indian nation is not a Hindu nation. The Indian nation is not a Mohammedan one either, nor is the Indian nation a combination of Hindus and Mohammedans alone. There are others... And these different cultures, all these different communities constitute the new Indian nation.'

Though Pal maintained that Hindu culture would remain the basis of Indian nationalism, his blueprint of an independent India was solidly grounded on the vision of secularism and he firmly believed in syncretic mix of different cultures evolved in different phases of Indian history. He said, 'The future of Indian nation will not be a nation that will profess one religion. The future of Indian nation will not be a nation that will accept one social code. The future of Indian nation will not be a nation that will submit itself to one particular set of spiritual or ethnical disciplines'.

Thus, it is crystal clear that Pal's position was associated with the cultural heritage of India. His political, social and economic ideas influenced the Indian National Movement and had its links with the cultural soul of India. In his view, European nationalism, being isolationist and materialist in nature, was anti-humanity, while the Indian nationalism represented a higher stage of group consciousness and was a positive step towards human brotherhood and spirituality.

Pal's views are relevant even in today's context, as he made a major contribution to the multicultural discourse both in terms of thought and action. Though today the theory of multiculturalism is facing a lot of critical attack, a multicultural approach has a great significance in the context of growing communal divide and religious fundamentalism in different parts of India.

In fact, true knowledge of religions will break down the narrow barriers and also help people of different faiths to understand each other's religion better. There is a need to find out the commonalities of various religions and promote mutual tolerance. The need of the moment is to foster mutual respect and tolerance of different religions. Some of the eternal values of our multifaceted scriptures as well as the views of our philosophers and saints have become a treasure for strengthening and keeping awake the foundation of multiculturalism in India.

Swami Vivekananda

Swami Vivekananda's views on the enormity of Indian philosophical advancements and its ethical values point to the magnitude of spiritual progresse the country has made to accommodate diverse cultural traits. 'This is the ancient land where wisdom made its home before it went into any other country and where the first enquiries sprang up into the nature of man and the eternal world', he said.

According to him, if a person has attained progress in terms of spiritual and ethical values, he or she is capable of accommodating persons of different religious and cultural background. 'Help if you can; if you cannot, fold your hands and stand by and see things go on. Do not injure, if you cannot render help', he maintained.

For Vivekanand, three things are necessary to make every man great, every nation great—conviction of the powers of goodness, absence of jealousy and suspicion and helping all who are trying to be and do good. He pondered: 'Are you unselfish? That is the question. If you are, you will be perfect without reading a single religious book, without going into a single church or a temple'.

Talking about India's multicultural traits, Vivekananda said, 'It is the same land, which has withstood the shocks of centuries, of hundreds of foreign invasions, hundreds of upheavals of manners and customs. It is the same land which stands firmer than any rock in the world, with its undying vigour and indestructible life. Its life is of the same nature as the soul, without beginning and without end, immortal, and we are the children of such a country'.

According to Vivekananda, India's life-blood is spirituality and the world is waiting for the treasures to come out of India, waiting for the marvelous spiritual inheritance of the race for completion of civilisation. 'We talk here, we quarrel with each other; we laugh at and ridicule everything holy. Little do we understand the heart pangs of millions waiting outside the walls; stretching forth their hands for a little sip of that nectar of love our forefathers have preserved in this land of India', he said.

He talked about the immensity of Indian thought, which encompasses the conflict among different racial and ethnic groups and has the potential of nurturing multiculturalism. 'Indian thought, philosophical and spiritual must once more go over and conquer the world. There have been great conquering races in the world. We also have been great conquerors. The story of our conquest has been described by the noble Emperor of India, Asoka, as the conquest of religion and spirituality. Once more the world must be conquered by India', he said.

RabindranathTagore

Nobel laureate Rabindranath Tagore believed that India had spiritual power that it could offer to the world in an hour of crisis and it would be a contribution to humanity. He said that Indian culture had taught the lesson of cooperation, morality and humanism to the whole world and people who were lacking in this higher moral power and who, therefore, couldn't combine in fellowship with one another must perish or live in a state of degradation.

Tagore warned the Western countries against using power for selfish needs and advised them to teach the ignorant and help the weak. Tagore wanted to keep India united, and rejected the concept of a Muslim or Hindu nation. He opined that India tolerated differences of races and religion and that the spirit of toleration has acted all throughout her history.

He advocated the theory of internationalism and equal opportunities for all, thus laying the foundation of multiculturalism in India after independence. Tagore went to Japan and invited Chinese scholars to Shantiniketan, which is a diverse institution. Tagore said that Indian culture gave the lesson of social adjustments and cooperation. In India, the production of commodities was brought under the law of social adjustment. Its basis was cooperation, having for its object the perfect satisfaction of social needs. 'The Spirit of India has always proclaimed the ideal of unity. This ideal of unity never rejects anything, any race or culture. It comprehends all, and it has been the highest aim of our spiritual exertion—to be able to penetrate all things with one soul, to comprehend all things as they are, not keep out anything in the whole universe, to comprehend all things with sympathy and love. This is the Spirit of India', he said.

Tagore said, 'So, in the centre of Indian learning, we must provide for the coordinate study of all these cultures—the Vedic, the Puranic, the Buddhist, the Jain, the Islamic, the Sikh and the Zoroastrain. The Chinese, Japanese, and Tibetan will also have to be added; for, in the past, India did not remain isolated within her own boundaries. Therefore, in order to learn what she was, in her relation to the whole continent of Asia, these cultures too must be studied. Side by side with them must finally be placed the Western culture. For only then shall we be able to assimilate this last contribution to our common stock'.

MK Gandhi

For Mohandas Karamchand Gandhi, plurality was the ethos of India culture and it was embedded in its history. Gandhi advocated that controversial issues that alienate Hindus and Muslims should be left to them for an amicable settlement. 'It was, therefore, necessary that the Hindus abandon the idea of compelling Mussalmans to stop cow-killing, and Mussalmans the idea of compelling the Hindus to stop music. The regulation of cow-slaughter and playing of music must be left to the good will of the respective communities. Each practice would assume a becoming proportion with the growth of the tolerant spirit', he said.

Gandhi also emphasised on intimate integration of different religious groups, especially the Hindus and the Muslims in India. 'The union that we want is not a patched-up thing but a union of hearts based upon a definite recognition of the indubitable proposition that Swaraj for India must be an impossible dream without an indissoluble union between the Hindus and the Muslims of India. It must not be a mere truce. It cannot be based upon mutual fear. It must be a partnership between equals, each respecting the religion of the other... We would ill learn our history if we conclude that because we have quarreled in the past, we are destined so to continue unless some such strong power like the British keep us by force of arms from flying at each other's throats.'

According to Gandhi, 'Love is the basis of our friendship as it is of religion. If love persisted even on the part of the one community, unity would become a settled fact in our national life.'

He further asserted, 'Hindu-Muslim unity is possible, if only we have mutual toleration and faith in ourselves and, therefore, in the ultimate goodness of human nature'.

He said, 'What, then, does the Hindu-Muhammedan unity consist in and how can it be best promoted? The answer is simple. It consists in our having a common purpose, a common goal and common sorrows. It is best promoted by cooperating to reach the common goal, by sharing one another's sorrows and by mutual toleration'.

'And mutual toleration is necessity for all time and for all races. We cannot live in peace if the Hindus will not tolerate the Mohammedan form of worship of God and his manners and customs, or if the Mohammedan will be impatient of Hindu idolatry or cow-worship... All the quarrels between the Hindus and the Mohammedans have arisen from each wanting to force the other to his view.'

He said: 'Let all of us Hindus, Mussalmans, Parsis, Sikhs, Christians, live amicably as Indians, pledge to live and die for our motherland. Let it be our ambition to live as the children of the same mother, retaining our individual faiths and yet being one like the countless leaves of one tree.'

Gandhi's concepts of *Sarvodaya* and *Sarva Dharma Sambhava* (Equal respect for all religions) augmented the process of multiculturalism in the country. The word 'Sarvodaya' constitutes 'Sarva' (All) and 'Udaya' (Uplift). The literal translation of Sarvodaya would then be the uplift of all. It has physical and material dimension but at its base is spiritual enlightenment that brings about changes in the physical and material aspects.

The notion of *Sarva Dharma Samabhava* goes far beyond the concept of multiculturalism. In fact, it could very well be taken as a positive and constructive multicultural approach which offers a way out of the present cultural, religious and ethnic conflicts. Gandhi's

Sarva Dharma Sambhava is based on the premise that the truth underlying all religions is one and the same though the pathways may be different. His attitude towards religion sought to develop the spirit of a fellowship which helps a Hindu to become a better Hindu, a Mussalman to become a better Mussalman, and a Christian to become a better Christian. Gandhi said that, 'I hold that it is the duty of every cultured man or woman to read sympathetically the Scriptures of the world. A friendly study of the world's religions is a sacred duty'.

Aurobindo

Aurobindo gave philosophical foundation to multiculturalism, saying that unity among antagonistic races was bound to be realised one day when there would be one country and one mother. He presumed that the 'one country' idea would unite the antagonistic cultures by a single thread when there was 'one-country' conviction among the people drawn from different cultures and religious beliefs.

'Religious beliefs may differ, religious communities may be in perpetual conflict, there may be no harmony but even so, there is no cause of alarm. A country may have many languages, brother may be unable to understand brother, impenetrable walls may stand in the way of uniting our hearts... still there is nothing to fear, where there is one country, one life, one stream of though running through ever mind, by the force of necessity a common language is sure to emerge', he said.

Thus, Aurobindo was of the opinion that despite plurality we could maintain unity and peace in a single country for the sake of our nationalism through sacrifice or any other method. He considered the country as important factor for nationalism. This was a very important message during the freedom movement for generating the spirit of cultural nationalism in the hearts of Indian masses.

According to Aurobindo, 'The fundamental idea of all Indian religion is one, common to the highest human thinking everywhere. Indian religion placed four necessities before the human life'. First, it imposed upon the mind a belief in a highest consciousness of state of existence, universal and transcendent of the universe, from which all comes, in which all lives and moves without knowing it and of which in all must one day grow award, returning towards that which is perfect, eternal and infinite. Second, it laid upon the individual life the need for self-preparation by development and experience, till the man is ready for an effort to grow consciously into the truth of this greater existence. Thirdly, it provided it with a well-founded, well-explored, many branching and always enlarging way of knowledge and of spiritual or religious discipline. Lastly, for those not yet ready for these higher steps, it provided an organisation of the individual and collective life, a framework of personal and social discipline and conduct, of mental and moral and vital development by which they could move, each in his limits and according to his own nature in such a way as to become eventually ready for the greater existence.

The first three of these elements are the most essential to any religion, but Hinduism has always attached a great importance to the last also, it has left out no part of life as a thing secular and foreign to the religious and spiritual life. Thus it is clear that Aurobindo opined that Hinduism practiced by the majority in India taught the lesson of universal brotherhood, happiness, peace, truth, ahimsa, morality, spiritual values, and above all, tolerance not materialism and unhealthy competitions. This view provided an ideal setting for all religions and communities to pursue socio-religious and economic activities and live in peace on single geographical entity.

Lala Lajpat Rai

Freedom fighter Lala Lajpat Rai observed that the edge of the communal hysteria could be blunted if people accepted religion in the ideal sense and were not carried away by narrow loyalties and fanatical consideration. He suggested people distinguish between essentials and non-essentials of religion to avoid conflict. Rai believed and advocated that patriotism should revolve around love for the nation as a whole, regardless of the various religious creeds and communities which it is internally divided. For him, patriotic feelings would blur the cultural fault lines and lead to a cohesive multicultural society.

In the Indian context, Rai admitted the existence of caste system based on the age-old Varna system but strongly refuted racial discrimination as Indians belong to the same racial stock. He acknowledged existence of religious conflict in India but said that it was more artificial than real, manufactured by the vested interests. Since India always has such diversity, it needed philosophies akin to multiculturalism. In this regard, Rai said that 'loyalties that are rational, reasoned and sincere' were best suited for multiculturalism in India.

Bal Gangadhar Tilak

A staunch nationalist, Bal Gangadhar Tilak always wanted to glorify the cultural heritage of India. Because of his spiritual approach, he regarded that *swaraj* was not only a right but a dharma and also gave a moral and spiritual meaning to it. Politically, swaraj meant Home Rule. Morally, it meant the attainment of perfection of self-control, which is essential for performing one's duty (swadharma).

Albert Einstein

The great scientist Albert Einstein did not use the word 'multiculturalism' but espoused the view that individual races and cultures should maintain their distinct identity and dignity and prosper together giving respect to each other in a unified society. Einstein was very conscious of the strong communal anti-Semitic feeling against Jews in Germany and some parts of Europe despite the fact that the Jews were assimilated in the German society. They did not regard themselves as belonging to the Jewish people but felt themselves as belonging to just a religious community. They went to mixed schools and had adapted themselves to German national and cultural life. Nevertheless, and despite equal political rights which they had secured, there existed in Germany a strong movement of social anti-Semitism.

Einstein said that it was deplorable to deny the Jew's nationality in the diaspora and championed the cause of Jewish nationalism. But his Zionism did not exclude a cosmopolitan view. He talked about tolerance towards other communities and creative fusion, which should enrich mankind at large.

'I believe in the actuality of Jewish nationality, and I believe that every Jew has duties towards his co-religionists... Zionism involves a creative fusion, which should enrich mankind at large. But the main point is that Zionism must tend to enhance the dignity and self-respect of the Jews in the Diaspora. I have always been annoyed by the undignified assimilationist cravings and strivings which I have observed in so many of my friends.'

S Radhakrishnan

Contemporary Indian philosopher S Radhakrishnan preferred religion of love and brotherhood, not power and hate. For him, any religious system is healthy and progressive so long as it is capable of responding creatively to every fresh challenge, whether it comes by the way of outer events or of ideas. When it fails to do so, it is on the decline. Radhakrishnan averred that the breakdown of society is generally due to failure to devise adequate responses to new challenges, to a failure to retain the voluntary allegiance of the common people who, exposed to new winds of thought and criticism, are destitute of faith, though afraid of skepticism. Unless religions reckon with the forces at work and deal with them creatively, they are likely to fade away.

'We live in an age of science and we cannot be called upon to accept incredible dogmas or exclusive revelations. It is again an age of humanism. Religions which are insensitive to human ills and social crimes do not appeal to modern man. Religions which make for division, discord and disintegration and do not foster unity, understanding and coherence, play into the hands of opponents of religion', he said. Thus, we can derive from his views that a multicultural social milieu provides a perfect setting for different religions to prosper, flourish and imbibe positive values from each other. This, in turn, also provides opportunities for synthesis of values of different religions.

All religions require us to look upon life as an opportunity for selfrealisation—*atmanastu kamaya*. They call upon us to strive incessantly and wrest the immortal from the mortal. God is the universal reality, wisdom and love and we are His children, irrespective of race or religious belief. Within each incarnate soul dwells the god-consciousness which we must seek out and awaken. When mankind awakens to the truth, universal brotherhood would follow—the atonement with the great fountainhead of all creation. One whose life is rooted in the experience of the Supreme, spontaneously develops love for all creation. He will be free from hatred for any man. He will not look upon human beings as though they were irresponsible things but boldly work for a society in which man can be free and fearless, a subject, not an object. This will eventually ready people to accept and respect other religious thoughts and foster multiculturalism. Thus, the philosophy of *atmanastu kamaya*, which is core of Indian philosophy, submits that religion in its highest form will automatically ensure multiculturalism.

Religion, in this sense, will be the binding force which will deepen the solidarity of human society. The encounter of the different religions has brought up the question whether they can live side by side or whether one of them will supersede the others. Mankind at each period of its history cherishes the illusion of the finality of its existing modes of knowledge. This illusion breeds intolerance and fanaticism. The world has bled and suffered from the disease of dogmatism, of conformity. Those who are conscious of a mission to bring the rest of humanity to their own way of life have been aggressive towards other ways of life. If we look upon our dogmatic formulations as approximations to the truth and not truth itself, then we must be prepared to modify them if we find other propositions which enter deeper into reality. On such a view it will be illogical for us to hold that any system of theology is an official, orthodox, obligatory and final presentation of truth. Rather, reality is larger than any system of theology, however large. So, dogmatism has to be removed or reformed, without tampering with the core values of any religion, to accommodate other theological views for the course of multiculturalism to be completed.

In all countries and in all religions, there are creative minorities who are working for a 'religion of spirit' that primarily aims at providing a path of spirituality to people. There are several organisations working in the world today—World Congress of Faiths (1936), World Alliance for Friendship through Religion and Church Peace Union (1914), World Brotherhood (1950), World Spiritual Council (1946), Society for the Study of Religions (1924).

American writer, scientist, philosopher and famous skeptic Sam Harris, in his book titled, '*Waking Up: A Guide to Spirituality Without Religion,* has provided a guide to meditation as a rational spiritual practice to millions of people, who follow no religion and want spirituality without religion. For the millions of Americans who want spirituality without religion, Sam Harris's new book is a guide to meditation as a rational spiritual practice informed by neuroscience and psychology. Inter-religious understanding, which is the aim of these organisations, is inherent in Indian society since ages. Emperor Asoka in his twelfth edict proclaimed:

> *He who does reverence to his own sect while disparaging the sects of others, Wholly from attachment to his own, with intent to enhance the glory of his own sect. In reality, by such conduct, inflicts the severest injury on his own sect.*
>
> *Concord, therefore, is meritorious, to wit, hearkening and hearkening willingly to the law of piety as accepted by other people.*

Thus, it is clear that multiculturalism had roots in the Indian society even during the Mauryan period when Buddhism flourished and Emperor Asoka preached to people about religious tolerance.

Religion reflects both God and man. As religion is the life to be lived, not a theory to be accepted or a belief to be adhered to, it allows scope and validity to varied approaches to the Divine. There may be different revelations of the Divine but they are all forms of the Supreme. If we surround our souls with a shell, national pride, racial superiority, frozen articles of faith and empty presumption of castes and classes, we stifle and suppress the breath of the spirit.

The Upanishads are clear that the flame is the same, even though the types of fuel used may vary.

Similarly, cows are of many colours but their milk is of one colour. Again, the Bhagvata Gita says even as the various senses discern the different qualities of one object, so also the different scriptures indicate the many aspects of the one Supreme. Therefore, religious beliefs are not opposed to each other but they work as guides to their believers to respect other faiths too as the ultimate reality is the 'milk' or the 'flame', not the varieties of cows or the firewood. This one supreme concept binds all religions and promotes multiculturalism.

True religious life must express itself in love and aim at the unity of mankind. Bead necklaces, rosaries, triple paint on forehead, or putting on ashes, pilgrimages, baths in holy rivers, meditation, or image worship do not purify a man as service of fellow-creatures does. The Hindu dreamed of universal peace and clothed his dreams in imperishable language:

> *Mata ca parvati devi pita devo mahesvarah*
> *bandhavah sivabhaktas ca svade so bhuvana-trayam.*
> *Udara-caritanam tu vasudhaiva kutumbakam*

(Mother is Shakti, father is shiva, friends and relatives are the devotees of Shiva and own country is all the three worlds. We are liberal in approach and believe in welfare to all.)

The goal of world unity is to be achieved by ahimsa which is insisted on by Hinduism, Buddhism and Jainism. Both Islam and Zoroastrianism promoted cooperation between different groups.

In Zoroastrianism there is dualism, an open struggle between two forces. Ahura Mazda and Angra Mainyu are the two warring principles and in their struggle is grounded the drama of cosmic life and human history. The one is the principle of light, justice and the good; the other is the principle of darkness, injustice and evil. The battle between these two is decided by the victory of the good. Before the triumph of light over darkness is complete, the universe and mankind must pass through endless cycles of exhausting torment and untiring strife.

In the strife between the good and the evil, the Zoroastrian holy text Zend Avesta talks about respect to other faiths throughout the globe. It talks about universal religious community which supersedes all distinctions of race, caste and nationality. 'A believer, wherever he be found, is an object of veneration and we worship the former religions of the world devoted to righteousness', the Avesta says.

In Islam, Prophet Muhammad affirms the unity of God and the brotherhood of man. The Muslim feels deeply man's insignificance, the uncertainty of his fate, and the supremacy of God. Muhammad recognised the fact that each religious teacher has faith in his own mission, and his vision and experience fulfill the needs of his people.

In Baha'i Faith, youngest of the world's independent religions, founder Baha'u'llah's central message was the oneness of God, the oneness of humanity and the oneness of religion. His message was that God had set in place forces to overcome barriers that divide societies such as race, class, creed and nation. The main principles of Baha'i faith focus on abandonment of prejudice, unity and relativity of religious truth, belief that true religion is in harmony with reason and the pursuit of scientific knowledge and establishment of a global commonwealth of nations among others. It mainly advocated multiculturalism with a message of universal peace and harmony.

Religion's main function is to make society cohere. The cooperation between different groups, as suggested by different religions, will certainly make multiculturalism easier to achieve. This is what Nicholas Wade in his book, *The faith instinct*, arguing that the horizontal function of religious faiths was to cement group identities and reflect group will. If there are similarities in the religious experience of mankind, it only means that a common humanity reacts in more or less similar ways to man's encounter with the Divine. The common points to be found in the different manifestations of religion should not lead us to think that they are organised in each religion in the same way. The manner in which these beliefs are correlated varies from one religion to another. Each religion is a living organisation of doctrine, worship and practice, has uniqueness and individuality of its own and changes as a whole in response to the needs of the age.

Therefore, while we indicate the area of agreement, the distinctive arrangement of the basic presuppositions gives the varying quality to different religions. For our present purpose, it is not necessary to stress the differences which are important and fundamental in some points. According to Radhakrishnan, even though each sect of a religion claims to be the true representative of its specific religious message, yet all the followers of all the sects feel that they are bound together in a unity.

As we are trying to overcome the conflict within each religion where every organised group claims to possess the truth by the recognition of the unity of religion, conflicts among religions require to be reconciled, if religion itself is not to be defeated since man needs a tradition to anchor society too and some explanation for his existence. A defeat will certainly have disastrous consequences.

The world has bled and suffered from the disease of dogmatism, of conformity, of intolerance. People conscious of bringing humanity to their own way of life, whether in religion or politics, have been aggressive towards other ways of life. The crusading spirit of some religions has spoiled the record of religions. What is needed is piety, good virtues and tolerance towards others. Osho rightly said, 'I teach religiousness not religion'.

It is no more possible for different cultures of different racial and religious groups, to live in ignorance of one another in today's world of fast communication. The scientific discoveries which have penetrated all parts of the earth are making the world one, though the different civilisations live by and cherish their distinctive principles of life. If the world is to be united on a religious basis peacefully, it will be not on the basis of this or that religion but by a cooperation among the different religions of the world. If the different religions strive to achieve their common ideals and seek to understand the differences in a sympathetic spirit, the world will be relieved of the misery and fear which now engulf it.

In his hypothesis, Samuel Huntington opined that people's cultural and religious identities will be the primary source of conflict after the Cold War era. But he also affirmed, 'This is not to advocate the desirability of conflicts between civilisations. It is to set forth descriptive hypothesis as to what the future may be like'. What is required, therefore, is that the tradition of opposition to one another should yield to cooperation. The conviction of superiority should not prevent appreciation of other faiths and cultures and fruitful interchange among them.

According to Erasmus, 'If the message of religions is to be articulated in relation to the problems of our age, we must give up the view that any one religion contains the final, absolute and whole truth, and adopt the Eastern attitude that the faith is realised in historical patterns, though no one of these patterns should regard itself as the sole and exclusive truth for all. We must be on our guard against the enemies of truth, men of fixed ideas and fanaticisms'.

Atheists and agnostics may differ but between the believers in the different historical patterns, there exists a hidden common substratum. If we overlook this, we will not be able to overcome nihilism, lack of faith and irreligion. If we seek for a joyous reconciliation of the members of the human family, we will acknowledge that even heretics have divined some aspect of the Godhead. Just as God lets his sun shine on good and evil, He pours forth His loving kindness on all the children of mankind. A perusal of the different major religions will strengthen the view that religion is the hope of man and sustain the new world.

Religion has many doors; the observance of its duties can never be useless. This view makes for the appreciation of religious knowledge, of the beliefs and practices of other peoples. This understanding makes for spiritual fellowship. Within this fellowship, each religion will have scope for full expression. Religious reflection will be stimulated by the knowledge and friendship of others of different religions.

We will also have to evolve universal ethical standards, even if they are opposed to theology of religions. Even as the interplay of Jewish, Christian and Muslim in the West has enriched the experience of the West and that of Hindu, Buddhist and Confucian has enriched the experience in the East, so the cross-fertilisation of ideas among the living faiths of the world will tend to foster and enrich spiritual life. The sign of hope is the perpetual youth of religions, as also the way in which they renew themselves as the world changes.

To quote Radhakrishnan from his book titled, *Indian Religious Thought*, 'The choice before humanity is either cooperation in a spirit of freedom and understanding or conflict in an atmosphere of fear, suspicion and jealousy. The future of religion and mankind will depend on the choice we make. Concord, not discord, will contribute to the establishment of spiritual values in the life of mankind'.

Thus, the cultural heritage of India is the backbone on which the whole structure and foundation of multiculturalism is based. Whenever there arose differences and turmoil among two different communities on the basis of their ideas, our cultural heritage becomes boon to calm the burning differences.

Culture is understood as a system of shared beliefs, values, customs and artifacts that the members of a society use. Cultural heritage is an expression of the ways of living developed by a community and passed on from generation to generation. Cultural heritage includes tangible culture (such as buildings, monuments, landscapes, books, works of art and artifacts), intangible culture (such as folklore, traditions, language and knowledge), and natural heritage (including culturally significant landscapes, and biodiversity).

'It stands for synthesis of the different cultures that have come to stay in India, that have influenced Indian life, and that, in their turn, have themselves been influenced by the spirit of the soil. This synthesis will naturally be of the spirit of the soil and of the *swadeshi* type, where each culture is assured its legitimate place', Gandhi had said.

The first lesson which our cultural heritage teaches is '*Atithi Devo Bhava*', a guest is God, which makes the base of multiculturalism strong. Our cultural heritage teaches us the lesson of mutual cooperation, mutual understanding, accommodation, tolerance, respect for each other feelings, and above all peace and harmony.

If we follow the lessons of Gita, Ramayana, Bible, Quran and Adi Granth, then we realise how pious our cultural heritage is. Ignorant people, in the name of religion, spread violence and distort the tender mind of ignorant youth. Our first spiritual training should be given to the youth about the treasure of our cultural heritage.

References

1. Gandhi, MK, '*Collected works of Mahatma Gandhi*', 100 volumes. *Hind Swaraj. An Autobiography*, Navjivan Publishing house, 1958. *The story of my experiments with truth*, Navjivan Press, Ahmedabad, 1927 *Hindu Dharma*, Orient Paperbacks. *The Bhagwad Gita*, Orient Paperbacks.

2. Pal, BC, '*An introduction to the study of Hinduism*, SC. Gupta, Calcutta, 1908. *His life and utterances*, Ganesh & Co, Madras, 1907. *The spirit*

of Indian Nationalism, 1910. *Indian Nationalism: Its principles and Personalities*, RS Murthi & Co, Madras, 1918. *Memories of my life and times*, Volume I, Modern Book Agency, Calcutta, 1932. *Nationality and empire: A running study of some current Indian problems. Swadeshi and Swaraj* (The rise of new patriotism), Yugyatri Prakashak Ltd, Calcutta, 1954. *The New economic menace of India*, Ganesh & Co., Madras, 1920. 'The New spirit', Sinha Sarvadhikar & Co., Calcutta, 1907. *The Soul of India*, Choudhary and Choudhary, Calcutta, 1917.

3. Radhakrishnan, S, 'Eastern Religion and Western Thought', Oxford India. *Indian Philosophy*, Vol 1 & 2. '*Hinduism: A way of life*'.

4. Rai, Lala Lajpat, *Call to young India*, Madras, 1921. 'Ideals of Non-cooperation', Madras, 1921. 'India's will to freedom', Madras, 1921. *The Arya Samaj*, London, 1915. *The Political future of India*, Renaissance Publishing House, Delhi, 1919. *Unhappy India: A reply to Miss Catherin Mayo's mother India*, Calcutta, 1928. *Young India*, New York, 1917. *National Education in India*, 1920.

5. Savarkar, VD, '*Hindutva*', Veer Savarkar Prakashan, Bombay, 1969. 'The Indian war of independence of 1857'. 'Hindutva', Hindi Sahitya Sadan. 'Some of the Basic principles and tenets of the Hindu movement: In Fred Dallmayr and GN Devy (eds), *Between tradition and modernity, India's search for identity: A twentieth century Anthology*, New Delhi, Sage Publications.

6. Tagore, Rabindranath, '*Nationalism*', McMillan & Co., 1917, London, Rupa & Co, reprint, 1991, New Delhi.

7. Tilak, BG, *Arctic home in Vedas*, Pune, Kesari office, 1903. *Arya Lokanche Mulasthana* (in Marathi), Bombay, Damodar Savtaram Yanede, 1910. *Bhagvadgitarahasya Athavakarmanya Shastra* (in Marathi), Ed.10, Pune, Lokmanya Tilak Mandir, 1953. *Chaldean and Indian vedas*, Pune, Bhandarkar Oriental Research Institute, 1917. *His writings and speeches*, Madras, Ganesh & Co, ' Lokmanya Tilak Tekhsangraha', (in Marathi), New Delhi, Sahitya Akademi, 1969. *Lokmanya Tilakanche Kesarintil Tevha*, Vol 1-4, Collections of writings in Marathi in Kesari, Pune, Kesari, 1922-30. *Brahmasutravritti*, Pune, Bharat Ithihas Sansodhak Mandal, 1957.

8. Parekh, Bhikhu, *Gandhi-A very short Introduction*, Oxford University Press, 1997.

9. Sandel, Michael J, *Liberalism and its Critics* (Oxford, Basil Blackwell, 1984).

10. Gauba, O P, *Dimensions of Social Justice* (New Delhi, National, 1983). *Reading Gandhi* (New Delhi, National, 2009). *Social and Political Philosophy* (New Delhi, National, 2007).

11. Roy, Ramashray, *Understanding Gandhi*, Delhi, Ajanta 1996.

12. *Secularism Islam and Modernity: Selected essays of Alam Khundmiri* (2001), edited with an introduction by MT Ansari, Thousand Oaks/ London: Sage Publications.

13. Prabhupad, Swami Vaktivedanta, AC, *The Science of Selfrealization*, The Bhaktivedanta Book Trust.

14. Varma, VP, *Modern Indian political thought*, Lakshmi Narayan Agarwal, Educational Publishers.

15. Aloysius, G, *Nationalism without a nation in India*, Oxford University Press.

16. Muller, F Max, *Ramakrishna: His life and Sayings*, Advaita Ashrama.

17. Paine, Jeffery, *Father India*, Penguin Books.

18. Griffiths, Bede, *A New vision of reality*, Harper Collins Publishers India.

19. *Holi Quran*, Motilal Banarasidas.

20. *Bible*

21. Damodaran, Edavana, *India the cradle of mankind*, Sahayog Publications.

22. Jaising, Indira, *Justice for women, personal laws, womens rights and Law reform.*

23. Awasthy, SS, *Indian Government and politics*, Har Anand Publication Pvt *Ltd.*

24. Lal, CK, *Human Rights, democracy and governance*, Pearson.

25. Pal, Bipin Chandra, *Nationality and Empire A running study of some current Indian problems.*

26. Eternal values, The Ramakrishna Mission Institute of Culture.

27. S Radhakrishnan, *Indian Religions.*

28. Madan Gopal Sinha, *Political ideas of Bipin Chandra Pal.*

Challenges of Multiculturalism

THE Vedic credo *Vasudhaiv Kutumbakam* (the world is a family) is one cardinal philosophy that underlines life in all its various hues in India. It also underlines the spirit of multiculturalism in India. Yet India continues to be beset with numerous challenges that threaten to derail the country's political life and institutions, if not urgently and satisfactorily addressed.

Both societal structure and political institutions are equally important in tackling the challenges of multiculturalism. Any shortcoming will have equal impact on both, social structure and the political institutions. Discourse and adaptation of innovative ideas keeps a system or a culture healthy and moving, as the banal saying goes—A Rolling stone gathers no moss. Different cultural groups should come on one platform to communicate with each other, understand each other and innovate their social system in the process in order to exist in a multicultural nation. This would augur well for multiculturalism. Ideas are never formed in a 'closed circuit'. They need input, output, a feedback mechanism as well as communication channels between different cultural groups as well as with the political system. This is the best mechanism for an all-round progress of a multicultural nation. If ideas are formed in a closed circuit they could be harmful for a system, even more so, for multiculturalism. The political and social system should act as 'problem solving' 'crisis-management' entities to prevent conflicting situations in a multicultural society. Barring a few odd, superficial instances of discord between some religious groups, the very foundation of our cultural heritage—spirituality, has proved strong enough to bind everyone in one single thread—the thread of love, peace, harmony, mutualrespect, accommodation and tolerance. Sometimes conflict also plays a positive role in the progress of society. As Ralph Miliband, a British sociologist, appositely elaborated in his classic *Marxism and Politics*, 'conflict is not only civilised, but also civilising. It is not only a means of resolving problems in a peaceful way, but also of providing new ideas, ensuring progress, achieving ever-greater harmony and so on. Conflict is "functional", a stabilising rather than a disrupting force'.

This is an age of interdependency and we have developed into a 'global village' where sustaining multiculturalism has become necessity and India has the potential to be a shining example to the whole world as to how multiculturalism can be sustained.

The Indian Constitution is, I believe, the other pillar that has helped India consolidate whatever gains that have accrued to traditional Indian society because of its adherence to the norms that govern multiculturalism.

Certain groups are against these principles, but that does not mean that multiculturalism has failed. One cannot conclude that a social club failed if one person refused to attend. Most Hindus, Muslims, Christians, Jews, Buddhists, Sikhs, Jains and many others manage to live together, respecting the rights of others to equal treatment. The fact that some groups don't accept this doesn't mean that the basic concept of multiculturalism is wrong.

Hinduism is part of India's multicultural society. It is there for all to see how the tolerance among groups within Hinduism is a model for inter-religious respect. If Vishnava, Shaiva, and other sects within he fold of Hinduism can hold their own views and respect others, then this attitude can also exist and be expected to exist among other faiths in society.

It is argued that if Hindus become a minority group, then multiculturalism might not be sustainable. But the concept of multiculturalism is having respect for other ways of life and beliefs, while holding one's own. It certainly works. We need to make sure that those who think that they should dominate and restrict other groups are not allowed to do so. We also need to keep an eye on the dialogue, and make sure that 'anti-extremism' is not hijacked by right-wing parties and changed to an 'anti-other culture' movement.

This restriction, preventing them from subjugating others and illegal acts, is no more a failure of multiculturalism like constitutionally preventing parties from ending democracy is not failure of democracy.

Democracy and legal legitimacy granted by India's Constitution as preservers of multiculturalism

A robust democracy and a vigilant constitution are the two guardians of the diverse groups that make up different sections of a multicultural India, allowing them to flourish in a cordial atmosphere. Though conventional exponents of democracy treated it as a mere form of government, the American philosopher John Dewey analyses democracy aptly as a way of life. In his celebrated and much acclaimed work, *Democracy and Education*, Dewey said: 'A democracy is more than a form of government; it is primarily a mode of associated living, of conjoint communicated experience.... The method of democracy is to bring conflicts out into the open where their special claims can be seen and appraised, where they can be discussed and judged.' Thus, Dewey's vision of a true democracy and a multicultural nation, both go along side by side. Democratisation at all levels is an all-important necessity for a successful multicultural nation. The concept of multiculturalism bears a discernible closeness to democracy which empowers and emancipates every citizen.

Deliberative democracy: *Another tool for making multiculturalism successful.*

The concept of deliberative democracy embodies an attempt to reconcile two different models of democratic thought: 'Democracy as a popular rule' and 'democracy as the bulwark of personal freedom'. Now, deliberative democracy requires that democratic decision-making should strike a balance between personal freedom and popular rule. It should be used as a means of encouraging public deliberation on issues that are best understood through open, deliberative processes. Deliberative democracy does not subscribe to the model of politics where each individual is fighting to secure his self-interest. Rather, it promotes a model of politics where each individual is trying to persuade others to find a reasonable solution of public issues of concern. People in a deliberative democracy try to influence each other through an accepted mode of reasoned argument, that is to win the heart through an appeal to the prevalent value system. At the same time, it pays due regard to personal freedom of every individual. Thus, autonomy doesn't simply consist in living according to one's own choice. It requires one to have a share in political decision also, which affects one as well as others. This is made possible only through the mechanism of deliberative democracy.

The successful, seamless working of democracy in a multicultural nation depends upon many factors like *national sentiment* (in spite of plurality and diversity there should be a sense of belonging to a single nation, inspired by feeling of common history, common way of life and common centre of loyalty towards nation), *spirit of toleration, high moral character, widespread education, economic security and guaranteed equality.*

Macpherson has developed a new, vibrant theory of democracy, based on a moralist viewpoint and a humanist vision: Democracy emancipates human beings and promotes creative freedom which can nurture multiculturalism in a cordial atmosphere without the loss of one's identity. In India, the concept of creative freedom has been the soul of multiculturalism. Macpherson draws a distinction between two types of power: (a) developmental power and (b) extractive power. Developmental power refers to man's ability to use his own capacities creatively, for the fulfilment of his self-appointed goals. Extractive power, on the other hand, stands for power over others—man's ability to use other men's capacities to extract benefits for himself. In India, developmental power is given greater emphasis rather than extractive power. This is one of the more important factors contributing greatly to the strength of the multicultural bond in India.

Bryce justifies democracy by the concept of relativity, that is by comparing its merits and demerits with other forms of government. The litmus test of any government, according to Bryce, is the welfare of the people. This is where other forms of governmentlag behind. Thus, for multicultural nations like India, democracy is the best way to foster brotherhood while ensuring the welfare of the people of diverse cultural, religious and ethnic groups.

Our vigilant Constitution is also a custodian of multiculturalism. It provides legal legitimacy by guaranteeing the fundamental rights of every citizen. The preamble of our Constitution, described as 'the soul of the constitution' by Earnest Barker and 'Key to the constitution' by KM Munshi, give supremacy and sovereignty to the people of India. It reads: We, the people of India, having solemnly resolved to constitute India into a Sovereign, Socialist, Secular, Democratic Republic and to secure to all its citizens justice, social, economic and political; liberty of thought, expression, belief, faith and worship; equality of status and opportunity; and to promote among them all fraternity assuring the dignity of the individual and the unity and integrity of the Nation.... Thus, the preamble of the Constitution clearly indicates the steps to be taken to foster multiculturalism in a healthy, conducive environment.

Our Fundamental Rights are the most important tools to secure multiculturalism legally. The Fundamental Rights are defined as basic human freedoms that every Indian citizen has the right to enjoy, for a proper and harmonious development of personality. These rights apply universally to all citizens of India irrespective of race, place of birth, religion, caste or gender. All people have been given the right to move to the Supreme Court of India and the High Courts if the state or any entity denies them or abridges their fundamental rights; nonetheless, poverty-stricken people may not have the means to do so. Therefore, in the public interest, anyone can commence litigation in the court on their behalf. This is known as 'Public interest litigation' (PIL), which has proven a boon for multiculturalism in India. The classification of Fundamental Rights in the Constitution which safeguard multiculturalism are as follows:

Right to Equality (Articles 14-18)

Art. 14 says that 'the state shall not deny to any person equality before the law or the equal protection of the laws within the territory of India.' Art. 15: Prohibition of discrimination on grounds of Religion, Race, Caste, Sex or Place of Birth. Art. 16: Equality of opportunity in matters of public employment. Art.17 : Abolition of untouchability. For the enforcement of this provision, Parliament had enacted the protection of Civil Rights Act, 1955 which was amended in 1976. Art.18: Abolition of Titles, which means no kings and emperors.

Right to Freedom (Articles 19-22) The six Fundamental Freedoms are:

(a) **Freedom of Speech and Expression** (b) **Freedom of Assembly** (c) **Freedom to form Association** (d) **Freedom of Movement** (e) **Freedom to reside and settle** (f) **Freedom of Profession, Occupation, Trade or** Business.

Right to Information (RTI): has been given the status of a Fundamental Right under Article 19 (1) of the Constitution in 2005. Article 19 (1), under which every citizen has the freedom of speech and expression, also bestows the right to know how the government works, what role does it play, what are its functions so on. RTI has proven to be a hallmark legislation for the securing of information and one's right in a multicultural land.

Art. 20: Protection in respect of conviction for offence.

Art. 21: Protection of life and personal liberty.

Art. 22 : Safeguards against Arbitrary arrest and detention.

The 86th Amendment, 2002 has inserted in the Constitution, a new Article 21 A, after the existing Article 21. The new Article 21 A deals with the **Right to Education**. It reads, 'The state shall provide free and compulsory education to all children of the age of six to fourteen years in such manner as the state may, by law, determine.

Right against Exploitation (Arts. 23 & 24) provides for prohibition of traffic in human beings and forced labour. No child below the age of 14 years will be employed in any hazardous work.

Arts. 25-28: **Right to Freedom of Religion.**

Arts. 29-30: **Cultural and Educational Rights** : *Art. 29* provides that minority communities/linguistic groups shall have the right to conserve their own languages, scripts, literature and culture. Admissions to any state-aided educational institution shall not be refused to anybody on grounds of religious, race, caste or language.

Article 30 says that all minorities, whether they have religion or language as their distinguishing feature, shall have the right to establish and administer educational institutions set up by them. The state shall not, in granting aid to educational institutions, discriminate against any educational institution on the ground that it is under the management of a minority community.

Article 30 does not say that minorities based on religion should establish educational institutions only for teaching their language or religion only. It could be a higher educational institution related to any field or discipline. However, such minority institutions can be acquired by the state after Article 30 (1A) was inserted in the Constitution by the 44th amendment in 1978. But such acquisitions require adequate and comfortable compensation.

Art.32: **Right to Constitutional Remedies:** It provides a guaranteed remedy for the enforcement of the above-mentioned fundamental rights. Under it, a person has the right to move the Supreme Court by appropriate proceedings, for the enforcement of his Fundamental Rights. The Supreme Court and the High Courts have been empowered to issue writs in the nature of Habeas Corpus, Mandamus, Prohibition, Quo Warranto and Certiori, whenever and wherever they consider appropriate.

Thus, India's Constitution is replete with ample provisions regarding the safeguards of the rights of an ordinary citizen, in a multicultural society. It gives a sense of security to diverse groups—both the minorities and the majority—to flourish without fear.

In the **Golaknath v. State of Punjab case, 1967**, the Supreme Court ruled that Parliament had no power to legislate a law that took away or abridge any Fundamental Right. Later, in the **Keshvananda Bharti v. State of Kerala case, 1973** the Supreme Court held that Parliament had wide powers of amending the

Constitution but the amending power is not unlimited and does not include the power to destroy or abrogate the basic features of the Constitution. This remarkable judgement has proven to be a boon for multiculturalism.

The Constitution has provided ample opportunities for SCs and STs to fulfil their desirable legitimate goals. The National Commission of SC/ST was set up by the 65th Amendment, 1990 (Art.338), in the Fifth and Sixth Schedules of the Indian Constitution as well as the Government. It is committed to the welfare and socio-economic integration of India's tribal communities into the national mainstream. Now it is the duty of every citizen to promote harmony and the spirit of common brotherhood amongst all the people of India, transcending religious, linguistic and regional or sectional diversities; and to value the rich heritage of our composite culture.

India, as an active member of the United Nations and an ardent champion of human rights, has given due recognition to the content of the Universal Declaration of Human Rights for the promotion of multiculturalism. This has been made clear in various parts of the Indian Constitution including its Preamble, the Fundamental Rights, Directive Principles of State Policy and Fundamental Duties. The Supreme Court of India has cited the Universal Declaration of Human Rights in quite a few of its judgements from time to time, in order to promote the democratic spirit and social justice in favour of sustaining multiculturalism. The Government of India had also set up a National Human Rights Commission in 1993 which is working towards fostering holistic justice to all sections of our diverse, multicultural society.

Human Rights are now classified into three categories:

(a) *First generation rights* including Civil and Political Rights;
(b) *Second generation rights* including Social and Economic Rights
(c) *Third generation rights* including the newly recognised human rights, such as Cultural Rights of minorities in a multicultural society or nation.

Now the protection of all the three generation of rights are a duty of state as well as every citizen.

A multicultural society is a society wherein people belonging to different cultural groups live together as equal citizens. These groups must have the freedom to preserve the salient features of their respective cultures ie. language, symbols of identity, religion, places of worship, custom, dress code, eating habits, styles of living, art and craft etc. within the larger society; none should be forced to assimilate into the dominant culture. Thus, to sustain multiculturalism, both normative and empirical methods are equally important. A normative statement serves an intrinsic value and an empirical statement serves an instrumental value. While an empirical statement is concerned with 'is', the normative approach is concerned with 'ought to be' or 'should be' and both are equally important to sustain multiculturalism.

Multiculturalism enables different cultures within a community to flourish and treat each other with mutual respect. Some writers have argued that this is a necessary condition of an individual's freedom. Joseph Raj (Multiculturalism: A Liberal Perspective, Dissent, 1994) observed that an individual's autonomy is intimately tied up with access to his culture. It enables him to make good choices befitting a good life if his culture is flourishing and getting respect from others. Hence the sense of identity is closely linked with an individual's self-fulfilment.

In a multicultural society, it is necessary to unite the individual's self identity and the community. It is now widely experienced that the sense of shared community in many other multicultural nations has largely eroded, leaving modern people without a clear sense of identity. Modern society, particularly the Western society, is characterised by the absence, breakdown, confusion or conflict of norms. In order to maintain peace and solidarity in a multicultural society, it is necessary that all cultural groups, as defined in the wider sense, get due recognition, enjoy due respect and rights as equal citizens and get representation in decision-making bodies. Multiculturalism has emerged and flourished as a response to this vital demand.

Maslow's Hierarchy of Needs, a theory proposed in his paper, 'A Psychological Review', is very helpful in understanding the psychological requirements of a multicultural society. This hierarchy of needs shows us that physiological needs are not the only requirement of an individual. A sense of safety, love, feeling of belongingness, esteem and self-actualisation are also important.

Maslow's Heirarchy of Needs, represented as a pyramid

A multicultural nation needs to fulfil all the aspirations and requirements of every citizen and cultural group, according to this hierarchy. A multicultural country that fails to cultivate the spirit of multiculturalism may eventually disintegrate. Fragmentation of Yugoslavia first into Slovenia, Croatia, Macedonia and Bosnia Herzegovina (1991-92) and later into Serbia, Montenegro (2006) and Kosovo (2008) is a case in point. The declining minority population in Pakistan and Bangladesh is a great concern which shows their growing intolerance and needs microanalysis.

One of the parameters to judge the strength and richness of a culture is the status of minority groups. Various government census data shows that after partition of India in 1947, the population of Muslims, the largest religious minority group grew from 9.8% (1951 census) to 14.23% (2011 census) in India over a period of 60 years. Whereas in Bangladesh, the population of Hindus, the largest religious minority group decreased from 22.05% (1951 census) to 8.5% (2011 census). Similarly, in Pakistan the population of Hindus, the largest religious minority group decreased from 16% (1947) to 1.6% (1998). These census data show the sustainability and accommodativeness of the Indian culture.

Siby K Joseph rightly said in his article, 'Gandhi, Religion and Multiculturalism: An Appraisal':

'It is important today to understand multiculturalism in the context of the changing character of nation states which is marked by the absence of any single national identity. While some view it as a panacea for the growing menace of divisiveness in the world, others take it as a challenge for their dominant culture and nationhood. More than any other country, India needs to grasp its full implications in view of its multicultural and multireligious character. Gandhi's concept of *Sarva Dharma Samabhava* (equal respect for all religions) goes far beyond the concept of multiculturalism. In fact, it could very well be taken as a positive and constructive multicultural approach which offers a way out of the present cultural, religious and ethnic conflicts and cleavages.'

A growing tendency to identify and segregate people along religious, ethnic and linguistic lines raises a real threat to the peaceful coexistence of divergent human groups. However, among these challenges, it is the religious divide which adversely affects the normal and tranquil life of people of many countries. This line of thinking has been given further momentum by fundamentalist attempts to use 'religious' identity to spread the venom of hatred and conflict among various communities. They even go to the extent of waging war against many nations which do not follow their faith. The attack on the WTC on 9/11/2001 and subsequent attacks in different parts of the globe have brought the issue of religious fundamentalism to centrestage of international affairs. All attempts to overcome this precarious situation by Western countries under the leadership of the USA, with the avowed purpose of eliminating religious fundamentalism and its concomitant cross-national terrorism, have failed. In fact, it has further exacerbated the situation, leading to mushrooming of such elements worldwide, including in India.

A number of thinkers are seriously concerned about finding ways and means to tackle this growing peril confronting mankind. Samuel P Huntington looks at the whole problem in terms of clash of civilisation: those of the West and the Islamic. He further avers that an idea like multiculturalism cannot meet the challenge. In fact, he argues that multiculturalism is essentially an anti-Western, particularly anti-American ideology. According to him, it denies the existence of a common American culture and it promotes racial, ethnic and other subnational cultural identities and groupings, a challenge to American identity. However, this has been widely contested by a number of scholars who look at multiculturalism as the only real antidote to religious fundamentalism and cross-national terrorism. Multiculturalism is being looked upon as the only practical option before humanity for responding to the challenge of diverse cultural, ethnic and religious identities. It is much more than mere toleration of group diversity. In essence, it stands for treating, accommodating and recognising all members as equal citizens whether they belong to minority or majority groups.

The concept of multiculturalism emerged in Western societies in the 1970s, especially in the context of the Canadian attempt to tackle the problem of immigrants. It soon became a part of Canadian official policy and even spread to Australia, USA, UK and some countries of the EU. Subsequently it has become a dominant political ideology in the West. There have been some other important factors contributing to its emergence as a dominant policy of various governments. The failed attempts at assimilation and homogenisation of various ethnic groups resulted in a search for a new policy which could preserve and promote the diverse identities without adversely affecting the overall unity of the nation's social fabric. In addition, there was also a new awakening among different groups towards their primordial consciousness and relative deprivation. What gave a new impetus to this trend was the predominance of human rights approach in the arena of public policy. Perhaps the bitter memories of ethnic cleansing during holocaust, collapse of colonialism and totalitarian regimes also contributed to the development of support for multiculturalism.

It is also relevant to mention that in a number of Western countries ethnic studies were introduced primarily with a view to underline the significant contributions made by minority groups. As a result, there was growing self-confidence and consciousness among the minorities about their distinct identities. All these factors made multiculturalism a dominant theme of political discourse towards the end of the 20th century.

The term 'multiculturalism' has been used in different contexts, with varying connotations. Will Kymlicka in his work, *Multicultural Citizenship*, uses this term in a restricted sense focussing on 'ethnic' groups and 'national minorities' and not marginal or disadvantaged groups like gays, the poor, women et al. According to him, 'a state is multicultural if its members either belong to different nations (a multination state) or have emigrated from different nations (a polyethnic state), and if this fact is an important aspect of personal identity and political life'. In this context, Charles Taylor emphasises the necessity of developing a 'politics of recognition' in favour of minority cultures, by the supposed links between recognition and identity. 'The thesis is that our identity is partly shaped by recognition and its absence, often by the misrecognition of others—non-recognition and misrecognition—can inflict harm, can be a form of oppression, imprisoning someone in a false, distorted and reduced mode of being.'

Amartya Sen, while discussing this term, makes a subtle distinction between multiculturalism and 'plural monoculturalism'. According to him, genuine multiculturalism is marked by the existence of a diversity of cultures, which tend to interact and even intermingle among themselves. On the other hand, existence of various cultural traditions co-existing side by side, without the twain meeting, could be nothing more than plural monoculturalism. Andrew Heywood underscores two forms of multiculturalism—descriptive and normative. According to him, the former refers to cultural diversity whereas the latter implies a positive endorsement of such a diversity. Most of the theorists of multiculturalism tend to focus their arguments on immigrants who constitute ethnic and religious minorities (eg. Latinos in US, Muslims in Western Europe), minority nations (eg. Catalans, Basque, Welsh, Quebecois) and indigenous peoples (eg. Native peoples in North America, Maori in New Zealand).

Bhikhu Parekh, a prominent political theorist and an extensive researcher on multiculturalism, defines it as follows: 'Multiculturalism is not about difference or identity per se but those that are embedded in and sustained by that culture; that is, a body of beliefs and practices in terms of which a group of people understand themselves and the world and organise their individual and collective life.' According to him, it could be virtually taken as synonym for cultural diversity. It is entirely of a different genre from other kinds of differences. He underlines three different types of cultural diversity: subcultural diversity, perspectival diversity and communal diversity. In his view, groups like lesbians, gays and the like could be put under subcultural diversity as they seek nothing more than to pluralise the existing dominant culture.

Some other groups, like the feminists seek to reconstitute the dominant culture in their own perspective. Hence, Parekh puts them under the category of perspectival diversity. But it is the religious diversity, Parekh emphasises, which constitutes the core of multiculturalism. He illustrates it by referring to well-established cultural groups like Jews, Gypsies and recent immigrant groups. While his views have been widely accepted as a major contribution towards political discourse, he has been contested by critics like Joshua Broady. Another line of attack on the concept of multiculturalism has been that in its attempt to replace the similies of the 'melting pot' by 'flower pot', it creates a very congenial ground for all kinds of conflict situations. This is so because multiculturalism goes against the nation state's attempt to cultivate ultimately a distinctive national identity. Siby Joseph rightly said that:

'The Indian society has been multi-cultural, multi-religious, multi-racial, multi-ethnic and multi-linguistic from time immemorial. However, India has also encountered various kinds of divisiveness. It is unfortunate that unscrupulous politicians, with an eye on vote banks, are indirectly supporting the force promoting narrow religious sentiments and linguistic and regional identity. Building bridges of solidarity among different religious communities in India is essential to preserve the pluralistic and multicultural credentials of the country. In the context of such a challenge, the initiative and concerted effort made by Gandhi may provide a framework for thought and action.'

In a multicultural country, national interest is superior to individual interests. This may sound like an inducement to totalitarianism, but there is a discernible contrast between the two. While totalitarianism calls for complete and compulsory renunciation of one's self interests, for the country's materialistic gains, a multicultural country calls for voluntary renunciations on part of its citizens, for the nation's integrity and welfare as well as for the common good of its population. No other example is more befitting than that of our brave soldiers who sacrifice their lives for the nation. It, therefore, follows that it is our duty to preserve and maintain the nation's integrity and actively pursue the policy of accommodation and tolerance in order to cope with the many socio-economic challenges that India is up against.

Among the most pressing of challenges that confronts India are issues like its numbing poverty, a skewed education system, illiteracy, unemployment, gender discrimination, wide-spread corruption, minority-majority discords as also those that exist between the country's upper and lower castes, regionalism, which gives a fillip to separatist politics besides such disturbing issues as terrorism from across India's borders and Left-wing extremism.

While many of them are related to economic disparities, others can be attributed to the government's failure to properly implement the programmes and policies. Some of them are rooted in social discrepancies while some are political and sponsored by forces from across the border to destabilise the country. Despite socio-economic and political problems in a multicultural India, s one truth that hold us is the feeling of the spirit of 'unity in diversity' that can provide strength to fight various challenges.

The socio-economic and political challenges to multiculturalism in India are as follows:

Poverty

Poverty is the one hurdle that has negated all efforts of the Indian administrators to fast-forward the country on the path of inclusive development in the past, and continues to do so even today. A hungry stomach needs bread first and foremost. However, instead of ensuring that each and every citizen has enough food, its citizens, particularly the majority Hindu and minority Muslim, are today joined in a battle of wits over proprietary rights to a place of worship—a battle that has indelibly and adversely affected the way the country thinks and behaves as a nation.

Recent data shows that 37 per cent people are living below the poverty line; 57.2 per cent people in Odisha and 48.6 per cent in Madhya Pradesh were found to be living below the poverty line. According to certain critics, every third person lives below the poverty line in India. A pertinent question at this juncture, is how does one make poverty eradication programmes successful in the face of so-much diversity.

Education

Education is another issue that continues to dog the ideals of multiculturalism in India. A value-based education can help unite a people into a nation. An education that either lays too much store on theory or which is based on false principles, on the other hand, can fragment a nation into States split along either religion, caste or some such social ill. The Indian state, therefore, should ensure that the education model it employs is rooted in the nation's traditional wisdom and values. Still further, it needs to be ensured that the education the state imparts to its people is compulsory and free, irrespective of the rich-poor divide.

Mahatma Gandhi suggested various healthy and sustainable methods of education for the well-being of the nation, which if adopted, would ultimately benefit not only the country's people but the larger humanity beyond.

He said: The object of basic education is the physical, intellectual and moral development of children through the medium of a handicraft. But I hold that any scheme, which is sound from the educative point of view, and is efficiently managed, is bound to be economically sound too. For instance, we can teach our children to make toys that are to be destroyed afterwards. That, too, will develop their intellect. But it will neglect a very important moral principle, viz. that human labour and material should never be used in a wasteful or unproductive way. The emphasis laid on the principle of spending every minute of one's life usefully is the best education for citizenship and incidentally makes basic education self-sufficient.

Employment
It would hardly be out of place here to mention the fact that there are far greater possibilities for jacking up employment levels in a multicultural set-up than one that denies any space to people of different castes, creeds and gender to exist peaceably side by side.

There will be demands for more by different communities, many revolutions within revolution but these are positive signs for a thriving multicultural society. VS Naipaul, in *A Million Mutinies* acknowledges, there is corruption and violence and excess, but, he says: 'Excess was now felt to be excess in India. What the mutinies were also helping to define was the strength of the general intellectual life, and the wholeness and humanism of the values to which all Indians now felt they could appeal. And —strange irony— the mutinies were not to be wished away. They were part of the beginning of a new way for many millions, part of India's growth, part of its restoration.'

The Gender Equation
Different personal laws of different religious groups sometime create hurdles in the path of the socio-economic reform movement. However, on the issue of women's upliftment, religious groups need to work towards evolving a common minimum understanding of the space that women need to occupy for them to grow unhindered as free, thinking individuals.

Regionalism and Ethnic Conflict
Minorities problems, Communalism, Terrorism
Regionalism, ethnic conflict and problems of the minorities such as communalism and terrorism are, by and large, interrelated and create hindrances in the evolution of a multicultural society. There are deep-seated conflicts between cultures embodying different values.

Different peoples and cultures have different values, beliefs and truths, many of which are incommensurate but all of which are valid in their own context.

There are examples of conflict between two separate racial identities like majority Sinhalese and minority Tamils in Sri Lanka. They lived together for centuries but once the trust quotient between them was lost, it led to a violent conflict claiming thousands of lives.

In several parts of the globe, including in India, such racial and ethnic conflicts continue to occur but they are mainly due to political reasons as communityr leaders want them to fight for their political survival. A positive approach by the state and the political leadership through measures of social justice is much needed. What is required is not just that individuals are treated as political equals, but that their cultural beliefs are also treated as equally valid, and indeed are institutionalised in the public sphere.

Multiculturalism, at one level, means the appreciation, acceptance or promotion of multiple cultures, applied to the demographic make-up of a specific place, usually at the organisational level. In this sense, multiculturalism approximates to respect for diversity. In a political context, the term has come to mean the advocacy of extending equitable status to distinct ethnic and religious groups without promoting any specific ethnic, religious, and cultural community values as central. Survival of the fittest may be the motto of Western countries but our goal is survival of all the creation of the almighty. Our cultural heritage teaches us to link our development with dharma ie. to sustain hold and integrate everyone in common thread of love.

References

1. Dewey, John, *Democracy and Education.*

2. Bryce, James, *The Amecican Commonwealth (1893) Modern Democracies.*

3. Macpherson,CB, *Democratic Theory-Essays in Retrieval.*

4. Walzer, Michael, *Spheres of Justice;* 1983.

5. Maslow, *A Psycological Review*.

6. Miliband, Ralph, *Marxism and Politics-The state in capitalist Society*.

7. Joseph, Siby K, Gandhi, *Religion and Multiculturalism: An Appraisal*, Gandhi Marg, Volume 33, No 4, January-March 2012.

8. Rawls, John, *A Theory of Justice*.

9. Sterba, James P, *Social and Political philosophy-Contemporary Perspectives*, (London & New York, Routledge 2001)

10. Schwartzmantel, John, *The state in contemporary society-An introduction*, (New York, wheat sheaf, 1994)

11. Rees, John, *Equality* (London, Pall mall, 1971)

12. Miller, David, *Social Justice* (Oxford Darendess Press, 1976)

13. Robertson, David, *A dictionary of human rights* (London & New York Europa publications 2004)

14. Wolkowitz Carole, Lovell Terry, Andermahir Sonya, *A Glossary of feminist theory*, (London Arnold, 1997)

15. Wollstonecraf, Marry, *Vindication of the rights of women* (1792)

16. Miller, John Stuard, *Subjection of women*.

17. Rousseau, JJ, *A discourse on the origin of inequality*.

18. Gauba, OP, *An introduction to Political Theory*.

19. United Nations Report.

20. Friedan, Betty, (1921-2006) *The Feminine mystique*.

21. Pateman, Carole, *The sexual contact*.

22. Woolf, Verginia, *A room of one's own*.

23. Beauvoir, Simone, *The second sex*.

24. Firestone, Shulamith, *The dialectric of sex*.

25. Millett, Kate, *Sexual politics*.

26. Young, Iris Marion, (1990) *Justice and the politics of difference*, Princeton, Princeton University Press.

27. Baumann, Gerd (1996), *Contesting Culture: discourses of identity in multi ethnic London*, Cambridge, Cambridge University Press.

28. Amin, Samir (1999), *Spectres of capitalism: A critique of current intellectual fashions*, New York, Monthly Review Press.

29. Sen Amartya, Dreze Jean, *India economic development and social development.*

30. *Gandhi for 21ˢᵗ century My views on Education*, Edited by Anand T Hingoani

31. *Fifty years of Indian parliamentary democracy* 1947-1997

32. *Yojana*, December 2009

33. Neera Desai and Usha Thakkar, *Women in Indian society.*

34. Jug Suraiya, 'Balkanistan vs India', *The Times of India*, December 23, 2009.

35. Bhave, Vinoba, *Talks on the Gita.*

36. Bhatta, Prem P, *Hindu gods and goddesses.*

37. Goswami Tulsidas, *Ramcharitmanas.*

38. *The Times of India*, Mumbai, Thursday, June 17 2010.

39. *Holy Quran*, Motilal Banarasidas.

Conclusion

Celebrating Indian Diversity: in Tune with Nature

DIVERSITY and sustainability is inherent in nature and Human being is also a part of the same nature. For our survival, it is imperative for us to respect this nature and follow the laws of nature. Disregarding it would only be detrimental for us because we are in no way empowered to proceed against the will of nature. Ultimately, we need to live in harmony with nature. Our *rishis* and *munis* used to reside in forests and synchronise their body and mind accordingly. Owing to this, they had full command over their physical and mental selves, inducing health and longevity in their lives. Thus, living in close association with the magnificently diverse Nature has been the core of India's philosophy. This very innate philosophy helps us to celebrate multiculturalism and to provide a conducive ambience for it.

Ever since the ancient period, there have been innumerable instances wherein Mother India welcomed different faiths, religions, travellers and traders, giving due respect and regard to them. My reading takes me back to the Chinese travellers like Fa Hien and Hiuen Tsang, who came to India, spent several years and amassed great knowledge. All sorts of faiths like Christianity, Islam and Zoroastrianism got acceptance in India and have flourished here. Even the British, French, Dutch and Portuguese came and stayed here for centuries. India believes in humanity, it believes in the concept of

'Vasudhaiva kutumbkam'. That is why every faith and every individual flourishes here, irrespective of their background. Multiculturalism thrives here because India does not believe in coercive assimilation. It fosters integration. It is here that the difference between 'melting pot' and 'salad bowl' culture becomes visible.

The virtue of tolerance, which enables us to accommodate everyone, runs in our veins. We believe in the unity of God and all places of worship—whether it be temple, church, mosque, synagogue or any other—are given equal importance. All religions are just different ways to worship the same God and their basic preaching and principles are the same. So we don't differentiate or discriminate between one man and the other, one faith or other. We treat everybody as equal, as our brothers. This concept inculcates accommodative nature and greater tolerance in every Indian. It is here that the greatest strength of Indian culture lies, enabling diversity to flourish.

Indian culture has been beautifully adorned with the efforts and sacrifices of our rishis and saints. They are the actual creators and perpetuators of India's cultural traditions. They have taught us the lessons of sacrifice, ethics, morality and tolerance. Their thoughts are holistic in nature. They considered themselves not the part of a certain community or society, but of the whole universe and for mankind. They imparted the lessons of identification, of individualism and of universalism for us. They worked for the welfare and well being of the whole universe. Their broad thoughts are the source of India's tolerance and the key to integrate peacefully with each other.

The Vedic vision envisaged the interdependency and inseparability of the physical, psychological and spiritual aspects. The whole universe was seen to be one, but manifesting at three levels. Nothing therefore, in the physical world was considered to be merely material. A major outcome of the development of Western sciences was the separation of the material from the psychological and the spiritual aspects. Materialistic phenomena came to be observed in isolation, separate from the psychological and spiritual aspects, so that science underwent incomplete development, merely on the lines of the quantitative aspect. This was valid in its way but it limited the investigator to a very narrow sphere of awareness and knowledge and when that narrow sphere was taken for the whole of reality, the result was a tragic illusion. This is known in Hindu tradition as 'avidya' (ignorance) and 'maya' and is exactly all that took place in Western society.

The Vedic understanding of the three integrated worlds, physical, psychological and spiritual was typical of the whole ancient world. The vision of an integrated universe was lost in the dark ages and instead of a magical revival during the renaissance, it succumbed to ignorance further; today we are trying to recover it. The Western School of thinking separates matter from mind and both matter and mind from the supreme reality, ie God, or whatever name it may be given. In the ancient vision, there could be no separation of matter from mind or of matter from the supreme spirit, which in India came to be known as *Brahman*—that which holds everything together.

According to the Vedic view, if we constantly keep returning things to their source, then only we can envisage a harmonious, rhythmic universe. Conversely, if we do not turn the wheel of the Law, if we only do the appropriate things for ourselves, then we are committing sin. Sin is separating our self from the order of the universe, making oneself an isolated entity and it is against the laws of universe. This Vedic philosophy perpetuates multiculturalism in India and diversity becomes a national treasure, rather than being a burden.

In Indian culture, we have given different names to the supreme reality. The Rig-Veda says, *Ekam sad viprah bahudha vadanti,* ie. the supreme existence is one, but scholars have described it in various ways. Different sects worship the same God, just through different names. Ramkrishna Paramhans used to say, *'jato mat, tato path'* (there are as many faiths as there are ways to God)). Swami Vivekanand further propagated this view at the world religion conference in Chicago, by explaining that each devotee, whatever be his method of worship, will definitely reach the same ocean. These thoughts stress on the value of Diversity.

India is multicultural, like no other country in the world. Multiculturalism in India is similar to, but not the same, as in other countries, say for example USA,UK, Australia etc. Other nations may also have different religions but the Indian story is different. We are majority Hindus but have the second largest Muslim population in the world. We are not a Hindu nation, nor a Muslim nation but secular as a nation. In addition to that, we have a sizeable population of Jains, Buddhists, Christians, Zoroastrians and Jews. That is, all the major religions of the world. Despite belonging to a multicultural society, all Americans dress the same, eat the same and speak the same. On the contrary, in India, a Tamil and a Punjabi are as different as a Spaniard and an Italian. A Tamil Muslim and a Tamil Hindu are culturally more akin than a Tamil Christian and a Mizo Christian. The difference in India is that each cultural entity retains its own identity. For example, a Bengali Hindu and a Marathi Hindu dress differently, eat differently and speak differently and for that matter a Bengali Muslim may have more in common to a Bengali Hindu. Another intriguing aspect is the celebrations of different festivals even within the same religion. In Bengal the pomp and gaiety surrounding Durga Puja surpasses even that during Diwali, while the same festival is not very common amongst say, Tamil Hindus. In the same way, Ganesh Chaturthi, such an important festival for Marathis is not a big thing in other parts of India. And all the while we have been talking of the same religion.

We have more than 30 languages, each with a different script. In this matter, India surpasses even the whole of the Europe since most of the European languages have the same script. For years, the Zoroastrians migrated from Persia to India to practice their religion freely, without persecution. They have become an integral part of our society and that too, without losing their identity. So, in India, Diversity is celebrated and not taken for granted.

Mill, a political scientist, was most sensitive to the value of diversity. He believed—the absolute and essential importance of human development is in its diversity. For Mill, the diversity of individual characters, lifestyles, and tastes was both inescapable and desirable, the former because each individual was unique, the latter both intrinsically and instrumentally. Diversity added richness and variety to the human world and made it aesthetically pleasing. It stimulated imagination, creativity, curiosity and love of difference. Diversity also led to progress because it created a climate, conducive to the emergence of exceptional original minds, provided new sources of inspiration and encouraged healthy competition between different ways of thought and life.

There are some other views on human nature too. Vico, another political thinker, was one of the first to take a historical view of human beings and emphasise on the uniqueness of every society. He believed: Human nature is a product of history... It was differently developed and expressed, in different epochs and societies; although all human beings shared a common nature.

For Herder, the influence of culture permeated the individual's ways of thinking. Since no man could be human outside his cultural community, membership of it was basic human need just as much as food and physical security. For him, all cultures were equal not only because they were equally good, but because they meant much to their members and were best suited for their needs. Therefore, a diverse society is a more successful society, with more satisfied members as compared to a unitary society, where all members may not be equally and fully comfortable.

Each culture, according to Herder, is valuable, because of what it is, and not as a stepping stone to an allegedly higher culture or as a stage in a grand historical teleology. A culture's sole concern should be to be true to itself and live by its own highest values. His theory of culture was a remarkable intellectual achievement. He rightly insisted that cultures were not results of geographical circumstances and stages of mental development ...but products of human imagination, creativity and the search for self-understanding. Cultural diversity was a permanent feature of human life and could never disappear as long as human beings remained what we have been always known them to be, playful curious, inventive, capable of dreaming dreams and probing the limits of knowledge and experience.

Human beings share a common nature, common conditions of existence, life experiences, predicaments and so on, to a great extent. They, however, conceptualise and respond to these in quite different ways, giving rise to different cultures. No theory of human beings can give a full account of them unless it is accompanied by a theory of culture. And since they face different natural and social circumstances, are heirs to different traditions, think and dream differently and so on, the cultures they create are inescapably diverse in nature. Therefore, cultural diversity is an integral feature of human existence.

The social movement that came to be known as multiculturalism seems to be associated with the projection of the rise of cultural studies in the Canadian, American and Western academies. Culture emerged as a catchword of public discourse in the 1980s and a new kind of cultural politics was built upon the phases of cultural difference and cultural relativism.

The meaning of culture, Turner says, is undergoing a historic transformation due to globalisatios, the information revolution, consumerism, and other such phenomena typical of this age. He argues that the 'culture', in multiculturalism, cannot be viewed entirely as a throwback to the romantics. The conscious creation of cultural identities within multicultural politics, and the political efficacy of the idea of culture itself suggests that the concept of culture that is emerging along with multiculturalism contains new elements which are connected with the context of its emergence.

Culture has come to serve as the basis of both imagined communities and individual identities, deemed to be authentic, in contrast to repressive, alien, or otherwise inauthentic normative codes, social institutions, and political structures. This historical unwedging of culture and society as political-economic structures has converged with, and greatly reinforced by, the idealistic culturalism...of the disciplines and thinkers primarily involved with multiculturalism.

A nation brimming with spirituality, like India, has never experienced civilisational discontinuity and for eons successfully maintained its identity. The modern understanding of what constitutes a nation is bewildered by the incomprehensibility of such great civilisations which constituted nations like China and India. India, and to some extent China, show a remarkable cultural continuity from the very ancient times to the present day. Other ancient civilisations, those of Egypt, Greece, and Mesopotamia were great, no doubt but in time they had to perish inevitably.

The sense of continuity, however, is not to be equated with inflexibility. On the contrary, if Indian culture has flowed over so many centuries, vibrant and alive, it is because it has shown a noteworthy ability to absorb and assimilate new ideas and influences. Let me quote AL Basham, who observed in *A cultural history of India*, that India has always been steadily changing and that has been for the benefits of both circumstances and the citizens—corelated by all means. This makes multiculturalism strong and powerful in India.

When we talk of India's culture, we take into cognisance the intellectual influences of various movements and cultures which seem to have been woven into a fabric of many hues. It incorporates cultures which were present in prehistoric India, those that had a temporary contact with the country, and those which came from outside and flourished in India permanently. S Abid Hussein in *The national culture of India*, writes: If we study the cultural history of India, we find that whenever any new movement or thought originated here or came from outside, it might have caused a temporary disapproval, but soon the Indian mind set into motion, its process of seeking unity in diversity, and after some time the conflicting elements were harmonised to lay the foundation of a new culture. India has been a remarkably ancient civilization with a deep historicity. Furthermore, it is a continuous flowing civilization and it is difficult to demarcate India's past into clear cut time boundaries. The diversity of Indian society and culture is stupendous, so much so that it would be difficult to speak of it in the singular, at the same time there is also a certain unity amidst the multiplicity.

Indian society, in general, has had a holistic aspect, concerning the relationship between the individual and the group, where the latter had primacy over the former. The wider interests of the community were always an important context, within which individuals were to perform their duties and claim their rights. These are the reasons for successful survival of multiculturalism in India.

The spiritual emphasis in Indian life was never lost sight of, whether men lived in it or left society, dharma is an important way of life. The stability of Indian life for long centuries rested on the firm foundation of dharma. Through the inculcation of the spirit of dharma, high standard of ethics, clear cut codes of behaviour and widespread acceptance of non-material values as of higher importance than possessions, came to be the expression of true Indian culture in ordinary society.

When we talk about dharma, first of all we must know the meaning of the word dharma. The word 'dharma' has been derived from the root '*dhri*' means to uphold, to sustain, to nourish. Dharma does not mean rituals, ceremonies, worship etc, but dharma means duty towards our life. Every human being has duty in every stage of life. To fulfil that duty is our dharma. The basic difference between dharma and religion is that dharma has nothing to do with any creed, dogmas, whereas religion is related to creed or dogmas. Dharma is above any creed or dogmas. It sustains everything. Dharma is a pious word which gives us the training of living a better life, making a better family, better nation and better world where only peace prevails. Thus, it is dharma which is sustaining diversity here.

The majority religion of India, ie. Hinduism, was and is essentially tolerant. It assimilated rather than converted other groups. Pluralism, as a value, implied tolerance of other styles of life, while preserving one's own. As Hinduism believes in the existence of numerous paths leading to the same ultimate reality, it was possible for rulers and people of diverse faiths to survive and even prosper for centuries, in India. Doctrines and rituals, certainly differed, but the followers of different religions lived in relative harmony in India. To quote Sir John Woodroffe, Hinduism is not a religion but a culture, which has produced, amongst other things, certain fundamental religion and philosophical beliefs on which have been superimposed a number of varying forms of particular philosophies and religions. Hinduism is unique in itself. Non-violence and dharma are the two hands of Hinduism. Its philosophy stands for *Vasudhaiva Kutumbakam* and the Vedic teaching, *Ekam sat Viprah bahudha vadanti*—truth is one, sages call it by many names. This gives strength to the multifaceted diversity, inherent in India.

Indian culture has been deeply influenced by Jainism in ideas such as *ahimsa* and in the development of language, literature, art and architecture. Indian culture got a fresh impetus from Buddhism in the intellectual, literary, artistic and architectural fields. Indeed, the missionaries of Buddhism spread India's culture beyond its boundaries, into Myanmar, Sri Lanka, China, Thailand and other places. The coming of Islam brought about a fusion of two vibrant cultures and the Indo-Islamic styles in art and architecture, music and literature evolved. A peculiar interaction between Islamic thoughts and the Bhakti movement in medieval India is said to have contributed to the Sufi movement in India.

Ramakrishna Paramhansa was an epitome of the tolerant and adaptable Indian, practicing different forms of worship, not only of the different Hindu sects, but also those of Islam and Christianity. From his experience, he came to the realisation that the goal of all religions is the same. Ramakrishna used to say, 'So one sweet Mother Divine is worshipped in different countries and ages, having different forms and names'.

Rabindranath Tagore expressed in his beautifully eloquent language, how different people came to India from pre-historic times right down to recent centuries (which brought to the shores of India the modern European people) and have cooperated in building up a great culture which does not seek to exclude anything, but is all-inclusive, and does not take up an attitude which would deny to any people its right of self expression. As a matter of fact, the great culture of India is basically a synthesis of not only different bloods and races, but also of speech and of ways of thinking (of which the different speeches are the outward expression) as well as of cultures—material, intellectual and spiritual—which give ideologies and determine attitudes and actions.

Though Lala Lajpat Rai said, 'There are no race conflicts in India'. Mother India recognises no race distinctions. If Mother India is proud of a Nanak, she is also proud of a Chisti. If she had an Ashoka, she had an Akbar too. If she had a Chaitanya, she had a Kabir also. If she had a Harsha, she had a Sher Shah too. If she had a Vikramaditya, she had a Shahjahan also. If she had a Mohammad Aladdin Khilji and a Mohammad Tuglaq, she had their Hindu prototypes as well'. For every Hindu hero, he cites a Mohammedan hero. He said that Hindus and Muslims must unite to remove all internal divisions based on relgion. All social barriers must be removed and the school, the college, the court and the council must be open temples for all to enter and worship, regardless of caste, colour and creed. He was of the opinion that no scheme of national education in India could be complete without including the active teaching of patriotism and nationalism as regular subject of study. He believed Indians should take a lesson from Europe, in this aspect. Every European country and United States also made it a point to cultivate the spirit of patriotism and nationalism though its schools. He emphasised on 'love for India' as a whole, as distinguished from love for village, town, city or province. He said, patriotism however does not include only the material and the physical aspects of a country. Patriotism should revolve around the love for the nation as a whole, regardless of various religious creeds and castes into which it is superficially divided. Every Indian child should be taught that every human being who is born in India or of Indian parents, or who has made India his or her home, is a compatriot, a brother or a sister regardless of colour, creed, caste or vocations.

Nature has blessed India with a bounty of resources. All sorts of geographical landscapes are available in the Indian subcontinent. From mountains and plateaus to vast planes and from glaciers, rivers to seas, everything is there. Similarly, all sorts of diversities like linguistic, ethnic and religious groups are present in India. These diversified groups are just like different kinds of flowers of different colours and different fragrances. A garden with only one type of flower is not as attractive as a garden with varieties of flowers, with a variety of look and smell. This is the beauty of our country.

Preserving this colossal diversity and beauty is a challenging task in itself but India has risen to it magnificently. It has preserved and accommodated its diversity for thousands of years, throughout the ages, thanks to her firm cultural and spiritual heritages. The deep-rooted Indian cultural values have taught us to become tolerant and accommodative.

The debate in India on 'cultural nationalism' has proceeded on the wrong premise that there exists an inevitable conflict between cultural nationalism and secularism, even democracy. This is incorrect since Indian culture is essentially accommodative of secularism and democracy. *Mother India is not just tolerant but accepts all other cultures, faiths and lifestyles with the same warmth as she would accept a homecoming son. In contrast, the cultures of countries and religions which seek to convert others are not accommodative of secularism and democracy. So, there is no scope of conflict between the Indian culture and secularism.* The idea of cultural nationalism in India is non-conflicting, inclusive and accommodative. These are fairly strong assurances which provide each religious community with a certain amount of space and autonomy to function vis-à-vis each other. As the father of the nation, M K Gandhi rightly said, 'eye for an eye will make the whole world blind'.

The ancient Indian epics of Ramayana and Mahabharata and the vast storehouse of puranic and vedantic literature have been instrumental in the education of masses about their country and culture. Their impact cannot be undermined. Such a highly developed patriotism and national consciousness is not available in the literature or oral traditions of any other ancient civilization. For treating all religious communities and individuals as members of one family despite of their different religious linkages, and as equal and providing liberty to propagate and practice their religions (Read Article 25 of the Indian Constitution), India has become the soul of 'humanistic virtuousness' worldwide.

The Constitution encouraged religions communities to group up and to set up their own charitable trusts and religious institutions (Article 26). Religious minorities received additional attention and were given the right to establish their own educational institutions for promoting their culture and language (Article 29, 30).

Caring for oneself is what comes naturally to everyone, but when we start caring for others, for our surroundings and the environment, we truly feel satisfied. Here it will not be out of context to narrate a beautiful didactic short story. A man died and the God asked him, if he would like to go to heaven or hell. The man requested God to show both the places before he could take a well informed decision. God took him to hell. There he saw a big hall containing a long table on which a variety of cuisines and foods were kept.. He saw the people sitting in rows but were very sad. They looked starved and there was no smile on their faces. He saw that their hands were tied to four-feet long spoons. They were trying to get the food from the centre of the table to put into their mouths, but they failed. When the man was brought to heaven, he saw a similar hall and table with lots of food. He also observed rows of people on both sides of the table with their hands tied to four-feet long spoons. But here people were smiling, satisfied and healthy looking. The people were feeding one another across the table. The result was happiness, prosperity and enjoyment because they were not thinking of themselves alone. They were thinking for the others, their fellow beings.

This story is applicable in our lives on earth too. When we care for others, it is automatically ensures that we are also being cared for. If every individual thinks for his own cause only, the social bonding becomes weak and the overall social climate is downgraded. When we care for others, it will in turn benefit us as well and the whole society gets benefited in the process. After all, how can one feel happy if there are sufferings all around? When we care for others, the social climate improves and the whole society lives in harmony. This is the driving force behind a vibrant multicultural society

Western culture believes only in the growth and development of the individual. On the contrary, Indian cultural ethos envisages a concept of togetherness, the concept of walking together, doing all the acts as a group, as a society and above all as a mankind. As the Rig-Veda says, 'O human being! Walk unitedly, speak unitedly, our mind should think unitedly'.

All the creatures of the world have been created by the same creator, we call him God. Conversely, all human beings are offsprings of the same God. From here comes the concept of universal brotherhood. According to latest discoveries in human genes, DNA of all human beings is common up to more than 98 per cent. It is a scientific fact that all human beings was derived from a single live cell. Every human on this globe, regardless of his caste, creed, gender, colour, language, religion and nationality, is related to the other. We need to accept this and realise that we are not enemies or competitors but like brothers and sisters. This is what the Indian cultural ethos believes in. All the people who may be coming from different cultural background are like our brothers and sisters and are respectable and desirable.

Let the nature of Nature shape us, guide us and help us to grow and gleam. Do not waste time before the mirror pondering on self. What we are from within is our real self, not the external demeanour. May God fill us with love for humanity, compassion and an urge to do good for all. Let there be universal brotherhood and let there be unwavering love for nature. That is what our Indian culture is! that's the reason we celebrate multiculturalism.

References

1. Beteille, Andre. Toleration and Exclusion, *The Hindu,* Thursday, March, 2003.

2. Mahajan G *Rethinking Multiculturalism.*

3. Modood, Tariq. *Multiculturalism: A Civic Idea Polity.* Oxford University Press, 2000.

4. Parekh, Bikhu. *Rethinking Multiculturalism: Cultural Diversity and Political Theory.* Macmillan Press Ltd, 2000.

5. Sreelekha Mishra, C Bharath Kumar. Understanding Diversity : A Multicultural Perspective, *IOSR Journal of Humanities And Social Science* (IOSR- JHSS) Volume 19, Issue 9,www.iosrjournals.org.

6. Bhabha, Homi. *The Location of Culture*, Routledge,1994.

7. Shende, Dharamdas M *Better Culture, Better Civilization : Rethinking Multiculturalism.*

Bibliography

1. Gandhi MK, *Collected works of Mahatma Gandhi*, 100 volumes.
   Hind Swaraj.
   An Autobiography, Navjivan Publishing House, 1958.
   The story of my experiments with truth, Navjivan Press, 1927.
   Hindu Dharma, Orient Paperbacks.
   The Bhagwad Gita, Orient Paperbacks.
2. Pal BC, *An introduction to the study of Hinduism*, SC Gupta, Calcutta, 1908.
   His life and utterances, Ganesh & Co, Madras, 1907.
   The spirit of Indian Nationalism, 1910.
   Indian Nationalism: Its Principles and Personalities, RS Murthi & Co.
   Memories of my life and times, Volume I, Modern Book Agency, 1932.
   Swadeshi and Swaraj (The rise of new patriotism), Yugyatri Prakashak Ltd, Calcutta, 1954.
   The New economic menace of India, Ganesh & Co, Madras, 1920.
   The New Spirit, Sinha Sarvadhikar & Co, Calcutta, 1907.
   The Soul of India, Choudhary and Choudhary, Calcutta, 1917.
3. Radhakrishnan S, *Eastern Religion and Western Thought*, Oxford India.
   Indian Philosophy, Vol 1 & 2.
   Hinduism: A way of life.
   Call to young India, Madras, 1921.
   Ideals of Non-cooperation, Madras, 1921.
   India's will to freedom, Madras, 1921.

The Arya Samaj, London, 1915.

The Political future of India, Renaissance Publishing House, Delhi, *Unhappy India: A reply to Miss Catherin Mayo's mother India*, Calcutta, 1928.

Young India, New York, 1917.

National Education in India, 1920.

Indian Philosophy: 2 Valumes –*An idealist view of life*.

'The Reign of religion in contemporary Philosophy'.

4. Savarkar VD, *Hindutva*, Veer Savarkar Prakashan, Bombay, 1969.

The Indian war of independence of 1857.

'Some of the Baisc Principles and Tenets of the Hindu Movement', in Fred Dallmayr and GN Devy (eds), Between Tradition and Modernity. *India's Search for Identity: A Twentieth Century Anthology*. New Delhi: Sage Publications, (1998).

Six Glorious Epochs of Indian History.

5. Tagore, Rabindranath, *Nationalism*, McMillan & Co, 1917,

Rupa & Co, reprint, 1991, New Delhi.

'Nationalism in India', in Fred Dallmayr and GN Devy (eds), *Between Tradition and Modernity: India's Search for Identity. A Twentieth Century Anthology*, New Delhi, Sage Publications.

The Message of the Forest', in Sisir Kumar Das (ed,) *The English Writings of Rabindranath Tagore*. Volume Three, A Miscellany, (1996), Sahitya Akademi.

Bhattacharya, Sabyasachi (ed.) (1997), *The Mahatma and the Poet. Letter and Debates between Gandhi and Tagore 1915-1941*, National Book Trust.

'The Way to Unity', in Sisir Kumar Das (ed.), *The English Writings, of Rabindranath Tagore*. Volume Three, (1996).

'The Union of Cultures (1921)', in Sisir Kumar Das (ed), *The English Writing of Rabindranath Tagore*. Volume Three, (1996).

'International Relations (1924)', in Sisir Kumar Das (ed), *The English Writings of Rabindranth Tagore,* Volume Three, (1996).

'National language of India', in Sisir Kumar Das (eds.), *The English Writings of Rabindranath Tagore*. Volume Three, (1996).

The Message of The Forest.

Sadhana: The Realization of Life, Cloucester: Dodo Press, (2005 [1913]).

The Religion of Man.

6. Tilak BG, *Arctic home in Vedas*, Pune, Kesari office, 1903.

   Arya Lokanche Mulasthana (in Marathi), Bombay, Damodar Savtaram Yanede, 1910.

   Bhagvadgitarahasya Athavakarmanya Shastra (in Marathi), Ed.10, Pune, Lokmanya Tilak Mandir, 1953.

   Chaldean and Indian Vedas, Pune, Bhandarkar Oriental Research Institute, 1917.

   His writings and speeches, Madras, Ganesh & Co,

   Lokmanya Tilak Tekhsangraha, (in Marathi), Sahitya Akademi, 1969.

   Lokmanya Tilakanche Kesarintil Tevha, Vol 1-4, Collections of writings in Marathi in Kesari, Pune, Kesari, 1922-30.

   Brahmasutravritti, Pune, Bharat Ithihas Sansodhak Mandal, 1957.

7. Kymicka Will (1991), *Liberalism, Community and Culture*, Oxford University Press, pp9-19, 176; also see by the same author (1995), *Multicultural Citizenship*, Oxford: Clarendon Press.

   Western Political Theory and Ethnic Relations in Eastern Europe, Oxford University Press (2002).

   Politics in the Vernacular: Nationalism, Multiculturalism and Citizenship, Oxford: Oxford University Press (2001).

   'Western Political Theory and Ethnic Relations in Eastern Europe', in W Kymlicka and M Opalski (eds), Can Liberal Pluralism Be Exported? *Western Political Theory and Ethnic Relations in Eastern Europe*, New York: Oxford University Press, (2002).

   'Multi-nation Federalism'.

8. Taylor Charles (1994), *The Politics of Recognition*, in Amy Gutmann (ed), *Multiculturalism and the Politics of Recognition*, Princeton University Press.

9. Marcuse Herbert (1966), *One dimensional Man, Boston*: Beacon Press.

10. Shachar Ayelet (2001), *Multicultural Jurisdictions: Cultural Differences and Women's Rights*, Cambridge University Press.

11. Okin Susan Moller (1998), 'Feminism and Multiculturalism: Some Tensions', *Ethics*, Vol.108.

12. Phillips Anne (2007), *Multiculturalism without Culture*, Princeton University Press.

13. Madan TN (1987), 'Secularism in its Place', *The Journal of Asian Studies*, Vol.46.

14. Engineer Asgar Ali (1998), 'Religion and secularism' and 'Secularism in India: Theory and Practice', in Asgar Ali Engineer and Uday Mehta (eds), *State Secularism and Religion: Western and Indian Experience*, Ajanta.

15. Singh Karan (1992), 'Secularism: The Right Approach', in MM Sankhdahar (ed.), *Secularism in India: Dilemma and Challenges*, Deep and Deep Publications.

16. Singhvi LM (1992), *Secularism: Indigenous and Alien*, in MM Snakhdhar (ed.), *Secularims in India: Dilemma and Challenges*, Deep and Deep Publications.

17. Carens Joseph (1997), Liberalism and Culture, *Constellations*, Vol 4, No1.

    Culture, Community, and Citizenship: A Contextual Exploration of Justice as Evenhandedness, Oxford University Press, (2000).

    Culture, Citizenship and Community: An Exploration of Justice as Evenhandedness, New York: Oxford University Press, (2000).

    Dimensions of Citizenship and National identity in Canada, The Philosophical Forum 28 (1-2), 1996-97.

18. Haksar Vinit (1998), 'Collective Rights and the value of Groups', *Inquiry*, Vol 41, No 33.

19. Kukthas Chandran (1992), 'Are There Any Cultural Rights', *Political Theory*, Vol 20, No1.

20. Fraser Nancy (1995), 'From Redistribution to Recognition? Delimmas of Justice in a Post-socialist Age', *New Left Review*, Vol 1, No 212.

21. Mahajan Gurpreet (1998), *Identities and Rights: Aspects of Liberal Democracy in India*, New Delhi: Oxford University Press.

    'Religion, Community and Development', in Gurpreet Mahajan and Surinder S.Jodhka (eds), *Religion, Community and Development: Changing Contours of Policy in India*, New Delhi: Routledge,(2010).

    Accommodating Diversity ideas and institutional practices, Oxford University Press.

    Multicultural Path, issues of Diversity Discrimination in Democracy.

22. Wilkinson Steven I (ed) (2008), *Religious Politics and Communal Violence*, New Delhi, Oxford University Press.

23. Sheth DL (2010), 'Political Communalisation of religions and the Crisis of Secularism', in Gurpreet Mahajan and Surinder S Jodhka (eds), *Religion, Community and Development*.

24. Bajpai Rochana (2010), 'Cultural Rights of Minorities During Constitution making: A Re-reading', in Gurpreet Mahajan and Surinder S Jodhka (eds), *Religions, community and Development,*

25. Guru Gopal (2010), 'Struggle for the Margin or from the Margin', in Gurpreet Mahajan and Surinder S Jodhka (eds), *Religion, Community and Development: Changing contours of Politics and Policy in India,* Routeldge.

26. Young *Policy and Group Difference.*

27. Weiner Myron (1978), *Sons of the Soil: Ethnic Conflict in India,* Princeton University Press.

28. Beteille Andre (1980), On the Concept of Tribe, *International Social Science Journal,* Vol XXXII, No 4.

    'The Idea of Indigenous People', Cultural Anthropology, (1998).

    Caste, Class and Power: Changing Patterns of Stratification in a Tanjore Village, New Delhi: Oxford University Press, (1965).

29. Haimendorf CF (1994), Problems and Prospects of Tribal Development in North-East India, *Economic and Political Weekly,* Vol 24, No13.

30. Scott Joan Wallach (2004), 'French Universalism in the in the 1990s', Differences: *A Journal of Feminist Cultural Studies,* Vol 15, No 2.

31. Young Iris Marion (1990), *Justice and the politics of Difference,* Princeton University Press.

    'Polity and group Difference, A critique of the ideal of universal Citizenship', *Ethics* 99 (2), 1989.

32. Baumann Gerd (1996), *Contesting Culture: Discourses of Identity in Multi-Ethnic London,* Cambridge University Press.

33. Abu-Lughod Lila (1991), Writing against Culture, in Richard G Fox (ed) *Recapturing Anthropology: Working in the Present,* School of American Research Press.

34. Asad Talal (ed) (1973), *Anthropology and the Colonial Encounter,* Ithaca Press.

35. Wagner Roy (1981), *The Invention of Culture,* University of Chicago Press.

36. Patnaik Prabhat (2008), 'The Ideological Hegemony of Finance Capital', manuscript;

37. Amin Samir (2000), Economic Globalism and Political Universalism: Conflicting Issues, *Journal of World-System Research,* Vol VI, No 3.

38. Ali Shaheen Sardar (2007),'Religious Pluralism, Human Rights and Muslim Citizenship Europe: Some Preliminary Reflections on an Evolving Methodology for Consensus', in Titia Leonon and J E Goldschmidt (eds),

Religious Pluralism and Human Rights in Europe: Where to Draw the Line, Antwerp.

39. Tezcan Levent (2009), 'Operative Kultur und die Subjektivierungsstrategien in der Integrationspolitik', in Ozkan Ezli, Dorothee Kimmich, Annette Werberger, and Mitarbeit von Stefanie Ulrich (eds), *Wider den Kulturzwang: Migration, Kulturalisierung and Weltliteratur,* Bielefeld, Transcript.

40. Battersby Christine (2007), *The Sublime, Terror and Human Difference,* Routeldge.

41. Chatterjee Margaret (2002), *Hinterlands, and Horizons. Excursions in Search of Amity,* Lanham: Lexington Books.

42. Geothe (1953), *Maximen und Reflexionen,* in Goethes Werke, Hamburger Ausgabe, Vol 12.

43. Das Sisir Kumar (ed) (1996), *The English Writing of Rabindranath Tagore.* Volume Three, A Miscellany.

44. Amin *Capitalism in the Age of Globalization.*

45. Cohn Bernhard (1985), 'The Command of Language and the Language of Command', in Ranajit Guha (ed), *Subaltern Studies IV,* Oxford University Press.

46. Nehru Jawaharlal (1989 [1936]), *An Autobiography,* London: Bodly Head.

    The Discovery of India, New Delhi: Oxford University Press, (1997).

    The Unity of India, (London, Undsay, Drummond, 1941.

47. Secularism, Islam and Modernity: *Selected Essays of Alam Khundmiri* (2001), edited with an introduction by MT Ansari, Sage Publication.

48. Arentd Hnnah (1978), 'Creating a Cultural Atmosphere', in Ron H Feldman (ed), *The Jew as Pariah: Jewish Identity and Politics in the Modern Age,* New York: Grove Press.

    Aufklarung and Judenfrage', in Hannah Arendt: Die Verborgene Tradition. Acbt Essays, Frankfurt am Main: Suhrkamp, (1976).

49. Jha Shefali (2002), 'Secularism in the Constitutional Assembly Debates', *Economic and Political Weekly,* Vol 37, No 30, pp 3175-80.

50. Chiriyandkandith James (1999),Constitutional Predelictions, *Seminar,* Vol.484, December, pp 50-5.

    'Unity in Divrsity' ? Coalition Politics in India with special reference to Kerala)', *Democratization,* Vol 4, No 4, (1997).

51. Ali Amir (2001), 'Evolution of the Public Sphere', *Economic and Political Weekly*, vol 36, No.25, 2419-32.

52. Minoo Masani, cited in Granville Austin, The Indian Constitution: *Cornerstone of a Nation*, Oxford University Press.

53. Diwan Paras (2002), *Law of marriage and Divorce*, Delhi, Universal Law Publishing Company.

54. Rudolph Susan and Lloyd Rudolph (2001) 'Living with Difference in India, in Gerald James Larson (ed.), *Religion and personal Law in Secular India*.

55. Das Veena (1994), 'Cultural Rights and Definition of Community', in Upendra Baxi (ed) *The Rights of Subordinated People*, Oxford University Press.

56. Oommen TK (2004), *Nation, Civil Society and Social Movement: Essays in Political Sociology*, Sage Publications.

57. E Annamalai (1997), 'Questions on the Linguistic Characteristics of the Tribal language of India', in Anvita Abbi (ed) *Languages of Tribal and Indigenous People of India*, Varanasi: Motilal Banbarsidass Publishers.

58. Robin Joan (ed) (1989), *Language Planning: Current Issues and Research*, New York, Cambridge University Press.

59. Dasgupta J(1976), 'Practice and Theory of Language Planning: The Indian Policy Process', in William M O'Barr and Jean F O'Barr (eds) *Language and Politics, Paris*.

60. Xaxa Virginius (2005), 'Politics of Language, Religion and Identity: Tribes in India', *Economic and Political Weekly*, Voi 40, No 3.

61. Brass Paul (1990), *The politics of India since Independence*, Cambridge University Press.

62. Forrester Duncan B(1970), 'Subregionalism in India: The Case of Telengana', *Pacific Affairs*, Vol 43.

63. Manor James (1982), 'The Dynamics of Political Integration and Disintegration', in AJ Wilson and Dennis Dalton (eds) *The States of South Asia: Problem of National Integration*, Vikas Publication House.

64. Dasgupta J (2003), 'Language Policy and National Development in India', in Michael E Brown and Sumit Ganguly (eds), *Fighting Words: language Policy and Ethnic Relations in Asia*, Massachusetts: MIT Press.

65. Parekh Bhikhu (1998), 'Cultural Diversity and Liberal Democracy', in Gupreet Mahajan (ed) *Democracy, Differences, and Social Justice*, Oxford University Press.

Equality in a multicultural society, in Jane Franklin (ed) Equality, institute for publ Policy Research, London 1997 and Will Kymlicka, *Multicultural Citizenship*, Qarendon Press, Oxford, 1995.

'Cultural Diversity and Liberal Democracy,' in Gurpreet Mahajan (ed), *Democracy Difference and social justice*, oxfered University Press, 1998.

Rethinkung Multiculturalism: Cultural diversity and political theory, Harvard (2002).

66. Sarkar JK (1982), 'The APHLC in Retrospect', in KS Singh (ed) *Tribal Movements in India*, Vol I, New Delhi: South Asian Publishers.

67. Gassah LS (1993), 'Regionalism and the HSPDP in Meghalaya: Some Basic Issues', in B Pakem (ed) *Regionalism in India* (with special reference to North-East India), Har-Anand Publications.

68. Sridharan E (1999), 'Principles, Power and Coalition Politics in India: Lessons from Theory, Comparison and Recent History', in DD Khanna and Gert W Kueck (eds), *Principles, Power and Politics*, Macmillan.

Principles, Power and Coalition Politics in India, p 280.

69. Griffin James (2008), on Human, Oxford University Press.

70. Indian Ronald (1990), *Imagining India*, Oxford: Basil Blackwell.

71. Appadurai Arjun (1993), 'Number in the Colonial Imagination', in C Breckenridge and Peter Veer (eds), *Orientalism and the Post Colonial Predicament*, University of Pennsylvania Press pp 314-39.

72. Cohn Bernard (1987) *An Anthropologist among the Historians and Other Essays*, New Delhi: Oxford University Press.

73. Kugle Scott Alan (2001), 'Framed, Blamed and renamed: The Recasting of Islamic Jurisprudence in Colonial South Aisa', *Modern Asian Studies*, Vol 35.

74. Bhargava Rajeev (ed) (2008), *Politics and Ethics of the Indian Constitution*, Oxford University Press.

75. Gitlin Todd (1995), *The Twilight of Common Dreams: Why America is Waracked by Culture Wars*, Henry Holt and Company, New York.

76. Hollinger David (1995), *Post Ethnic America: Beyond Multiculturalism*, New York, Basic Books.

77. Patterson Orlando (1998), *Rituals of Blood: Consequences of Slavery in Two American Centuries*, New York. Counterpoint.

78. Dirks Nicholas (2001), *Castes of Mind: Colonialism and the Making of Modern India*, Permanent Black.

79. Dalmia Vasudha and Heinrich von Stietencron (eds) (1995), *Representing Hinduism: The Construction of Religious Traditions and National Identity*, Sage Publications.

80. Bayly Susan (1999), Caste, Society and Politics in India from the Eighteenth Century to the Modern Age, *The New Cambridge History of India*, Vol 4, No 3, Cambridge University Press.

81. Kaviraj Sudipto (1992), 'The Imaginary Institution of India', in Partha Chatterjee and Gyanendra Pandey (eds), *Subaltern Studies VII: Writing on South Asian History and Society*, Oxford University Press.

82. Jaffrelot Christophe (2003), *India's Silent Revolution: The Fise of the Low Castes in North Indian Politics*, Delhi: Permanent Black.
    Dr Ambedkar and Untouchability, London: Horst & Co, (2005).

83. Nye Joseph and John Donahue (eds) (2000), *Governance in a Globalkizing World*, Massachusetts, Brookings Institution Press.

84. Nairn Tom (1977), *The Break-up of Britain: Crisis and Neonationalism*, London: New Left Books.

85. Kothari Rajni (ed) (1970), *Caste in Indian Politics*, Orient Longman.

86. Rudolph LI (2008), 'The Modernity of Traditions: The Democratic Incarnation of Caste in India', in Loyed and Susanne Rudolph (eds), *Explaining Indian Democracy: A Fifty Year Perspective, 1956-2006*, Vol III- *The Realm of the Public Sphere: Identity and Policy*, New Delhi: Oxford University Press, Original published in 1965.

87. Srinivas MN (1962), *Caste in Modern India and Other Essays*, Asia Publishing House. Also see Frankel, Francine and MSA Rao (eds) (1989), *Dmonance and State Power in Modern India: Decline of a Social Order*, Oxford University Press.

88. Jalal Ayesha (2001), *Self and Sovereignty: Individual and Community in South Asian Islam since 1850*, Oxford University Press.

89. Mitra Subrata and VB Singh (1999), *Democracy and Social Change in India New Delhi*: Sage Publications.

90. Rai Mridu (2004), Hindu Rulers, Muslim Subjects: *Islam, Rights and the History of Kashmir*, Permanent Black.

91. Kakar Sudhir (1996), *The Colours of Violence*, Penguin.

92. Sen Amartya (1999), *Development as Freedom*, Oxford University Press.

93. Bhargava Rajeev (2008), 'Introduction', in Rajeev Bhargava, *Politics and Ethics of the Indian Constitution*, Oxford University Press.

94. Jotirao Phule (2002), *Selected Writings of Jotirao Phule*, Delhi: Leftword.All references for Phule are from his texts, *Slavery and Cultivator's Whipcord*, as found in Phule, Selected Writing.

95. Deshpande GP (2002). 'Introduction', in Phule, Selected Writing.

96. O'Hanlon Rosalind (1985), *Caste Conflict and Ideology*, Cambridge University Press.

97. Nanda BR (1977), *Gokhale: The Indian Moderates and the British Raj*, Princeton University Press.

98. Chandra Bipan (1989), *India's Struggle for Independence*, Penguin.

99. Anglo Padma (2006), *The Emergence of Feminism in India, 1850-1920*, Aldershot, Hampshire: Ashgate.

100. Guha Ramachandra (2007), *India after Gandhi: The History* of the *World's Largest Democracy*, London: Picador.

101. Ambedkar BR (1989), 'Thoughts on Linguistic State', in Vasant Moon (ed), *Dr Baba Saheb Ambedkar's Writing's and Speeches*, Vol 1, Education Department, Government of Maharashtra.

102. Rajagopalachari C (1961), 'Majority and Minority', *Swarajya*, 22 July.

103. Von Herder JG, *On social and political culture*, translated and edited by FM Barnard, Cambridge University Press, 1969.

     'Philosophy of History, in outline of a Philosophy of History', translated by T Churchil, Bergman, Publishers, New York, 1966.

104. Kallen Evelyn, Multiculturalism, Ideology Policy and Reality, *Journal of Canadian Studies*.

105. Bhabha HK(1993), *The location of culture*, Routledge.

106. Fish S (1997), *Boutique Multiculturalism, or why are intellectuals afraid of Hate speech ? Critical inquiry.*

107. Gutman A (ed), *Multiculturalism in Princeton*, Princeton University Press.

108. Tayler C (1994) *The Politics of recognition in Gotman (ed) Multiculturalism.*

109. Kelkar NC, *Life of Tilak.*

110. Nevins HW, *The New Sprit in India.* (London)

111. Aurobindo Sri, *The Region of Religion. in contemporary Philosophy*, (London, Macmillan & Co(1920).

     The idal of Humanunity.

     The Riddle of this marked Dharma Aur Jatiyata.

     '*Ideas and progress*'.

Essay on the Gita.

112. Spengler Oswald, *The decline of the West,* Alfred A-Knopf (1926-1928).

113. Green TH, *Prolegomena to Ethics.* Oxford, the Clarenden Press.

114. The complete works of Swami Vivekananda.

115. Varma VP, *Studies in Hindu Policical thought and its Metaphysical Foundations.* (Banaras 1954).

     Hindu Political Thought.

116. Smith Donaled E, *India as a secular state.*

117. Khan Aga, *India in Transition.*

118. Khan Syed Ahmed, 'Essays on the life of Muhammad'.

119. Golwalkar MS, *We or our Nationhood Defined,* Bharat Prakashan.

120. Andrews CF, *Mahatma Gandhi's Ideals.*

121. Nevinsion HW, *The New spirit in India.*

122. Besant Annie '*Wake up India*', (Madras Theosophical publishing House)

     Ancient ileals in Modern life, The New Civilization.

     In Defence of Hinduism.

     India : A Nation

     Wake up India.

     Ancient Minds

123. Roberts PE, *History of Modern India.*

124. The Rama Krishna Mission Institute of Culture, *The Cultural Heritatges of India.* VI Volumes.

125. Paine Jeffery, *Father India.*

126. Woodreff John, *Is India Civilized.*

127. Huntington, *Clash of Civilization.*

128. Goswami Tulsidas, *Sri Ramcharitmanas.*

129. Bhagvatam

130. Bible

131. Quran

Index